Naomi Tucker
Editor

Bisexual Politics:
Theories, Queries,
and Visions

*Pre-publication
REVIEWS,
COMMENTARIES,
EVALUATIONS . . .*

"**T**he authors–a collection of the most influential bisexual activists, historians, and theorists of our time–simultaneously contextualize and deconstruct (often blurring) current notions of gender, sexual orientation, and identity politics. Historically grounded, collectively the essays inform, liberate, enlighten, excite, challenge–some even shock and upset. This anthology is crucial reading for anyone trying to make sense of shifting definitions of sexuality and politics in a post-modern age."

Warren J. Blumenfeld
Editor, *Homophobia: How We All Pay the Price*
Editor, *Journal of Gay, Lesbian, and Bisexual Identity*
Co-Author, *Looking at Gay and Lesbian Life*

The Harrington Park Press
An Imprint of The Haworth Press, Inc.

Bisexual Politics
Theories, Queries, and Visions

HAWORTH Gay and Lesbian Studies
John P. DeCecco, PhD
Editor in Chief

New, Recent, and Forthcoming Titles:

Bisexual Politics
Theories, Queries, and Visions

Naomi Tucker
Editor

Harrington Park Press
An Imprint of The Haworth Press, Inc.
New York • London

Published by

Harrington Park Press, an imprint of The Haworth Press, Inc., 10 Alice Street, Binghamton, NY
13904-1580

Excerpt from *The Fifth Sacred Thing* by Starhawk (New York: Bantam, 1993) reprinted with permission of author.

"Politics of the Bisexual Deep Fry" originally appeared in *Good Sense & The Faithless* by
Michèlle T. Clinton (Albuquerque, New Mexico: West End Press, 1994). Reprinted with permission of author.

Cover design by Freddie Baer.

Library of Congress Cataloging-in-Publication Data

Bisexual politics : theories, queries, and visions / Naomi Tucker, editor.
    p.   cm.
    Includes bibliographical references (p.) and index.
    ISBN 1-56023-869-0 (alk paper)
    1. Bisexuality. 2. Bisexuals–Political activity. I. Tucker, Naomi.
HQ74.B556   1995
306.76'5–dc20   95-3149
                                                                            CIP

Production/Editorial Staff

This book was dreamed, compiled, edited, and woven together by names too numerous to fit on its cover. These miracle-makers include:

Associate Editors
Rebecca Kaplan
Liz A. Highleyman

Assistant Editors
Judi Addelston
Dajenya
Rachel Kaplan
Susanna Trnka

Technical Assistants
Jill Nagle
Gerard Palmeri
Terri Rochelle

Advisors
Jane Felder
Lani Ka'ahumanu
Loraine Hutchins
Jill Nagle

Conception
Brad Robinson

. . . to the memory of David Lourea,
who inspired the revolutionary
in so many of us . . .

. . . and to all those who have struggled
and put their lives on the line
so that we could come out
and be free . . .

With pride, rage, sisterhood, and love

CONTENTS

SECTION II—CONNECTIONS: CAN WE WORK TOGETHER?

APPENDICES

Appendix A

Appendix B

ABOUT THE EDITOR

Naomi Tucker is a bilingual, bicoastal, bisexual activist, writer, public speaker, and workshop leader. She has been instrumental in organizing bisexual groups and events since 1985, including BiFocal, BiPOL, BiNet USA, the Bay Area Bisexual Speakers' Bureau, the 1990 National Bisexual Conference, and the Jewish Bisexual Caucus. Naomi's published works appear in *Anything That Moves: Beyond the Myths of Bisexuality; Bi Any Other Name: Bisexual People Speak Out; Looking Queer: Body Image and Identity in the Lesbian, Bisexual, and Gay Community(ies);* and *Bisexual Horizons: Politics, Histories, Lives.* She works in San Francisco as an elementary school teacher and counselor/advocate for battered women.

Contributors

Judi Addelston is a doctoral candidate in social psychology at the City University of New York Graduate School.

Elizabeth Armstrong is currently a PhD candidate in Sociology at U.C. Berkeley. She is working on a dissertation on the organizational history of the San Francisco queer community.

Freddie Baer is best known for her exquisitely detailed, surrealistic collages. Her illustrations are renowned throughout the small press and alternative communities. A book of her work, *Ecstatic Incisions: The Collages of Freddie Baer,* was published in 1992 by AK Press. Freddie lives in San Francisco where she works full-time as an administrative assistant; the rest of this stuff she fits in during her spare time.

Brenda Blasingame is an African-American, Jewish, Bisexual woman who works in the field of health education and prevention and is a consultant in the area of multicultural and organizational development. She lives in California with her life partner and their dog in the 'burbs. She is a community activist and committed to the pursuit of a joy-filled conscious existence.

Nishanga Bliss (aka Susan Carlton) taught the first university course on bisexuality at U.C. Berkeley. She is a writer, bodyworker, performance artist, and indiscriminate genital worshipper. She appreciates the help of Laura Weide and Paul Dalton on her piece, originally written for a reading at A Different Light Bookstore.

Mykel Board has been a controversial columnist for *Maximum Rock'n'Roll* for more than ten years. He has contributed freelance writings on sex, music, and travel to other publications. He also is a spoken/sung word performer.

Tamara Bower is a visual artist, radical feminist, and founder of the New York Bisexual Women's Support Group (January 1991). She also founded the New York Bisexual Women's Network (1982-1984).

Greta Christina is a white female lesbian-and-gay-identified bisexual pervert. Her writing has appeared in *On Our Backs* magazine, the *San Francisco Bay Times*, and the 1992 anthology *The Erotic Impulse*. Her fetishes include books, films, weird music, reference materials, baseball, and sex. She lives in San Francisco.

Michèlle T. Clinton, award-winning feminist poet/performance artist, has most recently published *Good Sense & The Faithless* (1994, West End Press), and *black sage: The Womb & The Water* (1995, Penny Whistle Press). "I believe in the ultimate transformative power of the word: I aim for an artistic vision that is a synthesis of radical politics and experimental spirituality."

Dajenya is a 40-year-old African-American/Jewish poet/writer and social worker-to-be. She lives in Richmond, CA with her two wonderful sons Bakari and Jelani. She does volunteer work with various agencies and is currently studying Spanish. She hopes someday to meet the woman of her dreams.

Stephen Donaldson founded the gay student movement (as an openly bisexual sophomore at Columbia University in 1966) and the Committee of Friends on Bisexuality, a pioneering bi Quaker group, in 1972-73. He is an activist on prisoner and male rape issues, editor (*Encyclopedia of Homosexuality,* 1990), writer, punk, and swami.

Elias Farajajé-Jones (aka Manuel Kalidas Congo) is a tenured Associate Professor at Howard University School of Divinity. Spanish-speaking African Native American queer theorist, AIDS terrorist, guerilla theologian, and performance artist, he has been involved since 1981 in the struggle against heterosexism, HIV/AIDS, and aparthAIDs, first in Switzerland and then in DC.

Sharon Gonsalves is an awesome woman who just keeps getting better. A member of the lesbian/gay/bisexual speakers' bureau at Lotus Development Corporation, her writing has appeared in *Sojourner, Gay Community News, Closer to Home,* and *The Femme Mystique.* She lives with her cat, Ida, in a limited equity co-op in Cambridge, MA.

Liz A. Highleyman is a writer, activist, and public health worker. She has been involved in bisexual organizing, AIDS activism, anarchist politics, sex worker empowerment, and various leather-s/m communities and organizations. She lives in San Francisco with her lover Jan and enjoys computer networking, travel, and photography in her nearly nonexistent free time.

Loraine Hutchins, co-editor of *Bi Any Other Name: Bisexual People Speak Out,* is one of six national coordinators of BiNet USA and co-founder of AMBi (the Alliance of Multicultural Bisexuals) in Washington, DC.

Orna Izakson is a nice Jewish girl who works at a small-town newspaper and has a passion for walking into political lions' dens. She thinks objectivity is outdated, sex is radical, and people need to recognize the interconnections among their issues and get down to business.

Lani Ka'ahumanu is a multi-ethnic indigenous queer mother who celebrates the complexities of her 51 years of life by cherishing the simple truth of her experience. A visionary who dances to the beat of different revolutionary drummers, she co-edited *Bi Any Other Name* and posed for *Women En Large: images of fat nudes.*

Rachel Kaplan is a dancer and a writer whose work frequently takes as its theme the relationships between the personal and social worlds. She is a pre-backlash feminist, published author, community organizer, critic, and teacher.

Rebecca Kaplan is a radical ashkenazi jewish reconstructionist ambi-sinister bi-dyke bi-national bi-lingual feminist eco-socialist postmodern brazen theory hussy. She is currently studying at Stanford Law School, striving to live happily and communally.

David Lourea was a therapist, preschool teacher, animal lover, and activist known for his pioneering community education efforts on bisexuality, s/m, HIV/AIDS, the Jewish community, safer sex, and human sexuality. His academic work appeared in the *Journal of Homosexuality* and *Medical Anthropology.* David dedicated much of his life to liberation struggles. He died on November 10, 1992.

Kory Martin-Damon is a Cuban-Venezuelan, female-to-male bisexual transsexual, aspiring to live in San Francisco one day. Kory hopes never to stop being challenged on matters of gender, sex, body, and other relevant realities.

Annie S. Murray is a 29-year-old graduate student in cognitive science and language acquisition at MIT who seems to be spending most of her mental energy discussing politics and feminism. She lives in Boston, where she is a not-active-enough member of GLIB (The Irish-American Gay, Lesbian, and Bisexual Pride Committee of Boston) and an active member of LABIA (Lesbians and Biwomen in Alliance) and BBWN (Boston Bisexual Women's Network). She can wiggle her nose.

Jill Nagle currently does Queer Jewishness, sex radical feminism, independent scholarship, poetry, and subversive philosophy. Hse (chosen pronoun) likes instigating inter- and intra-cultural education and love, justice, pleasure, and many other processes grounded in conscious, authentic presence. Hse enjoys writing, sexual pioneering, genderfuck, cooking, and just being fabulous.

Robyn Ochs, EdM, is a teacher, writer, activist, and speaker who has taught courses on bisexuality at MIT and Tufts University. She is a co-founder of the Boston Bisexual Women's Network and the East Coast Bisexual Network. Editor of the *International Directory of Bisexual Groups* and the *Bisexual Resource Guide,* her writings have appeared in several anthologies.

Laura M. Perez was born in Callao, Peru and raised in the U.S. She is a proud bisexual Latina who values self-identification and dislikes labels. Her passions are politics, chocolate, sex, sushi, motorcycles, and human liberation.

Mark Pritchard, co-editor of *Frighten the Horses,* is also a member of the Street Patrol, a group of queers who patrol San Francisco's Castro District and intervene in gay bashings. He is working on a collection of essays and stories about sex.

Carol Queen is a San Francisco writer, sex educator, sex worker, and sex radical/activist. She works at Good Vibrations and is on the training staff of San Francisco Sex Information. Her writing has appeared in *OUT/LOOK, On Our Backs, Taste of Latex, Frighten the Horses, Spectator, The Realist,* and other periodicals, as well as in *Bi Any Other Name, The Best American Erotica 1993, Madonnarama,* and *The Erotic Impulse.* She is working on a novel . . . or two. No, she never gets tired of it.

Dannielle Raymond is the founder of BLUR, a supportive social group for young bisexuals. Her contributions to this anthology are part of a national press kit she developed as a project of BiNet USA. Dannielle lives in San Francisco with her life partner and her two pet rats.

Indigo Chih-Lien Som is a garlic-chopping ABC born, raised & planning to die in the San Francisco Bay Area. Under the name *bitchy buddha press,* she makes one-of-a-kind, altered, letterpress & photo-copy edition artist's books. Her poetry has appeared in numerous journals & anthologies including *APA Journal* and *The Very Inside: An Anthology of Writing by Asian and Pacific Islander Lesbian and Bisexual Women.*

Starhawk is the author of *The Spiral Dance, Dreaming the Dark, Truth or Dare,* and *The Fifth Sacred Thing.* A feminist and peace activist, she is one of the foremost voices of ecofeminism. She contributed to the films *Goddess Remembered, The Burning Times,* and *Full Circle.* She works with the Reclaiming collective in San

Francisco which offers classes, workshops, and public rituals in earth-based spirituality.

Sunfrog is a polymorphous pervert, poetic terrorist, anarchist critic, drag queen, journalist & activist. He lives on the road in a motorhome with bi-artist & poet Lisa Lust, & their daughter Ruby Jazz.

Robin Sweeney is a San Francisco writer. When her life isn't being derailed by CFIDS, she is a pervert, troublemaker, and business manager of *Venus Infers.* She has published work in *Doing it for Daddy, Leatherwomen 2,* and *Dagger* and is co-editing an anthology of work by S/M dykes with Pat Califia.

Cecilia Tan knew she was bi in the 70s, came out to her parents (and the world) in the 80s, but didn't get a date with a woman until the 90s. She is a freelance writer specializing in alternative sexuality, science fiction, and erotica. She is the founder and publisher of Circlet Press, Inc. erotic science fiction book publishers, Boston, MA.

Susanna Trnka is a Czech-American, bisexual writer and poet. A former student in anthropology and women studies, she now works (temporarily) in the computer industry and spends her free time looking for more socially relevant things to do. She is the founder of a women's erotic writing group. Her writing has appeared in *Closer to Home, Anything That Moves, Socialist Review, off our backs*, and the Czech gay monthly *SOHO/Revue.*

Naomi Tucker is a teacher, public speaker, and community organizer with New York attitude and San Francisco politics. Heading into her second decade of bisexual activism, she writes and edits for *Anything That Moves,* surrounds herself with other progressive Jewish feminists, and devotes her soul to the battered women's movement.

Amanda Udis-Kessler is a writer, musician, sociologist, anti-homophobia/biphobia educator, and all-purpose queer nerd. She can be found in the Arlington Street Church choir, at video games in finer arcades everywhere, biking around Boston, and admiring her cat. She hopes to be a minister someday.

Stacey Young has been active in feminist and queer politics since 1981. Her other articles on bisexuality appear in *Closer to Home: Bisexuality and Feminism* (Weise, 1992) and Shane Phelan's forthcoming collection on queer political theory (Routledge).

Preface

WHY THIS BOOK?

It was a crisp March morning in San Francisco. I was milling about the registration area of the OutWrite '91 Lesbian and Gay Writers' Conference, clinging to my coffee as I nervously eyed the crowds of my literary idols. Although largely out of place amongst these famous writers from across the country, most of whom took comfort in their polite dismissal of bisexuality, I felt certain that some force had drawn me to this gathering for a reason. Amidst the crowd of famous faces I spotted my friend Brad Robinson, a comrade in bi-queer struggle. Bubbling with enthusiasm, he told me that he thought the time had come for a book addressing the politics of bisexuality–and that we should create it together. Certainly it was a book I longed to read myself. And so, taking a deep breath, not certain what I was getting myself into, I impulsively said yes. Thus this anthology was born.

Bisexual activists were craving a book that moved beyond the "bisexuality 101" level of discourse. Anthologies such as *Bi Any Other Name* (Hutchins and Ka'ahumanu, 1991) validated our experiences. Empowered by that support, out bisexuals were now ready for a body of literature that would challenge our thinking, formulate new bisexual political theory, document our activism in print, analyze our different organizing strategies, and provide a vision of future directions. We were outraged at the constant, intentional omission of bisexuality in gay/lesbian communities, HIV education, and hip hetero hangouts. We vowed to give voice to the theorists and political thinkers of the bisexual movement, to enrich the blossoming arena of bisexual writing.

As editors, Brad and I complemented each other well. He provided fearless initiative while I played the role of cautious, linear-thinking Virgo, and we grew tremendously. But in January 1993

Brad withdrew from the project, and I couldn't fathom carrying on by myself. The success of the anthology was a product of our partnership; it seemed impossible for me to fill that gap alone.

Ironically, the contract offer from The Haworth Press came during this time of uncertainty, perhaps one of the many signs indicating my path. Bi folks everywhere told me in no uncertain terms that the book had to go on; that there was a world of people waiting for it to appear on the bookshelves. So easy for them to say! The weight of that responsibility sat like lead on my shoulders. Yet their words hit home. Like it or not, the book was bigger than just my life and would outweigh this narrow little time of crisis.

Weeks before the March on Washington (for Lesbian, Gay, and Bi Equal Rights and Liberation) in April 1993, I spent a pensive weekend on retreat with other Bay Area bi activists. I looked to the fearless waves of the Pacific Ocean for guidance, and returned to anthologyland with a new plan. If the community wanted this book so badly, then the community would have to help piece it together. In this spirit came the idea for our editorial staff—a team of authors and other community members who would each be responsible for a part of the work. The astounding community effort that followed has carried the book through to its current incarnation.

COLLECTIVE VISIONS

This collection of essays represents many visions: my own, which flowed into the editing of each piece and formulated the initial structure of the book; the individual visions of each writer; the collective visions of the associate and assistant editors and production staff who formed a most amazing bisexual thinktank; the contributions of many bisexual activists and friends who gave me endless feedback and suggestions; and the web of communication amongst contributors who shared their writing and ideas with one another.

By no means is this book a definitive work. It is at best a starting point, scratching the surface of our movement. Its limitations are vast. Its composition underscores a shortcoming of the bisexual movement itself: in particular, that the majority of players are white, middle-class women. Many people with valuable ideas to contribute never found out about this anthology, or couldn't express their views in writing, or couldn't be included in this limited number of pages, or did not feel empowered to speak up, or could not afford the time to write.

No editor can deny the shaping of a project according to her own vision and experience. While I have tried to be as inclusive as possible in the variety of perspectives represented in the book, the overall flavor reflects my view of bisexual politics. My guiding principles are feminist, multicultural, inclusionary politics that embrace all forms of consensual sexuality and relationships—a bisexual movement whose mission is to fight for social justice and liberation for all. My experience is that of a second-generation American Jewish woman raised with a New York tongue and a San Francisco view of the world. White skin and upper middle-class resources have often afforded me privileges that shape my ability to be an in-your-face bisexual activist.

I grew up confronting dualities: sensing my cultural "difference" as a Jew yet passing for "white"; growing up with working-class parents who moved up into middle-class money. Even as a child I understood what it meant to be excluded from both sides, oppressed by one and not fitting in to the other . . . to live simultaneously with power and powerlessness. Perhaps because of those early experiences, it was not difficult for me to extrapolate to the realm of bisexual politics, where I again walked in more than one world.

Identifying as bisexual in a heterosexist, dichotomous, unfriendly world, shapes my politics. Conversely, my vision of social justice shapes the way I see bisexuality in the world. This book explores such symbiotic relationships between our experiences and the concept we call "bisexual politics."

Yet the anthology stands alone, beyond my personal perspective. From the time this baby was born it had a life of its own: a rebellious child with the tenacity to challenge me on my thinking.

The visions of the associate and assistant editors, who took on responsibility for specific sections, helped shape the final form of the book. Some of the essays were chosen because they captured the essence of our beliefs; others because they explained basic tenets of the bisexual movement; still others precisely because of how vastly they differed from our own viewpoints. I don't agree with everything said in these pages. But I do believe that for each idea expressed here, there is a larger constituency of bisexual people who hold those beliefs. And I also believe there are as many theories of bisexuality as there are bisexual people.

I intend this to be a politically progressive work, as well as a work-in-progress. I aim to reflect an agenda of social change, and to leave open more avenues for dialogue and opinion. I like to think of this anthology as a small section of a tapestry. Woven together are mini-treatises on particular aspects of bisexual political thought, personal experiences from underrepresented segments of bisexual people, and bite-size samplings from a wide range of topics within the rubric of bisexual politics.

By no means is everyone included in this tapestry. As the book goes to press, I cannot get my mind off all the queries, theories, visions, and pieces of history not touched on within these pages. In the book and in the bi movement, we need more analysis of issues of class, multiculturalism, and HIV/AIDS, more rural outreach and youth organizing. Yet one has to start somewhere. Comfort comes only from knowing that someone else will pick up the loom, continue to weave, embellish the tapestry with more colors and images.

Most of all, I am proud of the process by which this book has come into being. That process has confirmed the power of community and renewed my faith in collective spirit. From beginning to end, this project has been an act of bisexual politics itself.

Naomi Tucker
San Francisco, CA

Acknowledgments

When the time came within the bisexual movement to gather our political voices in print, people held hands from far and wide and breathed life into the center of an intangible circle, called community. They came bearing gifts, each offering what they could. Some brought the unseeable gifts of the wind, like knowledge, love, confidence. Others contributed their fiery talents—in writing, editing, organizing, managing the mysteries of technology. Still others came to the circle with gifts of the earth, sharing their food, flowers, phone, fax, photocopying, or finance. Some danced on the water in celebration, bearing the gifts of joy and laughter in times of need.

Testimony to the powers of a consensus-building process in a sea of widely divergent philosophies, our collective breath produced this offspring as a contribution to the bisexual movement. My deepest thanks to all whose breath created that circle. In particular, I thank the following people for their gifts:

- Editrix goddesses Liz and Rebecca, my muses and mentors: for their supreme wisdom, commitment, prophetic vision, eternal patience with me, and damn hard work. They devoted endless hours and resources to this book, and deserve more credit than can ever be given.
- All the authors, including those whose work is not in the final manuscript, who edited each other's essays, offered me immeasurable insight, and participated in a marvelous group process.
- The ones who danced with me: Dajenya, Judi, Liz, Rachel, Rebecca, Susanna, Jill, Gerard, and Terri Rochelle, the best staff one could ask for; Lani Ka'ahumanu, who saved me from existential hell; bodyworker supreme Ann McGinnis, who helped me through the worst of times and taught me to live in the land of "I don't know"; Karen Barnes, Josh, and my beautiful, fab-

ulous housemates Lydia, Ann, and Amanda, who probably hope I never edit another book again, but who put up with me nonetheless.

- My family, who believed in me always, and whose unconditional love is my cornerstone: my parents Harriet and Harvey, my brother Jeff, wondercousins Susan and Ilene (the West Coast crew), and the New York relatives, who never judged.
- The advice and technical support team: Pat Califia, Beth Elliott, Loraine Hutchins, Lani Ka'ahumanu, and Beth Weise were the voices of experience; Greta Christina, Autumn Courtney, Amanda Udis-Kessler, Ann Whidden, and Joe Wright lent me their sharp intellect; Gerard Palmeri, computer queen extraordinaire, transcribed and typed and converted disks for days without complaint; Amanda Tear and Rebecca Kaplan organized my office and therefore my life; Linda Hoagland graciously offered her copier and fax machine; Liz Echt sorted my finances and did the administrative work that no one else would touch; my father insisted that every good book editor deserves a computer; Jane Felder and the angels at Farella, Braun, and Martel reviewed my contract; and Bill Palmer, Dawn Krisko, and John DeCecco at The Haworth Press encouraged me at every turn.
- Lastly, I am grateful to everyone at the August 1991 Bi Writers Retreat (Pt. Reyes, CA); to the Jewish goddesses and faeries of Queer Minyan in San Francisco; to all the bi community members and allies whose input and encouragement were invaluable; and to Brad, for pursuing the dream.

Introduction

Naomi Tucker

It requires something more than personal experience to gain a philosophy or point of view from any specific event. It is the quality of our response to the event and our capacity to enter into the lives of others that help us to make their lives and experiences our own.

—Emma Goldman, 1934[1]

DID YOU SAY POLITICS?

Perhaps the greatest battle bisexual people have had to face is our invisibility and the pernicious invalidating of our identity. The bisexual movement of the 1970s to early 1980s therefore organized around the principles of visibility and support. But by the mid- to late 1980s bisexuals were seeking more than just the validation of our identity: we were defining political agendas, building a movement, participating in other social change movements as out bisexuals. In the mid-1990s we are beginning to shed the layer of identity politics altogether, seeking new organizing principles to guide us.

Ten years ago, when I came out to people, the word "bisexual" got stuck in their throat. Today, when I let the subject of my work slip into conversation with non-bi friends, a common response is: "Bisexual *politics?*" Hardly anyone bats an eyelash at the "b" word. But *politics?*

In 1989 Autumn Courtney and Lani Ka'ahumanu presented a workshop entitled "Bisexual Politics: What It Is" at an East Coast Bisexual Network Conference. Today, though the politicization of our identities is common knowledge within bisexual communities, we are still seeking a definition of bisexual politics.

WRITING OUR OWN HISTORY

Opinions about bisexuality are not difficult to find—from psychologists, talk show hosts, sex researchers, and right-wing fundamentalists; from lesbians, gays, and heterosexuals who compare our experiences to theirs; from non-bisexuals who attempt to define the social, political, or emotional contexts of bisexual experience. But how do bisexuals define our own place in the world?

This collection represents an effort by bisexuals to forge our own politics, from the inside. All the contributors self-define as bisexual, though that label may carry vastly different meaning for each individual. Together, their voices attempt to eke out a niche in the schema of sexual politics and progressive social movements. The writers examine the points of convergence between sexuality and politics. They explore the history, strategies, and philosophy of bisexual politics in the U.S. Their diversity presents a multi-faceted approach to defining bisexual politics.

The contributors address questions looming in the minds of many bisexual activists. How do our politics affect our sexual identity? Conversely, how does our bisexuality affect our politics? How does bisexual identity challenge our thinking? What are the sociopolitical roots of biphobia? How have the Black civil rights movement, the women's movement, gay liberation, lesbian feminism, and the HIV/AIDS movement influenced the evolution of bisexual politics? How is the "bisexual movement" similar to and different from other movements? Should we be a part of the lesbian/gay movement? How do we organize around our diversity?

Many of the essays emphasize a politics of inclusion, breaking down divisions and classifications. Other common themes include sexual liberation for all, combatting heterosexism and monosexism, and understanding the connections among all oppressions. The theories develop from each writer's personal history, as well as an intellectual knowledge of what has come before us.

BIRTHING A MOVEMENT

The face of bisexual politics has evolved tremendously in the last decade. Though pockets of bisexual organizing were visible as early as the 1970s, local groups did not begin connecting regionally and nationally until the mid-1980s. The 1987 March on Washington for Lesbian and Gay Rights [sic] brought bi activists together from across the country, leading us to ask the question: "Are we ready for a national bisexual movement?"[2] In 1990 BiPOL[3] in San Francisco hosted the first National Bisexual Conference, which changed the lives of many bisexuals from Houston to Hamburg who were hungering for a community and a movement. Energized from that momentum, pockets of local organizing crystallized across the country. The conference also paved the way for the first International Bisexual Conference in Amsterdam the following year.

And the crescendo continues: The 1993 March on Washington for Lesbian, Gay, and *Bi* [emphasis mine] Equal Rights and Liberation brought us into a new era of visibility. The victorious inclusion of bisexuals in the march title was actively supported by an unprecedented number of lesbian and gay leaders across the country (Braindrop, 1992). (See also Appendix A, this volume.)

Quietly, in the intervals between these milestone events, bisexuals have been busy organizing at home. College campuses have led the struggle for inclusion within the lesbian and gay community, with scores of queer campus groups adding the "b" word to their names. Bisexual movement hubs such as Seattle, Boston, Minneapolis/St. Paul, Washington, DC, and San Francisco now host dozens of bisexual groups where once there were one or two. Bisexual people are in high demand for speaking engagements, writing projects, and political campaigns. We are the subject of national media attention. In some contexts our presence is even considered a welcome diversity rather than the embarassment it used to be.

WHY A U.S. FOCUS?

Bisexual groups are flourishing around the globe, with a growing sense of international community. Yet as Liz Highleyman notes, bisexuals in many other countries do not base their politics so much on identity, instead forming political affiliations according to ideologies. What is political in one culture cannot be assumed to carry equal weight in another. Many cultures do not politicize their bisexuality. For these reasons, and for the sake of focus, I have limited this book to bisexual politics within the U.S.

A NOTE ON QUEER

Several essays explore the use of the inclusive label "queer" in answer to the problematic, ever-growing laundry list of terms required to describe the sexual minority community. Despite its virtues, however, the word "queer" is not entirely interchangeable with "bisexual, lesbian, gay, and transgender." Moreover, some people use "queer" to hide their biphobia or discomfort with the word "bisexual." Can we embrace the notion of queer community without supporting its use to downplay the term bisexual? While all sexual minorities may have some political and identity issues in common, it is equally important to recognize our differences. There is a value inherent in both: collapsing the labels to seize the power of our unity, as well as appreciating the qualities that distinguish us from one another.

Language is powerful, and even those of us who don't choose the bisexual label have a responsiblity to ensure that the world is safe for those who do. One way to accomplish that goal is to practice saying the word "bisexual." Say it again, "bisexual." Paint it on the walls; wear it on a t-shirt. Write it in toothpaste on your bathroom mirror; notice it as you stare at your beautiful self. Bisexual. Say it louder; say it in public; say it to someone who might not be comfortable hearing it. Let them begin to get over their discomfort. Begin to get over your own. Ask yourself: what *is* it about that word that is so frightening to people? How can we lower the fear content, undo the negative associations, create new meaning, open possibilities?

LOOKING INWARD, OUTWARD, AND FORWARD

The organization of this book follows a principle of self-examination. We begin by looking inward—reflecting on the history and present state of bisexual activism in the United States. Next we look outward, seeking to understand connections between bisexual organizing and that of other communities, and to locate our place within or alongside these movements. Finally, we look forward, creating bisexual political theory that will propel us into a new era of sexual politics.

Section one, *Reflections,* focuses on different segments of our movement in the U.S. The first four essays touch on the recent history and development of a bisexual political movement. The following eight contributors critically examine the ideological trends and political strategies of bisexual activism as we know it.

Section two, *Connections,* gives voice to those bisexuals who are invisible even within our own bisexual communities, or who often find themselves at a crossroads between two or more communities. They are bisexuals, but they are also lesbians, sex workers, people of color, SM dykes, transgendered people, swingers, anarchists, artists. Together, these writers explore the interconnections between bisexual identity and sexual choices, uncover the roots of the painful bisexuality debates within the lesbian community, examine how bisexuals exist within and alongside other communities, and suggest coalition-building strategies.

In Section three, *Directions,* contributors present their visions for the future expansion of sexual and gender politics and for locating bisexuality within the schema of broad-based liberation movements. They propel us beyond identity politics, beyond binary and categorical thinking. Without these old frameworks, we are compelled to invent new models of social, sexual, and political relationships. These essays are testimony to the many ways in which bisexual identity and experience serve as a springboard to cultivate political theory.

ONLY A BEGINNING

This is not a research book. It is a collection of opinions that paints a conceptual picture of bisexual politics, offering insights into various national, local, and individual political agendas for bisexuals. That is why you are holding before you an anthology of ideas that both complement and contradict one another. In this great entity we call our "movement," there is plenty of room for different philosophies and tactics. We do not all share the same goals. We do not even share the same definitions of bisexuality!

How, then, can we define bisexual politics? Not a simple question. Each potential contributor to this anthology submitted a brief "definition" of bisexual politics. It came as no surprise that those 70 people conceived of bisexual politics in 70 uniquely different ways.

Just as we are not a homogenous group of people, we are not a monolithic movement. This book will have accomplished its mission if it incites critical thinking, inspires dialogue and action. As you read through these pages, you may be challenged, joyful, angry. You may find words that move you, ideas that sing to your experience, stories that resonate deeply in your soul. You may also find words that do not speak to you, that offend you, that upset the balance of your visions, that are in opposition to your strongest beliefs. Revel in what nourishes you; seriously question what doesn't. Let your passions move you to action.

NOTES

1. Emma Goldman was one of the first 20th-century women to advocate for freedom of sexuality for all, and to critique the institution of marriage as a form of women's sexual slavery. She is quoted here in Alix Kates Shulman's "Was My Life Worth Living?" (1972).

2. National Bisexual Network flyer, designed by Boston Bisexual Women's Network activists Lucy Friedland and Liz Nania (See Hutchins and Ka'ahumanu, p. 364).

3. BiPOL, the first bisexual political action group, formed in 1983 in the San Francisco Bay Area.

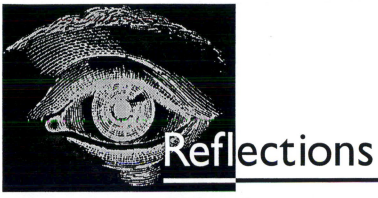

Reflections

A Look

in the Mirror

OVERVIEW

Susanna Trnka with Naomi Tucker

Spirituality which inspires activism and, similarly, politics which move the spirit—which draw from the deep-seated place of our greatest longings for freedom—give meaning to our lives.

—Cherríe Moraga, 1983

Wandering through a bookstore the other day, I came across a book that chronicles images of "life rituals" from around the world. Overflowing with photographs of various "rites of passage" —births, deaths, weddings, and even a few divorces—it included a single shot of a "gay wedding": two young white men kissing on the steps of San Francisco's City Hall. Obviously these two men don't *represent* homosexuality; many other images could do just as well or better. But this photo is at least *recognizable* as a "gay couple."

Could the photographer have captured a "bisexual wedding" on film? A "bisexual family," or a "bisexual political movement"? Or is bisexuality too young an identity to elicit such cultural images? Perhaps bisexuality is simply too complex to be portrayed by a single image? Bisexuality challenges our monosexual culture's assumption that sexuality can be identified by appearance, or by the gender of one's partners. So what kinds of images can we create for ourselves?

We begin our exploration of bisexual politics with reflections on the history and present state of bisexual organizing, known collectively as "the bisexual movement." This first section of the book contains both critical self-examination and proud recognition of our accomplishments, offering various explanations for where we have come from and assessments of where we are today. We celebrate milestones in bisexual visibility, remember the things we have done well, learn from our mistakes, hopefully develop new strategies and insights. These essays are a cross section of what we have done and what we have yet to accomplish.

Reflections is divided into two sections, the first documenting selections of bisexual history and the second analyzing the bisexual movement today.

A TASTE OF HISTORY

A complete history of bisexual politics would inevitably require its own volume. We have selected the work of four pioneering bi activists as samples, each chosen with particular intent: the first for its concise overview of our political roots; the next two for their unique personal stories from a mostly forgotten period of bi history; and the last for its historical importance in propelling bisexual visibility into a new era in the 1990s.

Anthropology and history document centuries of bisexual behavior across different cultures. Rather than attempting to resurrect the experiences of people long gone and define their identities in a context that is not theirs, we begin this story of bisexual politics in the U.S. from the perspective of the first bisexuals who organized around their identity as distinct from heterosexual and homosexual identities.

The roots of bisexual politics can be traced to feminism, lesbian activism, the Black Civil Rights movement, and the sexual liberation movement, as documented by the work of Amanda Udis-Kessler. The personal chronicles of Stephen Donaldson and David Lourea vividly reinforce that history, recounting the development of bisexual communities in the 1960s and 1970s on the East and West Coasts, respectively.

The early 1970s saw the first public claiming of the bisexual label to promote acceptance and visibility of bisexuals. In 1972 the

National Bisexual Liberation Group was founded in New York City; Chicago and San Francisco followed with bi groups founded in the mid- to late-1970s. The focus of this early activism ranged from challenging society's sexual stereotypes and combatting homophobia, to creating bisexual social spaces and fighting for recognition in the gay/lesbian community. In the late 1980s bisexual activism blossomed, with hundreds of new groups springing up in major cities and on college campuses everywhere.

Several key national events propelled bisexual organizing and visibility to new heights. The 1987 March on Washington for Lesbian and Gay Civil Rights motivated bisexual activists in Boston and San Francisco to create a national network. With the idea of holding a meeting to solidify the National Bisexual Network (later to become BiNet USA), BiPOL in San Francisco then organized the first national conference in 1990.

The conference mobilized 454 bisexuals nationwide to come out in pride. Participants took the energy inspired by the conference back to their local groups, which resulted in the formation of regional networks and a multitude of bisexual groups. Today there are bisexual gatherings for every interest under the sun, from specific ethnic, age, spiritual, recovery, professional, or political affiliations to bisexual ballroom dancers, science fiction fans, parents, and performance artists. It is significant to note that the bicoastal bias of bisexual organizing shifted in the late 1980s to early 1990s with the visibility and recognition of groups between the coasts, in states as diverse as Colorado, Indiana, Nebraska, New Mexico, Ohio, and Texas.

Bisexuals were instrumental in planning both the 1993 March on Washington for Lesbian, Gay, and Bi Equal Rights and Liberation, and the 1994 "Stonewall 25" celebration, the events in New York City commemorating the twenty-fifth anniversary of the Stonewall rebellion. The 1993 March was a major milestone in bi history for several reasons: the inclusion of "bi" in the title, the ways our struggle for inclusion fostered friendships and alliances with lesbian and gay activists, the subsequent national visibility of bisexuality, the numbers of bisexual people who marched because they felt included for the first time, and the outreach to heterosexually–identified bisexuals. And we had a bisexual speaker on the main stage—Lani Ka'ahumanu—whose passionate call to unity we include in this book.

A vital seed of bisexual organizing has come from college and university campuses, with strong lesbian/bi/gay coalitions as well as specifically bi-focused organizations and social groups. The resources, small community size, atmosphere of tolerance, and relatively privileged status of college communities all make bisexual organizing—both independently and in coalition with lesbian/gay groups—easier on campus than off.

Campus organizing has been pivotal to our movement in many ways. As Stephen Donaldson notes, student groups initiated some of the earliest bi activism. Campuses have bred a new generation of bisexual activists; they have brought bi groups to rural areas. Inside the classroom bisexuals are taking charge of defining their own experience, introducing bisexuality into academia. To date three universities have offered courses on bisexuality, with more in the planning stages.[1]

Far exceeding the pace of bisexual inclusion in the queer community at large, campus activism—along with other youth organizing—has opened doors for bisexual visibility nationwide. So-called "gay" student unions have experienced a relatively quick but often painful facelift, realigning with their lesbian, bisexual, transgender, and questioning members. Increasing numbers of campus queer organizations and youth groups now include bisexual in their names or have names which do not list specific words, such as "Alternative Sexualities at Swarthmore [AS IS]." This proliferation of inclusive groups is popularizing the "b" word, decreasing the lesbian/gay community's discomfort with the word itself as well as with the idea of bisexuality. In many parts of the country, campuses host the only bi or bi-inclusive group in the area. Most important, college campus and youth activism have created environments in which young people can come out—as bisexual, lesbian, gay, transgendered, or however they may define themselves—into a community of support that embraces, validates, and mirrors their experience.

ASSESSING THE STATE OF OUR MOVEMENT

As our movement expands exponentially, bisexuals are taking a necessary look at the institutions we develop and how they may or may not represent us. Liz Highleyman begins with a survey of bisexual organizing strategies, analyzing different strands of our movement. Laura Perez and Loraine Hutchins focus on mainstream bi organizing, examining ways to make those groups and their leadership more reflective of bisexual diversity.

In addition to specifically bi-focused agendas, bisexual activists have always been involved in broader political struggles. We have taken to the streets to protest homophobic legislation, government ignorance of AIDS, the reproductive rights backlash, U.S. military intervention abroad, and many other issues. Many of the essays underscore this progressive history, and point to ways in which bisexuals can direct their activism. For instance, Sharon Gonsalves and Elias Farajajé-Jones press the imperative of HIV/AIDS education and prevention. Tamara Bower argues for bisexual women to steer clear of possible political cooptation in coalitions with bisexual and gay men, refocusing instead on feminist politics.

Politics are inherently personal. As Indigo Som notes, we each craft our self-identity and choose words to describe ourselves according to our cultural and personal histories. The bisexual community, she writes, should be a safe haven that honors the fluidity of sexual identity. A place where people can choose the labels that fit them best—or choose no labels at all—without fear of losing the community they call home.

Bisexual politics is not just about the formation of bi organizations, classes, and conferences. It is also the history of conversations and longing glances; of sex, love, speeches, and demonstrations. Ultimately, we will each find our home in the place where we see our own reflection, mirrored in the very faces that challenge and embrace us.

NOTE

1. For syllabi and other information on university courses on bisexuality, contact either the Bisexual Resource Center, P.O. Box 639, Cambridge, MA 02140; or Robyn Ochs, P.O. Box 391611, Cambridge, MA 02139.

Part A

A Taste of History

. . . And the time came when the risk of remaining closed in a bud was more painful than the risk it took to blossom.

—Anaïs Nin, 1903-1977

Identity/Politics:
A History of the Bisexual Movement

Amanda Udis-Kessler

One muggy Spring evening in 1988, I sat in an Oberlin College Lesbian/Gay Union meeting and wondered why we were arguing over changing the name and the charter of the LGU to include bisexuals.[1] I had been a fairly active member of the LGU throughout my time at Oberlin, arranging a homophobia conference, serving as one of the first round of HIV test counselors, and helping to organize the Oberlin contingent for the 1987 March on Washington for Gay and Lesbian Rights. I had gotten arrested at the following Supreme Court civil disobedience with three other Obies, two of whom had at one point also identified as bisexual. Half of the regular LGU members in the room during this argument were bisexual. I was surprised and disheartened by the anger, fear, and resentment I heard on the part of some lesbians and gay men. The change finally did go through, leaving bitter feelings in its wake.

Today, I wonder about different questions. Instead of asking why the charter and name change was so difficult for lesbians and gay men, I have come to ask why the change was so important for those of us in the room who were bisexual. Or rather, I ask how lesbian/gay resistance and bisexual insistence are related to each other, and to larger social trends. The debate that Spring evening turned out to be merely a microcosm of a much larger set of trends affecting not just bisexuals in college lesbian/gay groups, but lesbian and gay communities around the country, feminism, sexual values, and even progressive political strategies. My goal in this essay is to situate the bisexual movement in its proper context, to locate it within this set of trends, and to understand how we arrived at our current status.

Part of my job as a sociologist is to refuse to take things for granted, and that must include both my own sexual identity and the

movement which I have come to call my own. There is no obvious
reason why the bisexual movement and the bisexual identity that
fuels it should exist *now* at this point in history, or why it should be
so important to some of us. Post-Stonewall lesbian and gay groups
got along fine for more than a decade without bisexuals insisting on
inclusion, and bisexuals presumably got along fine during that period without seeking it. What has happened in the past five years,
ten years, twenty years that caused some of us to become so invested, not just in our bisexual identity, but in the process of politicizing it? Given that the bisexual movement clearly owes its existence to lesbian/gay liberation and to feminism, we need to ask what
shifts in the social institutions, psychic lives, and systems of meaning within the lesbian and gay communities made our identity and
our movement not only possible but necessary. And we cannot
ignore the matrix of feminism within which lesbians and bisexual
women have come to differentiate ourselves from each other and to
contest the meaning of "real" woman-loving-woman identification. Ironically, we will see that a number of the strategies later used
by bisexuals to the annoyance of lesbians and gay men were derived
from lesbian-feminism or from choices made by the gay community.

The story I want to relate here is, like a good soap opera,
grounded in drama, basic social dilemmas, and, as C. Wright Mills
(1954, p. 9) put it, the intersection of history and biography. As I
was marching through Washington, DC with the Oberlin contingent
in 1987, I did not know that somewhere within the more than
500,000 marchers was the first ever nationally organized contingent
of bisexuals, nor did I know that this march would be considered a
turning point for the growth of a politicized bisexual movement,
that it would lead to the first national bisexual conference in 1990,
the first international bisexual conference in 1991, and the 1993
March on Washington for Lesbian, Gay, and Bi Equal Rights and
Liberation.[2]

What currents, tensions, compromises, and hopes brought us to
this point? Take the dance of solidarity and perceived betrayal
within feminism; add in the divisions between the values of culture
and community, liberation and freedom; mix liberally with debates
over allegiance versus membership, lesbian-feminism versus queer-

dom; situate the entire concoction within the context of increasingly fragmentary identity politics; and we begin to understand the stories, the stakes, and the priorities of bisexual activists—and of the feminist, lesbian, and gay communities with whom we are engaged in our uneasy tango.

There are many points where we could begin our story, but it seems to me that going back pre-Stonewall does not add much information or clear context. The word "bisexual" existed before Stonewall, and there were people who lived as bisexuals, even famous ones at times. However, the focus on bisexuality as a core aspect of one's identity does not seem to have arisen in any patterned way until after Stonewall. We may as well start, then, with the early 1970s.

The gay movement, heady with the sense of liberation following Stonewall, could afford to be utopian, and pronounced the goal of "free[ing] the homosexual in everyone" (Adam, 1987, p. 78). Gay theorist Dennis Altman argued that the gay movement would bring "the end of the homosexual" because "gay liberation will succeed as its *raison d'être* disappears" (Altman, 1971, p. 225). Such language and priorities created a climate in which bisexuality was not particularly problematized, though the only people calling themselves bisexual at that point were swingers and free love advocates. If you notice that I have not mentioned lesbians thus far, that's because many of them left the gay movement fairly early on in frustration over gay male sexism and turned to the burgeoning feminist movement (Faderman, 1991, ch. 8).

As it turns out, shifts in feminism explain much of bisexual history, which will turn out for the most part to be bisexual women's history. It is an often remarked upon fact among bisexual activists that many bisexual activists are women who formerly identified as lesbian feminists, that bisexual women's groups often have mailing lists ten times the size of bisexual men's groups, and that tensions between lesbian and bisexual women are understood as much more problematic than tensions between gay and bisexual men. To a large extent, these differences reflect the way lesbianism was politicized within feminism, such that a culture arose with clearly delineated norms of acceptability, norms which bisexual women—by definition—broke. Gay male culture did not become nationally politicized until the advent of AIDS, and life before AIDS in the baths and discos, at the bar or the opera, did not exclude bisexual men in the same way that lesbian space came to exclude bisexual women. When I talk about lesbian versus gay culture below, then, it needs to be clear how different the two were in the 1970s.

Let me begin by setting the stage of feminism.[3] The women's movement developed through women's experiences of sexism in Left political organizations at the end of the 1960s; radical feminist groups such as Cell 16 and Redstockings emerged at the beginning of the 1970s as the theoretical and intellectual wing of feminism. It is particularly important to understand that the earliest of these groups offered theories of patriarchy and resistance which belittled lesbianism as a personal cop-out to a political problem. Cell 16 called for celibacy, while Redstockings acknowledged that most women were in heterosexual relationships and claimed that such relationships should be the site of struggle. There were serious questions as to whether lesbians could be good feminists. Lesbian feminist groups such as Radicalesbians and the Furies turned the tables, arguing that lesbianism was a political choice indicating the willingness to prioritize women over men, and as such was exactly what feminism needed. Ti-Grace Atkinson had proposed that "feminism is a theory, lesbianism is a practice"; this aphorism spread in a slightly, but crucially, different form: "feminism is *the* theory, lesbianism is *the* practice." Over time, this idea was adopted among lesbian feminists, and came to permeate feminist culture to such an extent that it was questioned whether heterosexual women could be good feminists.

This early phenomenon of contestation over the sexual identity proper to true, real feminism had a number of unfortunate consequences. It led to a lesbian-heterosexual rift within feminism which, in large part, has never healed (Abbott and Love, 1978, chs. 5, 6; Weeks, 1985, p. 202; Wolf, 1980, ch. 2). Perhaps more pertinent to our story, it set up an understanding that feminism was dependent in some way upon sexual practices. I am not arguing that sexual practices ought to be exempt from critical examination and change if they serve to uphold sexist standards.[4] However, over time, one consequence of problematizing this most intimate form of personal behavior was resentment and resistance against what was perceived, ironically, as a form of social control. It was much less problematic for certain lifelong lesbians to adopt feminism as true to their experiences than it was for formerly heterosexual women to strive to become lesbians in order to be good feminists. For, as it turned out, the claim that feminists should be lesbians ultimately won the debate, sending some heterosexual feminists off toward more mainstream work and leaving some newly-identified lesbians within radical feminism. These particular lesbians represented a new trend in the relationship between desire and politics. Before second-wave feminism, homosexual desire generally led to a homosexual identity and whatever degree of political affiliation seemed appropriate. Within radical feminism, however, the expectation arose that a woman's political commitment could, and should, lead to her sexual desire for other women. This expectation is probably the single historical factor most responsible for the way that bisexual feminism was ultimately to define itself.

Another crucial trend within lesbian-feminism was the growth of women's culture in the early and mid-1970s. Feminism did not merely represent values and behaviors; it came to involve goods, services, artistic and intellectual work, and other cultural elements, often in places designated as women-only (Faderman, 1991, ch. 9; Phelan, 1989; Wolf, 1980, chs. 3-4). The rise of women's culture has a great deal to do with a shift from radical to cultural feminism, an account of which would take us too far afield. However, the place of women's culture, the growth of women's community in a geographical and cultural sense, becomes important down the line when lesbians would defend what they defined as theirs against bisexuals, claiming that the difference between lesbian feminism and bisexuality was the difference between a way of life, a political commitment, an entire culture, on the one hand, and a set of sexual practices on the other.[5] While lesbian culture did—and does—exist outside of feminism, as best represented by lesbian bars, these bars were not the arena of contestation; rather, women's bookstores, cultural spaces, artistic and intellectual gatherings would turn out to be the more problematic areas. These were acquiring deep significance in the early to mid-1970s. On a more individual level, lesbian feminists began to live out their political values more explicitly as a set of cultural norms. Today, Allison Bechdel's *Dykes to Watch Out*

For character Mo represents the personification of what she calls the lesbian feminist monoculture, a term I will use below. The seeds of this monoculture were sown by the mid-1970s.

During this period of gay male utopianism and lesbian feminist construction of community norms, bisexuals were not doing much, at least not in an organized way. The free love scene was in full blossom in a number of cities. Early social-only groups started forming in the mid-1970s; 1975 saw the formation of the Bisexual Forum in New York City, 1976 the inauguration of the San Francisco Bisexual Center. By "social-only," I mean that these groups were not political in their orientation; San Francisco, which later boasted some of the earliest political activism, was content at this point to speak of the need to recognize and value the natural androgyny of people. In a sense, there was a set of cultural values in place that might have been politicized, but the overwhelming theme among these early bisexual organizations was human freedom and potential, a clear recall of early gay liberation statements.

By the time bisexual organizations were making these statements publicly, however, the gay liberation movement had turned from human potential to gay consumerism amidst the growth of "urban villages" known as gay ghettos and the rise of businesses created to serve the gay community specifically (Adam, 1987, pp. 99-100; Altman, 1982, ch. 3; Epstein, 1990, p. 256; Levine, 1979a; Weeks, 1985, pp. 198-200). Altman's "end of the homosexual," mentioned earlier, could wait; for now, the priority was the pleasure and paycheck of the homosexual qua homosexual. Indeed, the sedimenting of gay male identity reached a new level with the rise of the clone look; not only had gay men adopted an "ethnic" self-identity as an oppressed minority group, but they also began to cultivate an ethnic chic. I do not mean to imply that gay culture was a new phenomenon in the mid-to-late 1970s, but there were clear ways in which gay culture and community, like lesbian culture and community, solidified during this time. Gay ghettos expanded and became considerably more visible following Stonewall, as thousands of gay men flocked to the coasts or, to a lesser extent, the major midwest cities, in search of community. Moreover, there was an explosion of academic research on gay men during this period which drew upon sociological and anthropological models in studying the gay male world. The writing generated during this time both encouraged and disseminated gay culture, and became a part of it.[6] Memories of earlier culture, and valuations of culture in process, took on a more explicit and political tone during this time, so that some gay men, like many lesbians, would later point to their achievements and ask what bisexuals had done in comparison.

Common wisdom has it that gay men in the 1970s were apolitical, focused on pleasure rather than changing the world. There is an important sense in which this notion is wrong, a sense directly connected to the later political claims of bisexuals. For it can be argued that what gay men were engaging in was a form of identity politics, a political strategy based on the celebration of one's distinct minority status, an assertive flaunting and reclamation of those very aspects of oneself for which one is disenfranchised [see Donaldson, this volume]. This way of engaging in political protest often involves being rather than doing, as in being oneself in an "in your face" way. Identity politics is, of course, much more complex than this brief description can begin to indicate, but perhaps even these few comments shed some light on the bisexual claim to political status. I will return to that claim later.

By 1978, the year that Chicago's Bi-Ways was founded, the definition of lesbianism had shifted somewhat. The cultural norms had solidified; proper dykes would not be caught dead in a dress, a Burger King, an MBA program—or in bed with a man. At the end of the 1970s, rather than being a woman-loving woman, a lesbian was a woman who did not sleep with men. Of course, some lesbians *did* sleep with men, and those who did kept this fact about themselves hidden. They were not newcomers to the fold; some had been lesbian-identified for five years or more. Many had been heterosexual prior to the women's movement and had come out as lesbians in the context of the lesbian feminist community and the subtle or not-so-subtle cultural pressure to be a lesbian. While these women did not come to love women grudgingly, they did not necessarily cease to be attracted to men; they simply stopped acting on the attractions, or began to hide the fact that they were acting on them. However, such secrecy was ripe for a new political analysis. Women in this situation in the late 1970s and early 1980s had a language to describe the discomfort, fear, and pain they felt, and it was the language of the closet.

Let me be very clear about what happened here: women who had grown up heterosexual and had come to lesbianism through feminism and through the idea that lesbianism could be a political choice began to apply insights developed by life-long lesbians and gay men about hiding a disapproved-of sexuality, and they applied it to their heterosexuality. Because they were deeply tied to lesbian feminist communities and had been for some years, their earlier societal norms of heterosexuality had essentially been replaced with the cultural norms of lesbianism. They began to experience the dictates of the lesbian feminist monoculture, especially its sexual dictates, as oppressive, and to ask whether both the lesbian/gay and heterosexual "communities" had equal social control over them. In one sense, this is surely a ridiculous question; feminist and lesbian-feminist analysis, such as that of Adrienne Rich, showed clearly that the social institution of heterosexuality was both compulsory and deeply damaging to women. Yet while these women knew the arguments of feminism where men were concerned and could debate them intellectually, they also knew that their desires for—or love of—certain men exerted an influence on them with which cognitive arguments and political theory simply could not compete.

Such "lesbians who fell in love with men" were in a bind, wanting desperately to remain within the community they had called their own for a number of years, sometimes having cut themselves off from heterosexual society with lesbian writing, music, or other cultural creations, yet unable to deny their politically devalued attractions to men. Such women would soon, or ultimately, become the leaders of the political bisexual movement: as they "came out" as bisexual; as they were castigated for doing so; as they reclaimed pride in their sexuality in ways taught to them, ironically, by lesbian-feminism and the gay movement. In 1980, the year the New York and Chicago bisexual social groups peaked in popularity, a lesbian activist in San Francisco went public with her relationship with a man and quietly initiated the process that led us to where we are today. In 1982, she ran an article in a Bay Area women's paper calling for bisexuals to become a political force within the women's movement (Ka'ahumanu, 1982); in 1984, she and a small group of bisexuals began engaging in the kind of guerilla theater now favored by Queer Nation; and in 1987, she wrote a piece on bisexuality for the March on Washington civil disobedience handbook that I read and pondered while preparing to get arrested.

Lesbians critical of bisexual demands have framed the problem as the bisexual desire to invade or infiltrate lesbian space, but hopefully it's now clear that for many bisexual women, there was no question of invasion; we had been a genuine part of lesbian feminism, and our call for explicit inclusion as bisexuals was meant to rectify what we perceived as an injustice of silencing. That this form of silencing was defined as so problematic indicated the effect that identity politics was having on these women, who had come to understand their situation as a political injustice, and the naming and claiming of their bisexual identity as a political act. And, in a way, this is not surprising: having focused for years on creating a political lesbian identity that played a crucial role in self-understanding, these women had in effect been resocialized to understand their sexual identity as core and as inherently political.

Elsewhere, "gaydom" was rapidly becoming "lesbian/gaydom." Lesbian cartoonist Allison Bechdel, as it turns out, was a member of the "Oberlin College Gay Union" in the late 1970s. Clearly, there were women in the various "gay organizations" of the 1970s, but this distinction became more explicit with the move to include the word "lesbian" in the titles of many gay organizations in the early 1980s, heralding a period of less separation by gender. This shift did not happen on all fronts. The debates between lesbians and gay men over gay male pornography, and over the display and valuing of male sexuality more generally, were rocking along in the early 1980s, with extraordinary amounts of anger and frustration on both sides. Lesbian communities were still separated in many ways from "the gay community," but there began to be more women in "the gay community" wanting recognition as women; a number of organizations, from college groups to the National Gay Task Force, changed their names (and, where relevant, charters) to clarify the valued place of women through inclusive language. This shift toward inclusivity, and the reconnection of women and men in lesbian/gaydom, were to have an impact on the sense of possibilities considered by the bisexual movement several years later (when, for example, Boston's bisexual community created a mixed-gender network in 1991, Biversity, in addition to its traditionally separate men's and women's networks).

Yet bisexual organizing in the early 1980s, like feminist organizing ten years earlier, was primarily a task undertaken by women. As the 1970s bisexual social groups began to fail—New York and Chicago in 1983, San Francisco in 1984—bisexual women were beginning to organize groups for support and social events, groups which would soon turn more explicitly "political" around the issue of including bisexuals within the lesbian/gay community. The Boston Bisexual Women's Network, the Chicago Action Bi-Women, and San Francisco's BiPOL formed in 1983, the Seattle Bisexual Women's Network in 1986. These groups were all composed of explicitly feminist women, in many cases "hasbians" (ex-lesbians). It is interesting to notice that the Boston group formed partly in response to an ad run in a Boston gay paper as a joke, advising lesbians to acquire "bisexual insurance" so they would not be burned when bisexual women left them for men. Yet bisexual feminist groups did not merely organize in response to such attacks, or even simply to defend their feminism. They also felt an absence of separate space and resented the advances of men in bisexual social groups, advances which seemed no less sexist coming from bisexuals. In a sense, the feminist networks were necessary, given that many bisexually-identified women came out of feminism, while many bisexual men at this point came from swinger scenes; the early to mid-1980s saw a recapitulation of both the male-female split in the Left, and the lesbian/gay-male split after Stonewall. These early bisexual feminists were also very conscious of the lesbian/heterosexual split within feminism in the 1970s, and tried to work out ways of living a commitment to feminism without excluding men from their beds or drawing rigid lines dividing their personal and political lives.

As bisexual women were trying to re-imagine ways of explicitly connecting feminism and their relations with (or capacity for relations with) men, the lesbian monoculture was losing ground; the cultural norms defining the real, true lesbians were not holding (Faderman, 1991, chs. 10-11; Phelan, 1989). Some lesbians were voting for Reagan, playing the stock market, or joining other lesbians at Boston Quality Women power lunches; some lesbians were buying sex toys, joining s/m groups, and subscribing to the sex magazine *On Our Backs,* and some lesbians—including cultural heroes Holly Near (Wofford, 1991, p. 37) and Jan Clausen (Clausen, 1990)—were getting involved with men. Put simply, the unified identity required (or thought to be required) by the monoculture was too monolithic, too uniform, to be tenable for a number of women. The exodus and fragmenting of the monoculture, with the extraordinary amount of betrayal involved, caused incredible pain for women who remained within lesbian feminism, pain that was dealt with in part through anger at the growing bisexual movement and its intrusion into lesbian cultural space. If most gay men have not been troubled by bisexuality because they didn't understand how it could pose a political threat to them (with the significant exception of some men deeply invested in gay culture), lesbians have been troubled precisely because they have understood the political threat involved. Nor have the lesbians been wrong in this instance; the bisexual movement really has represented a recasting of priorities in politicizing sexuality, and more importantly, in organizing community.

Thus far, I have primarily set the stage for the period of time in which the bisexual movement would truly take off: the late 1980s. By 1987, it became clear that there was considerably more interest in bisexuality than had earlier been surmised. Two new networks formed that year, one in Philadelphia, one in San Francisco. No longer were new members primarily feminist ex-lesbians. In San Francisco, Washington, DC, and New York, for example, an increasing number of sex-radical men and women became involved in bisexual groups. Some of the sex radicals were old free-love advocates, ex-hippies, or ex-feminists. A younger crowd also began to appear around this time, with some groups consisting almost equally of men and women, depending on the city. There began to be a greater interest in social events as networks became more mixed by gender, leading to "bi-friendly" groups and gatherings. The sex radicals also brought with them an explicitly political account of bisexuality, drawing from identity politics and anarchist writings. As the groups grew and were able to garner more publicity (due in part, ironically, to disastrous mainstream media coverage of bisexual men as AIDS vectors), more people joined, spanning a range of ages, political affiliations, and ideas for community direction. AIDS touched the networks, politicizing some previously inactive members.

The call for bisexuals to attend the October 1987 March on Washington was a success, setting off a number of new priorities within the movement, which was now beginning to look somewhat more like a movement. One focus which particularly picked up steam after the march was a form of bisexual activism strongly influenced by identity politics in general and the tactics of ACT UP in particular. The word "biphobia" had been used as early as 1982 (Ka'ahumanu, 1982); now it became a rallying cry as bisexual activists in newly formed bi-political groups (in New York, Chicago, Boston, and elsewhere) adopted a much more aggressive stance on visibility and inclusion of bisexuals, whether in AIDS information packets, college organizations, media coverage, or titles of national marches. The well-cultivated anger of bisexual feminists, bisexual AIDS activists, and a range of other bi-identified people, found its expression in a concerted effort to change names, charters, and other "exclusive" aspects of lesbian and gay institutions. These efforts have had a great deal of success from the perspective of bisexuals, but have increasingly alienated some lesbians and gay men, a point to which I will return later.

Another effect of the 1987 March on Washington was the sense of power bisexuals experienced walking with dozens of other bisexuals from around the country. This led organizers in a number of cities to envision a national bisexual network. After two years of work, in June 1990, activists convened the first national bisexual conference in San Francisco and formed a national network. The conference showed clearly how many people found their bisexuality to be an important matter; close to five hundred people managed to get to San Francisco and attend. The last day of the conference, June 23, was proclaimed "Bisexual Pride Day" by the San Francisco Board of Supervisors, and it seemed the bisexual movement had truly arrived.

Since that time, the movement has sought legitimacy in academic realms; bisexual studies courses have been taught at three universities (the University of California at Berkeley, MIT, and Tufts), and papers on bisexuality have been included in the major lesbian/gay studies conferences in the U.S. Bisexuals also turned to queerdom, finding affinity in the norms of androgyny, genderfuck, and "in your face" politics among a decidedly mixed-gender group of people.[7] Other bisexuals began or continued work toward the goal of a diverse but unified sexual minority community, the "lesbigay" community, joining lesbian/gay speakers' bureaus or starting bisexual speakers' bureaus to educate people about homophobia and biphobia.

Yet if some elements of the lesbian/gay/queer community have been welcoming to bisexuals, others have been decidedly more hesitant. Early in 1991, the queer New York journal *OutWeek* ran a cover article (Wofford, 1991) on "the bisexual revolution," asking whether bisexuals were "deluded closet cases or vanguards of the movement." And tensions between lesbians and bisexual women have remained problematic, focusing on contested definitions of whose community it is anyway, and who gets to count as lesbian, or gay, or as politically oppressed because of their sexuality. There have been extraordinary tensions over the Northampton, Massachusetts, Pride March since 1989 (Porter-Lara and McMaster, 1992; Young, this volume), and the Spring 1992 cover story of the national lesbian/gay journal *OUT/LOOK* asked "What do Bisexuals Want?" featuring (unsurprisingly) an article skeptical of the bisexual movement by a lesbian feminist (Wilson, 1992), and a personal account of the pain of growing up bisexual by a bi activist and writer (Queen, 1992).

Here we are, then, at a point of increasing bi-identification, working well with segments of the lesbian/gay/queer community and fighting constantly with other segments. I have tried to indicate some of the ways in which the current importance of bisexual identity, and the current presence of the bisexual movement, have their roots in feminism and lesbian/gay liberation, as well as why lesbian and gay communities occupy such a paradoxical role in the collective psyche of strongly bi-identified people. I hope that those of us in this movement can continue to wrestle with the problems and opportunities offered by remaining within, even if sometimes opposed to, this larger feminist and sexual minority community. For it is not just the source of our existence and power; it does not only have an effect on *us*. We, too, have an effect. We, too, have a valuable role to play in working toward the end of oppression on the basis of sex and sexuality.

NOTES

1. This chapter was first presented as a paper at Oberlin College on April 10, 1992. It draws on several earlier writings of mine (Udis-Kessler, 1990b, 1991b).

2. The following resources provided much of the information on the rise of the bisexual movement and its present trends: Barr, 1985; Hutchins and Ka'ahumanu, 1991, pp. 216-222; Ka'ahumanu, 1991; Margolis, 1991; Mishaan, 1985; Rubenstein and Slater, 1985; Sheiner, 1991; Tait, 1991; Weise, 1991.

3. This section of the chapter draws primarily on Echols, 1989 and Faderman, 1991, ch. 8.

4. In fact, elsewhere (Udis-Kessler, 1992) I have argued that our sexual practices represent a crucial locus of change, especially those of heterosexual and bisexual women involved with men.

5. The ways in which "women's communities" turned out to be resources for white women only has been addressed by Audre Lorde (1984).

6. Time constraints have kept me from including many examples of this writing, but two examples might be Levine, 1979 and Murray, 1979.

7. Coverage of "queerdom" is drawn in part from the *OUT/LOOK* Winter 1991 "Queer Nation" articles (Bérubé and Escoffier, 1991; Chee, 1991; Colson, 1991; Maggenti, 1991).

The Bisexual Movement's Beginnings in the 70s: A Personal Retrospective

Stephen Donaldson

Today the bisexual movement is commonly and erroneously thought to have begun in the mid- and late 1980s. Its history, however, actually goes back to a lively bisexual liberation movement which sprang up in the early 1970s, thrived in mid-decade, then stagnated and came close to extinction before reviving in the 1980s.

As one of the founders of that movement, I am concerned that the pioneering insights and achievements of those early years—almost all of them still relevant to the 1990s—not be lost. The period certainly deserves a thorough, carefully researched historical analysis, and it is my hope that someone will undertake that task, which is currently beyond my resources. Meanwhile, I have written this account based on the two sources which are immediately accessible to me: my own memory and the surviving contents of my personal 1970s files on bisexuality.[1]

How does a new movement get started? This perplexing question can be approached from the perspective of social history, examining large and impersonal forces that prepare the way. It can also be approached from the perspective of personal history, examining how key individuals were enabled to do what no one had done before. I begin with the latter, in this case autobiographical, approach.

THE PERSONAL JOURNEY

According to some sociologists, gay and lesbian identity is the end product of a socialization process shaped by a pre-existing gay or lesbian subculture and its articulation through the lesbian and gay movement(s). This theory raises the question: how did I arrive at a bisexual identity without a bisexual subculture or movement, and how did that identity lead to a movement?

As I grew into my teens in the early and mid-1960s I discovered, but did not consider unusual, the desire of the boys around me for blowjobs. I might have considered it on a par with my equally singular interest in collecting maps if I hadn't been summarily thrown out of the Scouts at age 12, a traumatic and totally unexpected rejection which taught me that giving blowjobs (but not getting them—the other boys weren't disciplined) was unacceptable to adults (including my parents) and had to be concealed.

At 18, however, I fell in love with a baseball teammate, and my casual sexual play with boys was transformed into a very serious matter which could dominate my whole life. I talked with a few trusted adults about it, and learned that if I loved another boy I had to be a "homosexual." (The sole dissenter was my coach, who told me I just hadn't met the right girl yet.) I could only find two books on the subject, which confirmed this label, and mentioned the Mattachine Society in New York as an organization of "homosexuals." So on a school expedition to the "wicked city," I slipped away, visited their office, and became a member (swearing I was 21, since Mattachine was deathly afraid of dealing with minors), thus giving my new identity official status. Then my homosexuality became a family issue, and I ran away from home. The gays of New York welcomed me enthusiastically, offered hospitality, and "brought me out" as a "butch" homosexual (in contrast to the "queens") in 1965.

In the summer of 1966 I fell in love with an extraordinary young woman, JD. On August 8, my diary notes: "How about Bisexual Society of America?" In the course of a year I had fallen head over heels in love with both a male and a female, so I stopped hesitating and began to identify myself as "a bisexual," as I have ever since. JD had enjoyed occasional lesbian encounters, called herself "bisexual," and said, "Why ignore half the world?" She introduced me to the Sexual Freedom League (SFL), led by the bisexual Jefferson "Fuck" Poland, whom I met in 1967. Based in a commune in San Francisco but nationally organized, the Sexual Freedom

League propogated the slogan "If it moves, fondle it," staged some memorable bisexual orgies, and in some ways was a predecessor of the bi movement. While the organization was not explicitly bi (most members identified as heterosexual), the SFL opposed boundaries on sexuality and encouraged experimentation with both genders. Primarily a social organization, the SFL also maintained an activist stance and participated in the sexual debates of the day.

Before encountering the SFL, as a bi-identified sophomore at Columbia I had founded the gay student movement as a vehicle for students of all orientations to combat homophobia.[2] I was heavily involved throughout the rest of the 1960s not only as national leader of the Student Homophile League but also as an elected officer of the North American Conference of Homophile Organizations (NA-CHO) and of its Eastern Regional subsidiary. (NACHO was an umbrella organization which united virtually all the homophile/gay/lesbian organizations on the continent from 1966 to 1970.) I also wrote a regular column for the New York newsmagazine *Gay Power* and occasional reports for the Los Angeles *Advocate.*

I took a lot of flak from the leaders of other homophile organizations for being bi.[3] For a couple of years I was having an affair with Martha Shelley, leader of the New York Daughters of Bilitis and later the Gay Liberation Front. As she described it, "We used to walk into these [homophile movement] meetings arm in arm. It was a scandal . . . but at the same time, because the two of us were so blatant and out there in public being pro gay, they certainly couldn't afford to throw us out" (Marcus, 1992).

Having been elected to NACHO office at the 1968 convention in Chicago, I was invited to appear as part of a small delegation from the convention on a local television show. But numerous delegates objected (unsuccessfully) to a bisexual representing the movement on TV, a then rare opportunity. My growing feeling of discomfort with biphobia in the homophile/gay liberation movement was a major factor in my 1970 decision to leave the movement behind and enlist in the Navy.[4]

After nearly two years as a sailor, I got kicked out for "homosexual involvement," a charge I received shortly after becoming a Buddhist Quaker and thus a pacifist.[5] Bitter at this second homophobic expulsion, which deprived me of the identity I loved more than any other—that of a sailor—and as a bisexual no longer feeling comfortable with the gay liberation movement, I found myself in June, 1972, attending the annual Friends (Quaker) General Conference (FGC)[6] in Ithaca, New York; its theme for the year was "Where Should Friends Be Pioneering Now?"

Contemplating that question, I organized an impromptu workshop on bisexuality and was astonished to find 130 Quakers, one of every ten General Conference attendees, overflowing into five meeting rooms and an auditorium for two days of lively discussion based more on experience than on abstract theories. Finally I was surrounded by bisexually-identified F/friends, formally considering the topic of bisexuality. Thus identity led me to activism.

This group adopted by consensus the "Ithaca Statement on Bisexuality" containing four queries to Friends everywhere. The fourth query asked, "Are Friends aware of their own tendency to falsely assume that any interest in the same sex necessarily indicates an exclusively homosexual orientation, and to further falsely assume that interest in the opposite sex necessarily indicates an exclusively heterosexual orientation?" The statement, which may well be the first public declaration of the bisexual movement, was printed in *Friends Journal* (the FGC monthly), and the *Advocate* (thus announcing bi consciousness to the gay world). It was certainly the first statement on bisexuality issued by an American religious assembly, at a time when the term "bisexuality" itself was still unknown to large numbers of people.

Bi Quakers met again at the next General Conference in Richmond, Indiana. After a series of meetings we decided to form an ongoing organization, the Committee of Friends on Bisexuality (CFB), the first bi religious caucus. I was its Clerk (chair) until 1977, when I left the Quakers.[7] During these years the CFB wrote to the various gay religious caucuses on the sensitive question of oppression of bisexuals by those who upheld an exclusively homosexual identity, but got little response (except from the gay Quakers) beyond exchanges of newsletters.

At the 1974 General Conference in a joint speech with his wife Berit, keynote speaker George Lakey, a leader of the Quaker-based Movement for a New Society, told over a thousand surprised Quakers, "I am a bisexual," and urged them to consider "the bonding power of eros . . . to enable us consciously to foster communities of awareness." John Paul Hudson of New York's Bi-Reach Information Center[8] delivered a speech to a CFB workshop entitled "Bisexuality and Gay Liberation." He dealt mostly with his personal odyssey, but critiqued narrowmindedness in the gay lib movement and sketched out a spiritual vision of bisexuality. Because Hudson had been strongly identified with the gay movement in the past, he, like me, could hardly be accused of taking refuge in a bisexual identity out of inability to deal with homosexuality.

With continuing workshops on different ideologies of bisexuality, such as rejecting the "point of equilibrium" definition of bi as having an exactly equal attraction to either gender, identity politics was already under discussion.

THE 1970s BI LIB MOVEMENT

In the mid-1970s I attended many bisexual events, spoke on panels, wrote articles, and kept in touch with the bi movement in New York, while receiving copies of articles on bisexuality from Quakers in other cities.[9] What follows is largely drawn from papers and clippings in my surviving files.

Bisexuality became "chic" in many circles (peaking in 1974) and was the subject of considerable coverage, often in an envious tone, in the mass media. In May, 1974, both *Time* and *Newsweek* ran stories on "bisexual chic." Helen Lawrenson (1974) wrote that bisexuality was "now the 'in' thing, the stylish, chic, trendy thing to be. The 'heads' who make the scene, the models, the young actresses, the social celebrities, the top pop musicians, the rich hippies, the avant-garde artists—take it for granted that you swing both ways." Most of the extensive media coverage focused on individuals' stories and such bi-accepting clubs as New York's Max's Kansas City, rather than on the new bi lib movement, but there was also considerable discussion of the historical, anthropological, biographical, and psychological dimensions of bisexuality. No doubt many readers exposed to this material decided that they, too, were bisexual.

The generation that came of age in the Psychedelic Sixties played a prime role in the birth of bisexual consciousness. The social historian may speculate as to why this was so. I suggest the following factors:

- The feeling among us was that all sorts of changes, even of the most fundamental nature—but especially changes in consciousness—were not only possible but inevitable.
- The end of the Vietnam War encouraged us to turn our attention to more personal issues (a trend that, alas, finally led to the Me Decade and then the Greed Decade).
- We were inspired by the proud, successful attempts on the part of blacks, women, and homosexuals/lesbians rallying around their own identities, to alter the national consciousness.
- We were dissatisfied with a fundamental shift in the burgeoning gay liberation movement, which emphasized the exclusivist culture of the gay ghetto rather than the previously articulated struggle for the rights of *all* people to engage in same-sex expression.
- The new visibility of homosexuals, and some lesbians, in the mass media, promulgating dualistic concepts of sexual orientation, made bisexuals feel excluded.
- Psychedelics broke down mental boundaries and gave many people a startling awareness of previously repressed gender attractions. The widespread use of psychedelics fostered a favorable attitude toward experimentation, inner exploration, self-discovery, and the debunking of previously accepted concepts. We simply applied these attitudes to our sexuality.

None of this, however, quite explains why bisexuality became chic. Maybe the slow-motion collapse of the criminal Nixon presidency was undermining all the verities; maybe bisexuality offered the mass media a way of approaching gay liberation while giving their heterosexual readers something with which they could identify at least in part. These factors may have motivated the surge of media attention, but do not explain its generally positive tone.

Those of us involved with the 1970s bisexual liberation movement spent a lot of time discussing what bisexuality was. Though never establishing a consensus definition, we tended toward a broad conception. Bisexuality was thought of as a basic capacity to respond erotically and/or emotionally/romantically to either gender, simultaneously or serially, not necessarily in equal measure, but at least enough to make one feel uncomfortable with identification as either heterosexual or homosexual. As far as I can tell, this sense of the term has remained with the movement to the present. Though there is considerable dissatisfaction with the "bisexual" label, no other term has gained wide acceptance.

Demographically, one major difference between the movements of the 1970s and early 1990s is the noticeable preponderance of men in the 1970s, whereas women now outnumber men by far both at the leadership and grass roots levels. The change may reflect how AIDS has decimated the male population and stigmatized bi men as AIDS infectors of the straight majority. The shift also reflects both the growth of lesbian awareness, and a subsequent rejection of lesbian separatism by "lesbians" involved with men.

This imbalance of gender is a problem. Bisexual leadership at all levels must reach out to men, and men in the movement must take responsibility for developing remedies. The intellectual discourse of the bi movement, which often appears to be dominated by "women's issues," must be broadened, or the movement may be perceived by men as primarily a vehicle for arcane intrafeminist controversies.

Much of our discussion in the 1970s involved a critique of homosexual attitudes toward bisexuality, what today we would call biphobia in the lesbian and gay communities. We recognized that the gay (a term which in those days also meant lesbian) movement was fostering an exclusively homosexual identity and promoting the growth of the gay ghetto. They were promoting gay power but alienating bisexuals, and nearly all of us with experience in the gay/lesbian subculture could recount experiences in which our bisexuality was devalued and disbelieved by homosexuals. Louise Knox (1974), describing the reaction of lesbian friends to her bisexuality, wrote, "I am told that what I think I am . . . doesn't exist. For all the credibility I get, I might as well be calling myself a centaur or a mermaid."

The pioneering feminist bisexual writer Kate Millet called bisexuality "the most friendless cause," with bisexuals "resent[ing] their position of double jeopardy, despised by the straight world as merely another species of 'queer' [!!] and dismissed by gay mili-

tants as mere 'swingers,' 'jet setters'—superficial and self-indul-
gent persons whose commitment to homosexuality is inauthentic."
She complained, "We are told to conform or go to hell by homosexual patriots who regard us as half-castes" and likened the position of bis in the "gay cause" to that of "gay women who helped to
build feminism, they were convenient and despised."[10] We often
wondered why there were no "bi bars" or other social sites specifically for bis, though New York and San Francisco certainly had
bi-friendly clubs. We were told that considerable numbers of homosexuals were claiming to be bi in order to escape the greater stigma
of homosexuality, but we seldom encountered such folk at our
gatherings, though we did encounter some self-designated homosexuals who were particularly sexually attracted to bisexuals.

Turning to the heterosexual world, we debated the implications
of bisexuality for marriage and the phenomenon of heterosexuals
(mostly women) claiming to be bi in order to appear liberated,
adventurous, or politically advanced. (Remember, bi was chic in
1974, and lesbian separatism had not yet raised its voice.) The
concept of the "political lesbian" had not yet appeared. Naturally,
we were also aware of how many bisexuals were "passing" as
straight.

In these discussions we were, however, handicapped by our very
parochial conceptual framework, inherited from nineteenth-century
Germans via the psychiatric establishment, which recognizes only
one type of homosexuality. This idea is based on the assumption
that the biological sex of one's partner, rather than the sexual role
practiced or the culturally recognized gender of the partner,[11] is the
most important factor in classifying sexual relationships. This perspective was derived from the Bible and religiously-inspired sod-
omy laws, rather than popular opinion or scientific criteria, and has
been rejected throughout most of European and American history
as well as by most of the world's population today.

Thus we were unable to come to terms with phenomena such as
the "straight trade" male: the guy who considers himself "straight"
and prefers females but is willing to have sex with other males so
long as he remains strictly in the penetrative role. The current U.S./
Western model which classifies sexual orientation by the biological
sex of one's partner would call this behavior "homosexual," or

perhaps "bisexual" by extension of his additional heterosexual activity. But in other models based on sexual role, which have been more influential among working-class Americans tracing their ancestry outside northern Europe, and which guide the conduct of most "straight trade," these same-sex acts are not considered "homosexual." In other cultures (and their American offshoots), penetrative male-to-male sex with a drag queen or a hairless boy is not considered to constitute sex with another "man" since both queen and boy are labeled "not-men." If there is no "homosexuality" there can be no "bisexuality" on the part of such a man.

In some ways we were bolder in the 1970s, many of us openly proclaiming that bisexuality was better, more flexible than either exclusive sexual orientation. Dr. Lonny Myers of the Midwest Association for the Study of Human Sexuality referred in a July, 1974 paper to exclusive orientations as "compulsively heterosexual" and "compulsively homosexual." Myers suggested that hostility to bisexuality was rooted in a perception that it was a serious threat to the ideal of monogamous marriage, which by extension can be seen to also apply to homosexual monogamy. Phil Mullen (1974) wrote "to be exclusively gay or straight is to be maimed."

Kate Millet concluded her December, 1974 talk by lauding "the very wealth and humanity of bisexuality itself: for to exclude from one's love any entire group of human beings because of class, age, or race or religion, or sex, is surely to be poorer—deeply and systematically poorer. And to be the group who opens up walls, who ignores and destroys the taboo, is surely to make all our lives broader and easier, full of new possibility, which is hope."

Louise Knox concluded her previously cited article by saying, "We can appreciate bisexuality as an oasis. It offers us a breather from either-or thinking. . . . And it is to be hoped that this new liberation movement will free us all from the need to cling to any label for an identity. Bisexual, homosexual, heterosexual, the terms are, even now, beginning to seem as irrelevant, as archaic as caste marks. Who needs them?"

Some of us were perceptive enough to recognize that bi chic wouldn't last. I repeatedly said that ultimately bisexuality would be perceived as much more threatening to the prevailing sexual order than homosexuality, because it potentially subverted everyone's identity (the idea that everyone is potentially bisexual was wide-spread) and could not, unlike exclusive homosexuality, be confined to a segregated, stigmatized, and therefore manageable ghetto.

Millet concurred, noting that straight had defined itself in nega-tive terms as "not gay"[12] and gay was imitating it by "mak[ing] it [gay] also an absolute. . . . But the lines between gay and straight are as nebulous, as ephemeral as a one-night stand." The experience of the bisexual, she continued, "defies the category of I am that whom I do *not* sleep with. Neither homo nor hetero, one is both and therefore neither—one's experience is a negation of these very strong categories by whom [which?] the others breathe and war." In other words, bisexual consciousness, because of its amorphous quality and inclusionary nature, posed a fundamental threat to the dualistic and exclusionary thought patterns which were—and still are—tenaciously held by both the gay liberation leadership and its enemies.

The bisexual liberation movement was quite concerned with the New York City Council fight over a gay rights ordinance (we did manage to get bisexuality into the proposed legislation), Anita Bry-ant, California's Briggs Initiative, and related gay rights issues. We saw ourselves as close allies of gay people in a common struggle against discrimination, rather than a part of their movement, and as forming a valuable bridge from the gay to the straight world.

Today, as in the 1970s, the lesbian and gay movement continues to promote a ghetto mentality and devalue all part-time participants in homosexuality, though the Kinsey data showed that part-timers actually form a majority of all participants in same-sex activities. In effect, by glorifying the "lesbian and gay identity" or the even less widely subscribed and generation-based "queer identity," the gay and lesbian movement's leaders are stealing the representation, and ultimately the practice, of homosexuality away from most of its practitioners. By maintaining narrow definitions of lesbian/gay identity, leaders further their vision of lesbian and/or gay power, but in a manner that consolidates their own personal political and cul-tural power at the expense of narrowing its base.[13]

The leaders of the bisexual political movement and its cultural auxiliary must also be wary of the perhaps unconscious tendency to limit bisexuality to those who subscribe to a "bisexual identity," or they will make themselves liable to the same charge. To paraphrase Shakespeare's *Hamlet*, there are more persons involved with both genders on earth than are dreamt of in your identity-politics philosophy.

Kate Millet described bisexuals as "the key, not merely to a new sexuality, but to a new sexual culture. For if we are to break down sex role, sexual stereotype and conditioning the answer does not, I think, lie in new constraints, new segregation. The bisexual is the leading wedge as well as synthesis. Like miscegenation, we're the center that unifies . . . a vanguard of sorts in the process of change." This challenge has scarcely been met, and perhaps it is unrealistic to expect it to be attempted in a time of sexual conservatism, but there it remains, waiting to be taken up again when conditions allow.

Historian Martin Duberman (now head of the Center for Lesbian and Gay Studies at the City University of New York) took note in 1974 of the new visibility of bisexuality (he said that in 1973 he had written in his personal journal, "Bisexuals seem to be popping up all over.") and insightfully declared, "It's easier, I believe, for exclusive heterosexuals to tolerate (and that's the word) exclusive homosexuals than those who, rejecting exclusivity, sleep with people not genders. . . . To suggest, as practicing bisexuals do, that each of us may contain within ourselves all those supposed diametric opposites we've been taught to divide humanity into is to suggest that we might not know ourselves as well as we like to pretend. It's to suggest, too, that the roles through which most of us define ourselves . . . represent transient and even foolish social values." Duberman, who said he'd been in love with a bisexual man, went on to criticize bisexuals for exhibiting "an incipient chauvinism of their own." He concluded that "the future will see many more people relating bisexually" (Duberman, 1974).

The famous anthropologist Margaret Mead (herself an unacknowledged bisexual; see Murray, 1990) sprang to the defense of bisexuality in 1974, writing, "The time has come, I think, when we must recognize bisexuality as a normal form of human behavior. . . . A very large number of human beings—probably a majority—are bisexual in their potential capacity for love." Despite the highly visible bi lib activities in New York, she said, "There is not, and it seems unlikely that there will be, a bisexual liberation movement . . .

since in fact we do not really recognize bisexuality as a form of behavior . . . in our society."[14] In a sense Mead was raising a chicken-and-egg question. She was probably correct in suggesting that recognition had to precede a movement, but a minimal level of recognition was in fact sufficient, given pioneers willing to explore uncharted territory, for the movement to get started. The movement then, with enthusiastic cooperation from the media, promoted bisexual visibility, which increased recognition and thus allowed for movement growth. What Mead usefully did point out was the vast gap between the level of recognition accorded gay and lesbian behavior by the majority culture and that given to bisexuality, with its correspondent consequences for the level of movement activity.

Dr. George Weinberg, author of *Society and the Healthy Homosexual,* ascribed the apparent increase in bisexuality to "the indifference to gender pushed by all the liberation movements" (Klemesrud, 1974). One unnamed critic attributed the increase in bisexuality to capitalist consumerism, presumably an attempt to create an exploitable bisexual market along the lines of the rapidly growing gay and lesbian markets, and even to seduce consumers away from them. This theory would suggest, I think, that a growth in bi consciousness would lead in early stages to bi journals, bi organizations, bi porno videos, and bi books, like this one, as products to be sold for profit to this created consumer class, and indeed, all of these are now extant. The next step would see bi bars, resorts, clothes, shrinks, and physicians, followed by bands, movies, cable networks, hotels, conventions, tourist agencies, and chambers of commerce.

The various media articles of 1974, the year homosexuals were "cured" by vote of the American Psychiatric Association, also commonly quoted psychiatrists who still maintained that bisexuality was a problem, often worse than homosexuality because it indicated "confusion," the inability to choose one's identity from the sanctioned menu of two. Bisexuals in the movement shrugged them off, feeling it was the psychiatrists who were confused.

The most prominent bisexual organizer of the time was Don Fass, a New York psychotherapist. In 1974-1975 his National Bisexual Liberation group was holding large monthly parties and weekly consciousness-raising groups (some of them for women only) in New York, along with occasional brunches and coffee-house-style socials, and published a pamphlet-sized magazine, *Bisexual Expression*. Fass was quoted in *New Times* newsmagazine as saying he'd been bi since March, 1972 (Greene, 1974), but in his own magazine (Fass, 1975), he wrote that he founded National Bisexual Liberation in February of 1972. If this claim is true, NBL preceded the Ithaca Statement by five months, but further investigation into the history of Fass' group is required before we can crown him the founder of the bisexual movement. (Perhaps there were others of which I have not yet heard, but we can be fairly sure there were no organized bisexual-identified groups in or outside the United States before 1970.) By winter of 1975, Fass claimed over 5,500 members in ten chapters in the United States, and said more than 4,000 people had attended NBL programs in New York alone. He had appeared on NBC's *Tomorrow Show* with Tom Snyder. In an article in *New York* magazine he claimed 800 members (500 men and 300 women) in New York (City or State is not clear). "We believe bisexuality to be the fullest expression of human liberation," Fass wrote. "Our emphasis is on growth, but we are aware of our political responsibilities."

Other information gleaned from my surviving copy of *Bisexual Expression*: "The first paperback on Bisexuality [was] published in October [1974], Bernhardt Hurwoods's *The Bisexuals* (Fawcett) . . . Julius Fast will be author of the first hardcover, *Bisexual Living* (Evans) in February" 1975. Jeff Davidson wrote in that issue that he founded a Bisexual Group in Philadelphia in the summer of 1974; either the City of Brotherly Love was unusually conscious about bisexuality, or the abundance of clippings on the subject from Philadelphia publications reflects its heavy concentration of Quakers, and therefore members of the CFB, who were sending them to me.

The pioneering and often courageous efforts of the 1970s movement have largely been forgotten. Its leaders have faded from view, and current writings often state that the bi movement began in the 1980s. It is a shame that our collective memory is so deficient, for so much of the intellectual spadework necessary for our existence today was done in the 1970s, and the questions we faced then still confront us today. I can only hope that this article will spur someone to do the necessary research and interviewing and come up with a good book-length history of the period or of the movement as a whole.

NOTES

1. The articles and texts quoted herein were found loose in my files, often without indication as to where or when they were published. I have provided the bibliographical information I have found.

2. This was the Student Homophile League, the first such group anywhere. It held its first meeting at Columbia on October 28, 1966, was recognized by the University as an official student group on April 19, 1967 (causing a front-page headline in *The New York Times* on May 3), and then organized additional chapters at New York University (under Rita Mae Brown) and Cornell University (under Jearld [sic] Moldenhauer). I became national chairman. The Columbia group survived under various names and recently celebrated its 25th anniversary.

3. Foster Gunnison, a prominent NACHO leader, head of the alumni auxiliary to the Columbia homophile group, and a fairly close friend of mine, told me once that he believed I was really heterosexual but involved in the gay scene in order to "be different." There may be a germ of truth to this observation, since I did relish the sense of non-conformity, idiosyncracy, and rebellion (and exploited the many advantages given by good looks in the gay scene). But more likely Foster was voicing his own reaction to my "butch" manner and appearance as well as my obvious involvement with women.

4. Had I known other bi-identified activists in 1970 interested in forming a bi group, I might have started one at that point and stayed a civilian, but I didn't. Martha identified as a lesbian.

5. There was a major fight over this discharge. The American Civil Liberties Union provided one of their staff attorneys as my lawyer at the hearings in Naples, Italy; political figures ranging from Rep. Bella Abzug to Sen. Sam Ervin protested to the Pentagon; and the official Armed Forces newspaper *Stars & Stripes* as well as gay papers like *The Advocate* provided extensive coverage. I was given a General Discharge, but continuing the fight in 1977, I became the first person to get a homosexual discharge upgraded to fully Honorable under the new Carter administration discharge review program, setting a precedent for future discharges. Later authors writing on the military policy struggle have overlooked this case.

6. Friends General Conference is the most liberal of three Quaker denominations in the United States; the same term applies to its annual convention, which in 1972 met at Ithaca College.

7. At this time I was using the name Bob Martin.

8. Hudson had been a well-known activist in the gay liberation movement since 1970, as well as a celebrated writer.

9. One such panel, for which I still have records, was sponsored by the New York Gay Activists Alliance on December 2, 1974, at the Church of the Holy Apostles. Panelists were writer Kate Millet, bi lib organizer Don Fass, psychologist Reesa Vaughter, bi activists John Paul Hudson and Kathleen Frazer, and myself.

10. All quotes from Kate Millet are taken verbatim and uncorrected from the unpublished text (which she gave me) of her talk at the Gay Activist Alliance-

sponsored panel of December 2, 1974. Her punctuation was obviously meant for oral delivery, not a written text. Note her application of "gay" to women.

11. E.g., a transvestite or a member of any of the "intermediate genders" recognized by various cultures around the world.

12. That is, the straight is one who never allows erotic contact with the same gender.

13. Political scientists borrowed the term *granfalloon* from Kurt Vonnegut to describe the outcome of a process by which giving people who originally have little or nothing in common a label causes them to act as if they were a real group, ready to declare "I'm really proud to be an A." The next step is "We As have to stick together and follow our leaders because the Bs are going to get us." Studies have shown that people who feel they are in a group will agree with what the leader of the perceived group says in order to stay within the group. A close study of the history of ideas relating to "homosexuals," together with the absence of any scientific evidence for a common element (other than the definition itself) among the great diversity of people around the world who are so labeled, strongly suggests that the groups "homosexuals," "gays and lesbians," and "queers" are indeed granfalloons.

14. Unfortunately, my copy of Mead's article does not contain a reference to the journal in which it was published.

Bay Area Bisexual History:
An Interview with David Lourea

Naomi Tucker

Editor's note: Alone in my car after David's memorial service, I cried as I wrote in my journal about what he meant to me and to so many other people. His absence was incomprehensible. The eclectic crowd of those who had come to mourn his death—teachers, young children, AIDS activists, bi activists, leather daddies, sex radicals, therapists, rabbis, and family members—was testimony to how instrumental David was in bringing communities together.

David's contributions to the world were numerous—from pioneering bisexual activism in the 1970s, to developing some of the earliest safer sex information, to healing people as a therapist. And David touched my life . . . a kindred spirit who also juggled roles in counseling, teaching, bisexual activism, and Jewish organizing. Always true to himself and his vision of social justice, he wore all of those hats and then some. His activism never ceased for a moment.

David would have written for this book were he not too ill by the time it was underway. Knowing he would not be around to see the book to press, he agreed to be interviewed and gave us permission to edit and print his words as a final contribution to the bi community. On June 27, 1992, the day before David rode on the Clean and Sober float in his last San Francisco Lesbian/Gay Freedom Day Parade, Brad Robinson, Cris Gutierrez, and I had the pleasure and honor of conducting the following interview. David gave his love and wisdom freely to everyone around him, in the spirit of Tikkun Olam—the healing of the world. Thank you, David. We miss you.

47

*Can you tell us how you became involved
in bisexual organizing?*

For me, being bisexual has a lot to do with being Jewish. I was
born right after the Holocaust and lived with my grandmother who
experienced the loss of her whole family. We grew up in Philadelphia, which was vehemently anti-Semitic, like the rest of the world
in the 1950s. I grew up as a minority in a Christian world. If you
grow up a privileged WASP, thinking that who you are is the dominant life form on the planet, that you have the right to take that for
granted, it's harder to suddenly see yourself as a minority. I've *only*
experienced myself as a minority. I know I'm white and I'm not a
minority in that. I'm male and in terms of dominance, I'm not a
minority. But I've always experienced myself as a minority in being
Jewish. My grandmother taught me that I'm okay for being Jewish
even though the rest of the world doesn't think that, which made it
easier to get that I'm alright for being a minority even within a
minority–although I don't think my grandmother was trying to
make me feel better about being bisexual!

There's so much confusion in literature about bisexuality. In the
Library of Congress there was a subheading for bestiality, for SM,
for transvestism, but not for bisexuality. That said we didn't exist.
There were no books written on bisexuality except for garbage.
There were no courses about bisexuality. Books on human sexuality
had listings of bisexuality under "The Causes of Homosexuality."
That's what we were dealing with back then.

The late '60s and early '70s were exciting times. During the
Sexual Freedom movement, swingers were exploring their sexuality
and challenging the stereotypes within the context of group sex scenes.
In the process, many people began to open up to bisexuality. If you
were lying down blindfolded and a number of people were touching
you, you couldn't tell whether they were male or female. . . . Oh! A
light bulb goes on! Maybe there isn't a difference!

Also, within the San Francisco SM world people began to take a
look at bisexuality. Women pushed their way into the male-dominated heterosexual SM clubs. It was a safe place for gay men to play
with women and for lesbian women to play with men. Suddenly
there was another world where bisexuality started becoming the

norm. The issue was not so much "Are you gay or straight?" but "Are you a top or a bottom?"

Except for Maggi Rubenstein,[1] there was no immediate intellectual understanding of bisexuality. Many people were experimenting with group marriages. With Kinsey and Masters and Johnson, people began to question their sexual assumptions. It was an easy, nonthreatening way to explore and to experience bisexuality. I don't think the label "bisexual" became political at that time.

San Francisco Sex Information (SFSI), an outgrowth of the Sexual Freedom League, formed in the early '70s to answer questions and dispel myths around sexuality. SFSI was a haven, the primary community in San Francisco for people who were bisexual.

Were you involved in founding SFSI?

No. Maggi Rubenstein, Toni Ayres, and Carolyn Smith got together. I think all three of them were nurses and swingers. They were in the Sexual Freedom League and the National Drug and Sex Forum. That's part of the history, too. Maggi had been talking about bisexuality for a very long time before anybody else had, but nobody was listening. She tried to get a bi movement started in the early '70s just as SFSI was starting, but it didn't go anywhere. For whatever organizational reasons, people just couldn't deal with it, and the emphasis was on the gay community at that time. But after about three or four years there was a strong enough core of people within SFSI who felt comfortable with their bisexuality, that an organization could start.

My wife and I had moved out to San Francisco from Philadelphia. We were looking for a bisexual, nonmonogamous community. About 22 of us got together and started planning [the Bi Center]. This was, I think, September of 1975. We were politically unaware and naïve, hoping for acceptance. "We're nonthreatening. We're nondemanding."

The Bi Center started six years after the Stonewall riots, when the gay community was in its infancy. Shortly after we started, a whole wave of stars like David Bowie came out as bisexual; it became very fashionable to be bisexual. I remember saying, "Well, you know, it's real nice that my sexual orientation is in fashion right now, but when it's not in fashion, it's still going to be my sexual orientation." Still, it was a very exciting time. Betty Dodson was part of the early group, and we were doing something brand new. We thought that we'd give ourselves a couple of years and pretty soon we'd be this huge, enormous bi movement, probably larger than the gay movement. *That* was our naïveté.

The first wave of people who started the Bi Center were political radicals and highly motivated people. The group was based on inclusivity . . . for example, in the women's groups, anybody who identified as a woman had the right to be there, so a lot of transgender people started coming to the Bi Center. We were a social and political organization fighting for recognition within the gay community, working on the concept of "make love, not war." We knew that there had been bi organizations before which fell apart because they were strictly social, without any political cohesiveness or sense of a higher purpose to hold them together. Even the Sexual Freedom League had a political sense.

We battled constantly between "Are we a social organization or are we a political organization?" and "To what degree are we each?" We'd put on a social event and people would come. We'd put on a political event and nobody would come.

Why was the political aspect important at the time?

Because we were dealing with sexual freedom. When the Briggs Initiative [in California] stated that gay teachers didn't have the right to be teaching, were they just going to let bisexuals teach *half* the day? We were being invalidated by the gay community because our lives were not at risk when we were within the straight community, but we knew that the same kinds of oppression applied to bisexuals because the rest of the world did not make the distinction.

Did the fight against the Briggs Initiative politicize the Bi Center?

The Bi Center took a very active part in that and other battles against homophobia. I want to acknowledge the contribution of Alan Rockway, an activist who left the area specifically to join the fight in Florida against Anita Bryant. He got no recognition as a bisexual. He was viewed as gay [though] he kept talking about bisexuality. What we needed was about two dozen people like him. He had all these great ideas and a lot of political savvy.

We kept giving our lifeblood, our energy, to gay and lesbian liberation, yet we were still being discounted. I remember we were marching once with the gay community on Martin Luther King Day, and the gay papers listed every single organization that was part of the march, except for the Bi Center. That happened constantly. Alan Rockway, my wife Lee, Maggi Rubenstein, and I wrote letters to the editor of the *B.A.R.* [*Bay Area Reporter*, a San Francisco gay newspaper]. They would invalidate whatever we wrote by some stupid [headline] like "Bis feeling offended" or ". . . feeling left out." There was a conspiracy of silence within the gay papers about our presence.

We wanted the Coalition for Human Rights to take a position against the *B.A.R.* [for] excluding us. It became apparent that the Coalition needed to be educated about bisexuality, and so Maggi and I put together this incredible three-hour workshop with 20 different people speaking. From the Coalition, which had about 56 different organizations, three people showed up. It was a real clear signal. "You don't count. You don't exist. We're not interested."

How did that invisibility within gay communities affect the direction of the Bi Center?

Well, we had one more thing to fight. It was so absurd. We would say we'd like to join forces, that we don't want to use our energies to fight the gay community, and yet the gay community would put us in a position where that's what we had to do.

There were just not enough of us. There was so much work for the handful of us that we could no longer do it. We were working to encourage people to come out of the closet, and until vast numbers of people came out, we would be thwarted. The mistake that Maggi and I and a few other people made was that we loved the community and the Bi Center so much, that we didn't transition the power. We kept doing [all] the talking, and the discrepancy between us and the newer members in the community widened.

Why was it difficult to get bisexuals to come out?

In some ways, I think it's easier to come out as gay than as bi. If I'm a gay man and I come out and the heterosexual world rejects me, there's a loss . . . but I'm not invested in it in the same way as a bisexual. While for some gay men and lesbians it's significant to lose a heterosexual support system, it's a lot harder for people who are bi—a lot harder.

One of the problems for bisexual people is that they lead enormously isolated lives where no one else knows who they are. The other thing that makes it hard, as bisexual activist and sexologist Margo Rila always says, is that there are a lot more people who have the capacity to be bisexual than there are people who have the energy and ability to manage that lifestyle. I think people who identify as bisexual are comfortable dealing with multiplicity in their life. People who have trouble with multiplicity find it much easier to say, "Well, I'm gay or I'm straight."

A woman who used to come to me for counseling would fly in once a month from Texas. She said, "You know, if you could give me a pill that would make me either straight or gay, I would take it. It would be easier for me to be either, and I don't care which it would be. I just can't deal with the complexity of feeling both. I don't have time to work out both."

With all of this complication, and for someone like you who felt such a strong connection to the gay community, why identify as bisexual?

Well, to not identify as bi would be antithetical to what we were trying to do. I feel great saying "I'm queer" because there's room for me to love women. When I say "I'm gay," there's no room for me to acknowledge that women are important parts of my life. We wanted to include same sex partners in our lives, not give up heterosexual partners. There was strong commitment to be part of the gay movement, but to be part of that movement in honesty, not in a lie.

When you're dealing with bisexuality you're dealing with such a broad spectrum of people and behaviors and needs. For instance, there are some people who are basically straight and occasionally like same sex contact, and that's valid. If they can identify as bi, I can give them credit for that. But their main interest is heterosexual, with the freedom to occasionally have sex with someone of the same sex. Then there are people at the other end of the continuum who are more lesbian- or gay-identified. And many people who are bi are defensive and hostile towards people who are gay. They've been invalidated and trashed and laughed at and ridiculed when they've tried to come out and be supportive. So we have enormous diversity . . . it's unrealistic to expect any one group to meet the needs of all these different people, which adds difficulty to organizing bisexual communities. We are not homogenous.

What factors besides the sexual freedom movement influenced the direction of bi politics?

Quite frankly, after eight years of doing Bisexuality 101, it was boring. We started pushing for acceptance in other places. Ahavat Shalom [a local alternative synagogue] was the first organization in San Francisco I know of that voluntarily, without bi instigation, changed their name to include bisexuals. It was a momentous occasion for us.

Then, in the early '80s, we began to notice that there was something unhealthy and frightening happening out in the world. The Bi Center frequently did workshops on venereal disease and health. We felt that a positive sex attitude and a sense of responsibility around venereal disease were important. We had [gay HIV+ spokesperson] Bobby Campbell come and talk about KS [Kaposi's Sarcoma]; this was before the term AIDS and even before the term GRID, gay-related immune deficiency.

In 1982, there was a "wellness" conference at UC Medical Center. At that time the Bi Center was a very small organization; we had maybe 600 members, but only about 50 active members. Out of that, we had maybe twelve people putting on presentations at the wellness conference, [yet] every single one of the people on the main platform refused to say the word "bisexual." Over and over and over again, we were contributing a major amount of energy and had speakers refusing to say the word "bisexual." We were furious, but we still went on.

Maggi, Steven Brown,[2] Margo, and I were all sexologists. We

had been out there pushing people to be sexual, advocating for
personal and sexual liberation. With increasing awareness of GRID
and eventually AIDS, we had a responsibility to take a look at that.
We also knew it would be very easy to blame diverse sexualities.
But the problem was not sexuality; the problem was a disease and
sex-negative attitudes.

We pulled back from the Bi Center at that point. Seventy percent
of our personal lives, energy, and finances were going into supporting the Bi Center. And suddenly there was something else; our
energy *had* to shift into AIDS work. Because we had not nurtured
and developed a strong group behind us, the Bi Center changed.

**So you took your bisexual politics into the AIDS activist
community?**

Yes, absolutely. It was terrifying because I knew there were huge
numbers of gay men having sex with women on an occasional to
frequent basis, and a huge number of lesbian women having sex
with men, which made talking about AIDS as a gay issue a serious
problem. There were large numbers of people engaging in bisexual
behavior regardless of what they were calling themselves. The label
didn't matter; it was the behavior that was going to transmit the
disease. Sex was going to get blamed and bisexuals were going to
get scapegoated.

I remember in 1980, I had a venereal wart on my lip. The doctor
asked me, "Are you gay?" and I said, "No." That wasn't to hide
the fact that I had sex with men. No, I'm not a gay man. I'm
bisexual. The question he needed to ask was, "Do you have sex
with men?" Doctors and researchers needed to think of other ways
to question people.

As horrible as it is, I think AIDS brought bisexuality out of the
closet. Those of us at the Bi Center who were sexologists were
involved in that early educational process. I was part of the Mayor's
AIDS Educational Advisory Committee back in '83. Steven Brown
and I were part of the very first program with the Public Health
Department on "Sex in the Age of AIDS." We put on workshops in
the bathhouses. During AIDS Education Week in San Francisco
[1984] the Bisexual Center was directly responsible for seven of the

twelve presentations, and again we got no recognition. Maggi Rubenstein and Margo Rila did the first "Women and AIDS" program. Autumn [Courtney] was part of that. We were the first ones to put on a workshop for heterosexual behavior and AIDS. "Behavior" was the important part because we wanted lesbians and gay men to feel comfortable coming to that workshop.

We spent hours designing programs, fighting with the Health Department to bring up the issue of sexuality. Because we were sexologists we knew how to help people change attitudes and behavior around sexuality, but they wanted to deal with AIDS without ever having to use the word "sex." Well, the gay community gets a great deal of its information via sexually explicit material; it's the most effective way for people to learn. We wanted to make films and videos showing people having safe sex. Rather than developing fear tactics, we wanted to give them something positive to move towards. Safe sex can be fun. It can be hot. It can be enriching. But they just weren't ready to spend public dollars doing that.

So much of the AIDS suffering comes from homophobic and sex-negative attitudes: people don't have the right to be sexual with anybody in the first place, and, if they do something wrong and get in trouble because of their sexuality, well, they deserved it.

Sex with men became dangerous. Some bi men were pulling back from relating to men, and some bi women were pulling back from relating to men.

How do you feel about the "bisexuality is not about sex," or "it's certainly not just about sex" response to stereotypes about bisexuals?

It's certainly not *just* about sex. Sex is an important part of it, but it's a great deal more than that. The gay community has a huge number of people who are only interested in partying. They're interested in going to the gym, to the bathhouses, or the sex clubs, and they wouldn't lift a finger to get involved in gay politics. They're in it for the good time. Fortunately, there's a large number of people who care about much broader issues than that. Probably in the same proportion, that's true within the bi community–there are people out there just for fun. We're a much smaller group and so the number of people who are willing to give time towards political issues is smaller. There's just not enough of us to sustain everything we need to.

Of course it's not just about sex. It's about a way of being. It's about the right for us to be different, the right for us to express who we are. You can't have any liberation as long as somebody's being oppressed. The political issues are far greater than just our sexuality; they involve issues of power and dominance. They involve issues of misogyny . . . of class struggles. . . . [If] I ignore women's issues, as a man, then the straight community has the right to do [the same thing] to me, and they will. My belief is that the gay community will sow the seeds of their own destruction if they use their dominance to silence the bi community.

How do you personally choose your battles?

That's a good question. Well, I try to lend support where I can, and in choosing my battles, I have to see where I would be the most effective. I am a sexologist. I work most effectively in AIDS education. What do I get pleasure out of doing? I don't think that there's a whole lot to be gained from giving your life away and being miserable about it. If you're going to give your life away, at least enjoy it. That's where you're most effective and conscious.

What do you get back as a personal reward for doing HIV education?

I feel alive! I feel that I contribute, and it's exciting! I like going to demonstrations sometimes. But that's what I do; that's fun for me. Someone who hates it shouldn't be doing it. There's other ways that they can contribute. Some people are political, and some people are not. I don't know how to inspire people to take responsibility in the world, but it helps me feel better to know that I would not have changed my life in the least.

How were you received as an out bisexual within the HIV education community?

People were frightened. We were so radical to begin with, because we wanted to talk about sex specifically, that it was hard for people to hear us as bisexuals. I remember one of the owners of the bathhouses saying, "Well, you're not going to try to make us all bisexual, are you?" But mostly there was an appreciation that we were willing to talk about it.

Now that you are well known and respected as a knowledgeable HIV educator in the Bay Area and in the gay community, has that fostered a greater acceptance of bisexuality?

I would love to say "Yes." If any of that is true, it's at an infinitesimal level. The reason that there's more acceptance is because life moves on and because more and more of us have been putting the word out. [Bisexual] is not a new word now. I give a lot of credit to the younger generations who are not threatened by the word.

You're a long-time employee of the San Francisco Unified School District. How did that interact with your bisexual activism?

My life has been incredibly blessed. Coming out was very easy. People who are bi do get pressures from their employment and are discriminated against. But more often it's the fear of it than [the] reality. I had a strong support group within San Francisco Sex Information. I had personal support. My wife was incredibly supportive of me coming out. So I could go to the School District and talk about the fact that I was doing a radio show on bisexuality. I never ever got any kind of negative feedback. Not from parents, not from the administration, not from anyone. And some of that may have been the fact that my attitude was "of course, this is normal. Of course, you wouldn't be upset about it."

Is the School District still having the gym teacher teach AIDS education?

The San Francisco Unified School District's position on AIDS is that the only effective form of AIDS prevention is monogamy. I keep arguing with them: if you believe monogamy is an effective form of AIDS prevention, why do you have programs for unwed mothers? If [teens were having safe sex], you wouldn't have all these teenage pregnancies. It's incredibly primitive. We don't want to honestly address the fact that kids are sexual.

I work with young children. Children are sexual. That's what we should be. Sexuality is healthy. It's viable. It's exciting. It's an important part of who we are. We want to pretend it doesn't exist. We certainly don't want to think in terms of our children exploring their sexuality, but they do. Human life doesn't care about shoulds. It will be what it wants to be. Unfortunately a lot of young children are going to lose their lives. You know, I feel horrendous being 47 years old and facing my death due to AIDS. It's just mind-boggling to think of a 16 year old in that position, and this is happening more and more.

Have you gotten any support from the bisexual community either in terms of your work with HIV, or in terms of living with HIV and being active in the bi community?

Yeah, I feel really wonderful about the bi community's contribution to AIDS education in San Francisco. We haven't done enough, but certainly we have done an enormously disproportionate degree of education compared to the smallness of our community. Personally I feel, again, incredibly blessed. I feel really loved. I feel supported by the community. I think Alan was supported. Cynthia was supported by the community.[3]

Is there anything further that the bi community should be doing around HIV education?

Oh, G-d, yes! There's still very little understanding around bisexuality, around diversity. The consequences of AIDS are so frightening. We need to continue having forums; we need to be politically active. The issue's not just bisexuality. The issue is broadening people's concept of human sexuality and putting bisexuality within that context.

*What is the relationship of people of your generation
with the younger generation of bisexual or queer activists?
Are they learning from you? Are you passing something on?
Are they revolting against your methods?*

Well, I hope they're revolting against our methods. I think it's the duty of every generation to revolt against the older generation and to go further. My expectation is that they ought to have a higher level of consciousness than I did, because they're standing on our shoulders. I didn't have me as a mentor!

Imagine if you had!

If I hadn't had Maggi as a mentor, I could not have gone further. The world is not stagnant. We don't have all the answers. We're in a bad place if, 20 years from now, the next generation comes along and they're saying exactly what we said.

We weren't as political . . . in the way that I love seeing [younger bisexual activists] being political today, but we were fighting overwhelming odds back then. We didn't have the political savvy they have today. I adore Queer Nation. I love and totally support their mistakes. I support their actions, and if we had not stepped back, we would have strangled their young creative energy. It's really wonderful to see [their] excitedness and vitality. I feel awful that AIDS has jarred us out of bisexual myopia, but if bisexuality is going to become a viable reality, it has to be in the context of our lives and not the only focus of our lives. I guess that's one of the things I like about Queer Nation. I like the fact that the word "bisexual" is not even used. There's problems with that, but what I like is that they [see] bigger issues and are totally intolerant of exclusion. I love the fact that they cause problems and they're obnoxious and disruptive to the extent I wouldn't be. I'm glad they're a pain in a lot of people's asses.

*What about young bisexual activists who are riding on the
coattails of the education you've been doing for the last 20 years,
but who think they invented bisexual politics?*

Well, that's the arrogance of youth. We had it, too. I mean, there were people before us. Sometimes I get angry; sometimes I feel invalidated. But mostly I really love that somebody, anybody, is doing anything and I don't have to. I've been around long enough to feel secure in what it is I've contributed.

One of the reasons that the younger gay and lesbian population today is more accepting of bisexuality is that they have a great deal more support. Today, while the world is still hostile, there's also a very strong gay and lesbian community for young kids coming out. That gives people who are bi the freedom to come out and be more honest and self-accepting, *as* bisexuals, since bisexuality is no longer merely the coming-out bridge towards lesbianism or homosexuality.

Also, the younger generation has a much broader perspective. They have learned that this is not just about bisexuality. I'm delighted with the freedom with which they put out, "This is who I am, and this is not the main issue." [For us bisexuality] *was* the issue, because we couldn't get anyone to even say "bisexual." I never heard the word "bisexual" until I was 26 years old. So we needed to harp on just the word: bisexual, bisexual, bisexual. We couldn't get on to the next issues.

What will the future bi movement look like?

I think it's within the queer movement, which is what we really wanted in the beginning. The issue is not gays or bis. The issue is joining together to fight for sexual freedom and for sexual rights–human rights.

*   *   *

Epilogue: The Bi Center opened its doors in 1976 as a primarily social organization. By the late 1970s it was a thriving institution providing support groups and groundbreaking workshops. In response to a growing need for feminist political organizing around bisexual invisibility, the first meeting of BiPOL was held at the Bi Center in 1983. As energy was diverted to fighting AIDS and political repression, the Bi Center eventually folded in 1984. Twelve years later, BiPOL is still going strong. BiPOL's founding members were David, Autumn Courtney, Lani Ka'ahumanu, Arlene Kranz, Bill Mack, Alan Rockway, and Maggi Rubenstein. The five who are still alive today remain active voices for bisexual liberation.

NOTES

1. Maggi Rubenstein is a San Francisco therapist, educator, and sexologist who has been promoting bi visibility as an out bisexual since the 1960s.

2. Steven Brown is a sex educator who served on the board of the Bi Center and is on the training staff of San Francisco Sex Information.

3. Alan Rockway and Cynthia Slater were bisexual activists who died of AIDS. Alan co-authored the Dade County, Florida gay rights ordinance as an out bisexual. Cynthia founded the Society of Janus, a pansexual SM support group and the first SM group in the nation to march in a gay pride parade. Cynthia was instrumental in promoting bi acceptance in the SM community, and was one of the first HIV-positive women to speak out publicly.

It Ain't Over 'Til The Bisexual Speaks

Lani Ka'ahumanu

The following was Lani's speech delivered on April 25, 1993, at the March On Washington for Lesbian, Gay, and Bi Equal Rights and Liberation. Lani was one of 18 people, and the only out bisexual, chosen to speak at the March. The last speaker of the day on the afternoon stage, Lani was told to cut her speech at the last minute due to time constraints. We present here her original text in full.

Aloha, my name is Lani Ka'ahumanu,
   and it ain't over 'til the bisexual speaks . . .

I am a token, and a symbol.
Today there is no difference.
I *am* the token out bisexual asked to speak, and
I *am* a symbol of how powerful the bisexual pride movement is
   and how far we have come.

I came here in 1979
   for the March on Washington for Lesbian and Gay Rights.

I returned in 1987
   for the March on Washington for Lesbian and Gay Rights.

I stand here today
   on the stage
   of the 1993 March on Washington
   for Lesbian, Gay, and Bisexual
   Equal Rights and Liberation.

In 1987 I wrote an article on bisexuality
   for the Civil Disobedience Handbook
   titled, "Are we visible yet?"

Bisexual activists
    organized on the local, regional, and national levels
    to make this March a reality.

Are bisexuals visible yet?
Are bisexuals organized yet?
Are bisexuals accountable yet?

You bet your sweet ass we are!

Bisexuals are here,
    and we're queer.

Bisexual pride
    speaks to the truth
    of behavior *and* identity.

No simple either/or divisions
    fluid–ambiguous–subversive
    bisexual pride challenges both
    the heterosexual *and* the homosexual assumption.

Society is based
    on the denial of diversity,
    on the denial of complexity.

Like multiculturalism,
    mixed heritage and bi-racial relationships,
    both the bisexual and transgender movements
    expose and politicize the middle ground.

Each show there is no separation,
    that each and everyone of us
    is part of a fluid social, sexual, and gender dynamic.

Each signals a change, a *fundamental* change
    in the way our society is organized.

Remember today.

Remember we are family,
    and like a large extended family,
    we don't always agree, don't always see eye to eye.

However, as a family under attack
    we must recognize the importance of what
    each and every one of us brings to our movement.
There is strength in our numbers and diversity.
We are every race, class, culture, age, ability,
    religion, gender identity, and sexual orientation.

Recognition of bisexual orientation and transgender issues
    presents a challenge to assumptions
    not previously explored
    within the politics
    of gay liberation.

What will it take
    for the gayristocracy to realize
    that bisexual, lesbian, transgender, and gay people
    are in this together,
    and together
    we can and will
    move the agenda forward.

But this will not happen
    until public recognition
    of our common issues is made,
    and a sincere effort to confront
    biphobia and transphobia is made
    by the established gay and lesbian leadership
    in this country.

The broader movement for our civil rights and liberation
    is being held back.

Who gains when we ostracize whole parts of our family?
Who gains from exclusionary politics?

Certainly not us . . .

Being treated as if I am less oppressed than thou
    is not only insulting,
    it feeds right in to the hands
    of the right wing fundamentalists
    who see *all* of us as queer.

What is the difficulty
   in seeing how my struggle
   as a mixed race bisexual woman of color
   is intimately related to the bigger struggle
   for lesbian and gay rights,
   the rights of people of color and
   the rights of all women?

What is the problem?

This is not a competition.
   I will not play by rules
   that pit me against any oppressed group.

Has the gayristocracy
   bought so far in to the either/or structure,
   invested so much in being
   the opposite of heterosexual
   that they cannot remove themselves
   that they can't imagine being free
   of the whole oppressive heterosexist system
   that keeps us all down?

Bisexual, gay, lesbian, and transgender people
   who are out of the closet,
   who are not passing
   for anything other than who and what we are
   all have our necks and our lives on the line.

All our visibility is a sign of revolt.

Bisexuals are here to challenge the bigots
   who have denied lesbian, gay, *and* bisexual people
   basic civil rights in Colorado.[1]

Yes, Amendment 2 includes bisexual orientation.
Yes, the religous right recognizes bisexuals
   as a threat to "so called" family values.

Bisexuals are here to protest
   the military ban against lesbians, gays, *and* bisexuals.
Yes, the Department of Defense defines bisexuals separately
   as a reason to be dishonorably discharged.

And yes, out bisexuals are not allowed
  to be foster or adoptive parents,
And yes, we lose our jobs, our children, get beaten and killed
  for loving women and for loving men.

Bisexuals are queer, just as queer as queer can be.

Each of us here today
  represents many people
  who could not make the trip.

Our civil rights and liberation movement
  has reached critical mass.

Remember today.

Remember that we are more powerful
  than all the hate, ignorance, and violence
  directed at us.

Remember what a profound difference
  our visibility makes
  upon the world in which we live.

The momentum of this day
  can carry us
  well into the 21st century
  if we come out wherever and whenever we can.

Remember assimilation is a lie.
  It is spiritual erasure.

I want to challenge those lesbian and gay leaders
  who have come out to me privately over the years
  as bisexual to take the next step, come out now.

What is the sexual liberation movement about
  if not about the freedom to love whom we choose?

I want to encourage bisexuals
  in the lesbian, gay, and heterosexual communities
  to come out now.

Remember there is nothing wrong with love.
Defend the freedom to express it.

We cannot be stopped. We are everywhere.
We are bisexual, lesbian, gay, and transgender people.

We will not rest
    until we are all free,
We will not rest
    until our basic human rights
        are protected under federal law,
We will not rest
    until our relationships and families
        are not just tolerated,
        but recognized, respected, and valued,
We will not rest
    until we have a national health care system,
We will not rest
    until there are cures for AIDS and cancer.
We deserve nothing less.

Remember we have every right
    to be in the world
    exactly as we are.

Celebrate that simply and fiercely.

I love you.

Mahalo and aloha.

NOTE

1. In 1992 Colorado voters passed an amendment to Article 2 of their state constitution prohibiting "any law or policy which provides that homosexual, lesbian or bisexual orientation, conduct, or relationships constitutes or entitles a person to claim any minority or protected status, quota preferences, or discrimination." Amendment 2 repeals existing protections and prohibits the passage of future protections for lesbians, gays, and bisexuals in Colorado. Anti-gay/lesbian/bisexual initiatives are currently being fought in nine states.

Part B

The State of Our Movement

If you are free, you are not predictable and you are not controllable. To my mind, that is the keenly positive, politicizing significance of bisexual affirmation.

—June Jordan, 1991

We Claim Our Own

Dajenya

We claim our own:
Sappho
Bessie Smith
Anaïs Nin

We claim our own:
Walt Whitman
Navratilova
Langston Hughes

Keep them in your archives
yes
you're welcome to them
as you are to us

I am bisexual
I am gay
I am a lesbian

Count me in your history books
fighting side by side
for the right
to love a same-sex lover
and not be persecuted for it

Surely, swell the ranks
Elton John
Virginia Woolf
James Dean

Boast about
Vita Sackville-West
Colette
Djuna Barnes

Whisper rumors
document
the (often hidden) gay lives
of famous people
who have given to the world

But don't then
turn around and tell me
I don't belong here.
If you claim bisexual cannot mean gay,
then purge your history books
of so many names
that swell your breast with pride—
names of people who have also loved
both sexes.

November 1991

Identity and Ideas:
Strategies for Bisexuals

Liz A. Highleyman

The bisexual movement has grown and evolved greatly in the past decade and many bisexuals are beginning to rethink old assumptions. Now is a good time to examine where we have come from and where we are going as bisexuals—as individuals, as communities, and as a movement. Is there (and should there be) a specific politics, culture, or lifestyle that goes along with a given sexual orientation? Is sexual identity a sufficient basis for political solidarity or social cohesion? What are the most useful strategies for bi organizing and activism? Should bisexuals integrate into the gay and lesbian movement, work to build an independent bi-focused movement, or aspire to create a broad sexual and gender liberation movement? Is our goal to build a strong, coherent movement based on sexual identity, or to break down identity-based distinctions altogether?

THE POLITICS OF IDENTITY
AND THE POLITICS OF IDEAS

Today's gay and lesbian movement reflects the emphasis on identity politics which is common among contemporary progres-

Many thanks to Muffy Barkocy, Loraine Hutchins, and Rebecca Kaplan for their helpful comments, and to the members of the BI*-L electronic mail lists where my ideas about bisexual politics and theory have been developed and honed over the years.

sive movements. *Identity politics* refers to political organizing based on membership in a group or class, usually defined according to some immutable (or believed to be immutable) characteristic. Alliances tend to be based on similarity of oppression.

The flip side of identity politics might be called *idea politics*; that is, communities and activism based on shared beliefs, commitments, values, and goals rather than on shared immutable characteristics or oppressions. A sexual and gender liberation movement based on ideas could encompass everyone who shares the goal of free choice in sexuality and gender expression, regardless of their personal sexual or gender identity.

Essentialist Versus Social Constructionist Notions of Identity

An emphasis on immutable or inherent characteristics makes identity politics in some ways related to *essentialism*. In terms of sexual orientation, the essentialist view holds that there are universal (perhaps biological) characteristics common to all people of a given sexual orientation. Essentialists see sexual identity as constant across eras and cultures, for example, equating Native American berdaches or ancient Greek pederasts with modern day gay men and lesbians. The opposing view, known as *social constructionism*, holds that our concepts of sexual identity are shaped by the society we live in, and that people cannot accurately be classified using the concepts of another society, even if their behaviors appear similar. The difference between essentialism and social constructionism is not one of "nature versus nurture." While it has probably always been the case that different people have had different attractions, constructionists believe that the *meaning* attached to those attractions is culturally specific. In a society in which the sexes were seen as equal, or in which a binary conception of sex and gender did not exist, people might not feel the need to classify themselves according to the sex/gender to which they are attracted (just as today someone may prefer people with blue eyes, yet not identify as a "bluist" nor feel they are part of a "blue-sexual community").[1] If people with similar sexual attractions share characteristics, values, customs, or lifestyles, it is because of similar experiences and the similar positions they occupy within the social hierarchy, not because of anything inherent to the nature of their sexual orientation.

The Pitfalls of Identity Politics

People who see the world in terms of identity politics often expect that all people with a given identity characteristic will share certain moral values, political beliefs, and cultural tastes which are not shared by those who lack that characteristic. An example is the surprisingly common belief that everyone with same-sex attractions must be politically and socially progressive, while those with other-sex attractions are necessarily politically and morally conservative. Identity politics is grounded in oppression and marginalization. Members of non-marginalized groups generally do not organize explicitly around identity characteristics, nor do they expect to find common political ground on the basis of these characteristics. It would be absurd to expect Ronald Reagan and a poor black teenage mother to empathize with one another on the basis of their shared attraction to the other sex. Yet many people do not find it odd to expect a wealthy conservative gay businessman and a working-class leftist lesbian to feel solidarity based on their shared attraction to the same sex. Proponents of identity politics may have difficulty seeing things from a non-identity-based perspective. For example, they may define their enemy as "straight white men" rather than attitudes of homophobia, racism, sexism, and intolerance. They may be unwilling to take into account differences in beliefs and behavior among members of an identity group. Identity-based movements have too often abandoned a broad social change agenda in favor of reforms that benefit members of a specific identity group (for example the focus on gay participation in the military). There is often little to hold identity-based communities together other than a common oppression. If an identity-based community is highly valued, there is a danger that its members may perpetuate their status as victims in order to avoid the loss of community that might accompany a reduction of oppression.

Identity politics is a response to an oppressive reality, and it is perhaps unlikely that most people will see beyond their need for it until society changes. It is no accident that liberal heterosexuals and bisexuals with only other-sex relationships seem more eager to do away with sexuality-based categorization than are gay men and lesbians and gay/lesbian-identified bisexuals: it is easy to say "sexual orientation doesn't matter—we're all just people" when you are not regularly treated as inferior because of your sexuality! Identity politics undoubtedly provides for many people a useful basis for solidarity and a haven against a hostile world. But it can become detrimental when labels are seen as more important than people, and when people are pressured to limit what they think, say, and do in order to fit into identity-based categories.

These comments about identity politics apply to the predominantly white, middle-class gay/lesbian and bisexual movements in the United States. Many people of other cultures and ethnicities conceive of their sexuality in different and often less identity-based ways. People may engage in behavior that is associated in the U.S. with being gay or bisexual without adopting a gay or bi identity. This does not mean that they are "in the closet" or *refusing* to adopt a gay or bi identity, but rather that these particular constructions of sexual identity are foreign to them. Because the gay/lesbian and bi movements are based on conceptions of sexual identity that are culturally specific, the participation of people of many ethnicities tends to be low. It remains to be seen to what extent conceptions of sexual identity can be broadened before they lose their meaning altogether and call into question the very idea of classifying people based on sexual behavior or sexual identity.

THE COMPOSITION OF THE BISEXUAL MOVEMENT

While there have been communities over the years that have consisted largely of bisexuals, and while bisexuals have long been active members of many different movements, a self-conscious, organized bisexual movement really began to develop in the 1970s. Some early bisexual groups tended to focus broadly on sexual liberation, while others were more closely aligned with the gay and lesbian or feminist movements. The earliest groups began in large U.S. cities, and many groups started throughout the U.S., Europe, and elsewhere in the 1970s and 1980s. Widespread national and international networking and organizing began in the early 1990s.

I find it useful to think of the contemporary bisexual movement as comprising people in several broad categories: (1) those that came to the bisexual movement through the gay liberation and lesbian-feminist movements, (2) those who came to a bi identity from a sexual liberation perspective, (3) those whose first conscious self-identification was bisexual, (4) those who primarily identify with various alternative political, sexual, or other subcultures that contain a large proportion of bisexuals, and (5) those whose primary interest is gender issues and those who want to deconstruct or go beyond binary gender and sexual orientation categories. Although individuals within the movement will often fall into none or more than one of these categories, such a breakdown may nonetheless help explain why the strategies and goals of bisexual communities and the movement as a whole are so varied.

The Gay/Lesbian Legacy

The organized bisexual movement is and always has been closely associated with the gay and lesbian movement. Ronald Fox's study (1993) of 900 self-identified bisexuals indicated that 35% currently or previously identified as gay or lesbian. Many bisexual women have a history of involvement with lesbian-feminist communities and consider their bisexuality to be closely integrated with their feminist politics. Despite their alienation from some aspects of gay and lesbian communities, many bisexuals retain a strong sense of affiliation with gay and lesbian culture and identity.

The Legacies of the Sexual Liberation Perspective

Many bisexuals became aware of or began to create their bi identity during the "sexual revolution" of the 1960s-1970s. In this era of "bisexual chic" it was considered uptight to rule out relationships on the basis of sex/gender (although it was fine if one "just happened" to always end up with members of the other sex). Many of these people had previously identified as heterosexual, and same-sex relationships or sexual explorations were often much more accepted between women than between men. Fox's study showed that 45% of bisexuals in his sample had previously identified as heterosexual. A common thread can be found connecting the sexual revolutionaries of the 1960s-1970s and later with earlier proponents of free love and sex radicalism dating back to the late 1800s and early 1900s.[2] Though the early sex radicals did not identify as bisexual (the classification of "the homosexual" as a distinct type of person, rather than a type of behavior in which anyone might potentially engage, was brand new), some were open to relationships with both sexes, and they tended to question male-dominated sex acts, uncontrolled reproduction, traditional gender roles, the institution of marriage, and the possessive commodity nature of compulsory monogamy (see Murray, this volume). Both the early sex radicals and the later sexual revolutionaries were often political radicals as well, with many being anarchists, socialists, libertarians, or utopianists.

Some people who are primarily attracted to the other sex may call themselves bisexual to express their support for sexual and gender liberation or as a rejection of heterosexual privilege. Bisexuality is sometimes seen as a "default" identity for those who are not gay or lesbian, but who do not wish to label themselves as heterosexual either. Some people view bisexuality as part of their struggle against sexism. They may feel that it is as wrong to discriminate on the basis of sex/gender in erotic relationships as it is in other areas of life. Some view sex/gender-based preferences as a product of patriarchal conditioning that can be altered with conscious effort.

Bisexuality as a Primary Identity

Some bisexuals have never consciously identified as anything other than bisexual, having either identified as bisexual early in life or having previously had an unspecified or "none of the above" or "heterosexual by default" identity. Fox's study revealed that 10% of his respondents claimed bisexuality as their first sexual identity. This is apparently becoming more common and seems especially prevalent among younger bisexuals who may become aware of the existence of bisexuality earlier in life due to the greater visibility of the bisexual label and bisexual communities.

Bisexuals in Alternative Subcultures

A sizable and increasing segment of the bisexual movement is made up of people who are part of various alternative subcultures that contain many bisexuals. Examples include pagan and alternative spirituality communities, progressive political milieus, various art, theatre, and music scenes (such as some punks, ravers, and neo-gothics), science fiction and fantasy fandom, and some computer network communities. It may be that for members of these subcultures, bisexuality, as a challenge to traditional notions of sexuality and gender, is part of a more general challenge to social and cultural norms. It is not uncommon to find people identifying as bisexual after becoming involved in these communities even if they had not previously shown any evidence of bisexual attraction. It is possible that some of these people come to identify as bisexual because it is a group norm, or because they feel a political or cultural affinity for bisexuality.

A number of "leatherfolk" (those affiliated with leather, s/m, or fetish subcultures) have come to associate with bisexual communities because their preferred erotic activities are not based on genital sex, and they may enjoy playing (doing s/m activities) with members of more than one sex, which may not be acceptable in strictly homosexual or strictly heterosexual spaces. Polyamorists (those who favor sexual and/or romantic relationships with more than one person) have often gravitated toward bi communities, especially when their relationships include members of different sexes, again because they may not be accepted in either strictly homosexual or strictly heterosexual milieus (even if the individuals involved are in fact homosexual or heterosexual).

Bisexuality and Gender

Some people come into bisexual communities because they are concerned with issues of gender. Many bisexuals minimize the emphasis on sex and gender, and bisexual spaces may be more welcoming to people of nontraditional, indeterminate, or uncertain gender identity than are strictly heterosexual or strictly homosexual spaces (which are often segregated by sex). Many transgendered people cannot be unambiguously classified in traditional sexual orientation terms because such terms presuppose a fixed binary notion of sex and gender. Even if they do not identify as bisexual (many feel that the very term is too binary!) they may feel more comfortable in a bi community in which attraction to all sexes and genders is accepted. Bi spaces tend to be among the few contexts in which people of varied sexual and gender identities can interact with one another socially, sexually, and politically.

ORGANIZING STRATEGIES FOR BISEXUALS

Given the broad diversity among bisexuals, what might be our best organizing strategies? Is there a common agenda that we can agree on? Bisexual activists and the organized bi movement have tended to embrace four broad strategies. The first is to seek inclusion within the existing gay and lesbian movement; this strategy addresses the immediate need to fight homophobia and gain acceptance for same-sex relationships. The second is to build a strong independent bi-focused movement, emphasizing the unique concerns of bisexuals while working in alliance with gay men and lesbians and others when our issues coincide. The third is to create a broad sexual and gender liberation movement that will encompass the concerns of all sexual and gender minorities as equals. The fourth strategy works toward breaking down and moving beyond identity-based categories in favor of more fluid conceptualizations of sexuality and gender. These strategies overlap and are in no way mutually exclusive, but they may provide a useful framework within which to examine the evolution and future directions of the bi movement.

INCLUSION WITHIN THE GAY AND LESBIAN MOVEMENT

From Gay to Queer: A Brief History

The modern gay movement is often said to have begun with the riots at the Stonewall Inn in New York City in June, 1969. Drag queens, hustlers, and at least one he-she dyke fought back after their hangout was raided yet again by the police. The post-Stonewall gay liberation movement had a broad agenda and an affinity for the leftist politics of the day (for example Marxism/Leninism/Maoism and opposition to the war in Vietnam). Many gay liberationists saw a strong connection between sexuality and politics, and believed that the experience of sexuality-based oppression would naturally lead to the desire to radically transform society. This movement embraced sexual minorities of all sorts and promoted free choice in the areas of sexuality and gender expression (though some expected that "after the revolution" everyone would be bisexual and androgynous).

As the social movements of the early 1970s fell apart or lost their radical edge in the 1980s, the gay liberation movement, now known as the gay and lesbian movement, followed suit. There was a growing emphasis on an identity politics model that likened gays to oppressed racial and ethnic minorities. Sexual identity was increasingly seen as an immutable characteristic without sweeping social or political ramifications. The movement became more focused on civil rights and assimilation into mainstream society. Many people with same-sex attractions wanted well-paid professional jobs and had no interest in abolishing capitalism. Many wanted access to positions of power in the legislature or the military and had no interest in overthrowing the government. Many wanted long-term monogamous partnerships and children and had no interest in challenging traditional ideas about relationships and families.

In the late 1980s a new current of gay and lesbian activism sprang up in opposition to the assimilationist trend. Often calling themselves "queer" to emphasize their outsider status, this tendency burst onto the scene with the formation of the AIDS Coalition to Unleash Power (ACT UP) in 1987, Queer Nation in 1990, and the Lesbian Avengers in 1992. The queer movement had many similarities to the post-Stonewall gay liberation movement (for example, its more diverse composition, in-your-face attitude, and direct action tactics), but it was heavily invested in identity politics. Several queer groups have experienced deep tensions (sometimes to the breaking point) about whether to focus on specifically gay/lesbian or AIDS-related concerns, or on a broader agenda of sexual liberation and social change.

Bisexuals Within Gay, Lesbian, and Queer Movements

Bisexuals were generally included in the early gay liberation movement (one might even argue that bisexuality as a concept was favored), but began to feel excluded as many gay men and lesbians came to adopt essentialist notions of identity and identity-based organizational strategies. Some gay men and lesbians see bisexuals as partakers of heterosexual privilege; bis may be regarded as unreliable or uncommitted allies at best, and traitors to the cause at worst. Bisexuals may be resented for seemingly not having suffered as much for their sexual identity. In some circles, bisexuals (along with drag queens, leatherfolk, and others) are seen as a threat to assimilation because they seem to reinforce stereotypes that non-heterosexuals are amoral, confrontational, and promiscuous. In the 1980s there was a furor within the lesbian-feminist community known as the "sex wars" (disagreements over issues such as pornography and s/m) which was often cast in terms of "male-identification" and "consorting with the enemy," leaving many bisexual women feeling caught between warring factions. Previously, a woman could be a lesbian if she loved and was committed to women, but by this period lesbianism seemed to become more defined in terms of *not* loving or having sexual relationships with men.

The position of bisexuals within the queer movement is unclear. Various groups and individuals disagree about just who should be included under the queer umbrella. Some maintain that "queer" applies only to gay men and lesbians (and perhaps gay- and lesbian-identified bisexuals who are willing to keep quiet about their other-sex attractions). In fact there may be a growing tendency for some gay men and lesbians to use the term "queer" to minimize the visibility of those who aren't gay or lesbian—by using "queer," they don't have to mention bisexuals, transgendered people, and others by name. Others insist that queerness has a large ideological component—it is as much about how you think and what you believe as it is about what you do in bed or who you do it with. Some see the queer movement as a sexual and gender liberation movement that includes all sexual and gender minorities and their supporters, rather than as a homosexual identity-based movement. Still others think of queerness as a cultural construct, which includes specific styles of dress, body piercings, genderfuck, and certain types of music. The evolution of the concept of "queer" has had a reciprocal effect on the concept of "straight." If "queer" implies radical politics and sexual and social liberation, then "straight" implies conservative or reactionary politics, boring whitebread culture, and a resistance to sexual and social diversity. Thus it is possible to speak of such seemingly oxymoronic concepts as a "straight homosexual" or a "queer heterosexual."

The Pros and Cons of the Les/Bi/Gay Strategy

Bisexuals who came from the gay and especially the lesbian-feminist movements have done a great deal of the organizing, writing, and speaking about bisexuality in recent years. They retain close ties to gay and lesbian culture, are well-versed in identity politics, and are eager to see bisexuals included in what has come to be called the LesBiGay movement (an increasing number are including transgendered people as well). They feel their oppression is based on their same-sex rather than their other-sex relationships, and they share the gay and lesbian movement's focus on eradicating homophobia and heterosexism. Many gay/lesbian-identified bisexuals are not seeking inclusion as outsiders, but have long been a part of the gay and lesbian movement (sometimes as closeted bis, sometimes before they identified as bi); to them, the failure of gay men and lesbians to include bisexuals feels like exclusion or expulsion. Many bisexuals seek to take advantage of the size and infrastructure of the gay and lesbian movement that many bisexuals helped to build. Within the gay and lesbian movement, bisexual activism is often centered around getting the word "bisexual" included in group names and statements of purpose.

There is a question about which bisexuals can be encompassed within a LesBiGay strategy. Will it be all bisexuals? Or only those who have same-sex partners, fit into gay and lesbian culture, or consider themselves gay/lesbian-identified (the "good bis")? Many gay men and lesbians and some gay/lesbian-identified bisexuals consider non-gay-identified bisexuals or those in other-sex relationships (the "bad bis") to be less dedicated and less genuine—they are seen as closet-cases or thrill-seekers, not as a distinct but equally authentic sexual minority. It is common for many gay men, lesbians, and even some bisexuals to regard bisexuals as substandard or "failed" gay men or lesbians. There is a well-founded concern among some bisexuals that LesBiGay groups may be inclusive in name but unconcerned about bisexual invisibility or bi-specific issues.

It is often proposed that bisexuals should deal with issues concerning same-sex relationships and express same-sex attractions within gay and lesbian environments, and deal with issues concerning other-sex relationships and express other-sex attractions within heterosexual environments. Yet many bisexuals do not see their sexuality as "half gay and half straight" and cannot neatly divide themselves this way. They do not want to always have to hide part of who they are according to context. True inclusion of bisexuals requires the acceptance and validation of both our same-sex and our other-sex attractions and relationships, for that is what bisexuality *is*.

Many adherents of identity politics believe that their demand for equal rights is stronger if their identity characteristic is inborn or unchangeable (as it is for racial or ethnic groups). The contemporary gay and lesbian movement is increasingly reliant on the claim that homosexuals are "born that way." Since gay people cannot help being the way they are, they should not be discriminated against. It is scientifically unclear whether there is a biological basis for variations in sexuality and gender identity, though some evidence indicates that there may be genetic, neuroanatomical, or hormonal correlates. Yet there is no evidence that societies in which a majority of people behave homosexually or bisexually are genetically different from our own. Many people are able to adopt different sexual behaviors and attractions in different circumstances (for example, single-sex schools or prisons) and stages of life, indicating that sexual orientation is to a large degree socially conditioned. Some bisexuals have hopped on the "born that way" bandwagon, but in general bis tend to be more amenable to the idea that there is flexibility and some degree of choice in the realm of sexuality. There is a serious strategic flaw in seeking equal rights because "we're born that way"—it implies that those who *choose* to love the same sex or who voluntarily adopt a queer identity deserve to be oppressed.

Many gay men and lesbians maintain a firm belief in the divisibility of the world into those with same-sex attractions ("us") and those with other-sex attractions ("them"); they may believe that these groups are fundamentally different and that their interests are necessarily and perpetually in conflict. Gay men and lesbians often build solidarity by naming heterosexuality and heterosexuals as the "enemy." Some bisexuals readily accept the "us" versus "them" paradigm as long as they can convince the world that bisexuals—or at least the "good bis"—are part of the gay/lesbian "us." Yet the very existence of bisexuality can throw a wrench into this neat two-camp system. Bisexuality combines the defining features of both homosexuality (same-sex attraction) and heterosexuality (other-sex attraction), which makes it difficult to maintain that the two orientations are separate and distinct. Some gay men and lesbians feel that the acknowledgement of bisexuality makes their own homosexuality less visible or less valid. It is the threat that bisexuals pose to a dualistic view of sexuality and to identity-based foundations for organizing and community-building that cause many gay men and lesbians to be so profoundly opposed to bisexuality. This opposition has much less to do with how individual bisexuals behave in relationships or how much or how little dedication bisexuals devote to gay and lesbian causes. There has been too much time spent chastising bisexuals who behave in "stereotypically bisexual" ways, and too much denigration of bisexuals by bisexuals in an effort to gain gay and lesbian acceptance. Attempts by bisexuals to attend more meetings, stuff more envelopes, and donate more money to gay causes in an effort to "earn" the respect and recognition of the gay and lesbian community (a respect and recognition that gay men and lesbians are accorded automatically, regardless of their degree of outness or activism) are ultimately futile as long as this clash of worldviews prevails.

It seems to me that trying to build a LesBiGay (or LesBiGay-Trans)[3] movement is misguided. If we want our issues as bisexuals to be addressed, we should build an independent bisexual movement and work in coalition with others when our concerns coincide. Likewise for the gender community: gender issues are different from sexual orientation issues (though many people confuse them), and these concerns will not get the attention they deserve if they are tacked onto the end of a gay and lesbian agenda. If we want large numbers and inclusiveness, we should create a broad-based liberation movement that includes all sexual and gender minorities and their supporters. A specifically LesBiGay movement seems to provide the disadvantages of both strategies (exclusion and invisibility) without the benefits of either.

CREATING A BI-FOCUSED MOVEMENT

Because organized bisexual communities often exist on the margins of gay and lesbian communities, it is sometimes easy to forget that many bisexuals do not consider themselves part of the gay and lesbian community or even particularly closely allied with gay men and lesbians. It may be just as appropriate to regard those for whom sex/gender is a deciding factor in selecting or ruling out partners (homosexuals and heterosexuals, sometimes collectively referred to as monosexuals) as more similar to each other than either is to those bisexuals for whom sex/gender is of little or no importance or relevance to their relationship choices.

Whereas it was once all but universally assumed that bisexuals should naturally seek inclusion within the gay and lesbian movement, more and more bisexuals have decided to put their energies and resources into the creation of an independent bi-focused movement. Several factors have influenced this shift. More young people have come into the movement, many of whom have always identified as bisexual and never as gay or lesbian. The organized bi movement has increased its outreach beyond the gay and lesbian milieu. The mainstream gay and lesbian movement has grown to the point where it is now part of the establishment and is no longer on the cutting edge of sexual and gender liberation. At the same time, the bi movement has grown to the point where many people believe that bisexuals are numerous enough and strong enough to accomplish things on our own and to maintain a unique bi identity while working in coalitions with others. Finally, many bisexuals have become frustrated and discouraged by the reluctance of gay men and lesbians to accept bisexuals as equal partners in a LesBi-

Gay movement; they feel they have achieved only half-hearted tolerance rather than real acceptance. They have decided they would prefer to be part of a strong empowering bisexual movement rather than second-class members of a LesBiGay movement.

Building an independent bi movement need not lead to divisiveness between bisexuals and gay men and lesbians. Making bisexuals stronger does not make gays and lesbians weaker, but rather increases our combined strength when we work as allies against a common enemy. An alliance of empowered, focused communities can be more powerful than a least-common-denominator movement that overwhelms minority voices. Bisexuals and transgendered people will only get respect from gay men and lesbians when we approach them as equals, not as subordinates pleading for a token mention or a glimmer of recognition.

Oppression of bisexual people is based in part on heterosexism and in part on monosexism, the belief that people can or should be attracted to only one sex/gender and that there is something wrong with those who cannot or will not choose. Whether bisexuals feel more oppressed by heterosexism or by monosexism depends on many factors, including how they identified before they called themselves bi and the sex/gender of their current partner(s). Bisexuals experience monosexism both from heterosexuals and from gay men and lesbians. Bisexuals can address heterosexism within a LesBiGay movement, but cannot address monosexism. Not only do gay men and lesbians have little reason to prioritize the struggle against monosexism, they often actively support and benefit from it; homosexuals are privileged by monosexism even as they are oppressed by heterosexism.

Being bisexual is not the same as being gay or lesbian despite some important similarities. We are not defined solely on the basis of our oppressions, but also on the basis of our aspirations. Invisibility is an important issue for bisexuals, as is the failure to recognize bisexuality as a unique sexual identity. Bis are generally perceived to be either gay/lesbian or heterosexual, often depending on the sex of their current partner(s). Gay men and lesbians are inclined to divide their spaces, activities, and political causes into male and female, and they are often not eager to do away with binary conceptions of sex/gender—in fact their very identity may depend on such conceptions! This may not be acceptable to those bisexuals and transgendered people who either identify as "none of the above" or who seek spaces where people of various genders and sexualities can interact.

Ideally, an independent bisexual movement would work in alliance with others on issues of mutual concern. Bisexuals share with gay men and lesbians the desire to fight homophobia/heterosexism and eliminate violence and discrimination based on sexual orientation. Bisexuals in relationships with members of the other sex share some issues with progressive heterosexuals, such as the desire to create egalitarian, non-sexist intimate relationships between women and men, and the desire to alter society's outmoded concepts of other-sex relationships. Many bisexuals and progressive heterosexuals want to do away with heterosexual "privileges" based on economic and social hierarchies that they reject (for example a tax system which favors couples with stay-at-home wives but penalizes two-career marriages with similar incomes). Many bisexuals seek social equality for same-sex and other-sex relationships and for relationships that include more than two people (whether it be increased benefits for same-sex or multiple-person relationships, or getting public institutions and employers out of the business of granting privileges based on relationship status altogether). Bisexuals have played a pioneering role in the budding polyamory/polyfidelity movement. Many bisexuals share with some transgendered people the desire to de-emphasize binary gender categories and to deconstruct inflexible gender roles.

CREATING A SEXUAL AND GENDER LIBERATION MOVEMENT

Another strategy favored by many bisexuals is the creation of a broad, inclusive sexual and gender liberation movement that welcomes sex and gender radicals of all sorts, including bisexuals (both the "good bis" and the "bad bis"), transsexuals and transgendered people, genderfuckers, androgynes, leatherfolk, fetishists, body modifiers, boy lovers, sex workers, nonmonogamists, polyamorists, their friends and lovers, and those of all sexualities who reject sexism, heterosexism, compulsory relationship models, restrictive sex/gender roles, and sex-phobic morality. Such a movement would be based on a radical, choice-based, consensual, sex-positive, diversity-valuing ideology rather than on any specific characteristic-based identity. Some proponents of sexual and gender liberation have coined terms such as "pansexual" and "omnisexual" to describe their aspirations, but no term for this movement has so far achieved common usage.

Some have argued that a movement of this type should be built upon the foundations of the existing gay and lesbian movement, with demands that gay men and lesbians should expand their movement to include every group with an interest in issues of sex or gender. The early gay liberation movement had many of the characteristics of a broad sex and gender liberation movement, as did the "sexual revolution" of the same era, but both were too limited and fell short of achieving their goals. A number of people have looked to the modern queer movement as the broad and inclusive movement they seek, but this movement seems to have imploded under the weight of identity politics. Gay men and lesbians deserve their own space in which to focus on their unique issues. Many sexual and gender liberation proponents believe it is both wrong and futile to demand inclusion in the gay and lesbian movement if a substantial segment of that movement does not want to expand in this way—a community cannot be forced to accept people against its will. While many gay men and lesbians do indeed share the broad goals of sexual and gender liberation, others emphatically do not, being concerned only with issues that will directly benefit those with gay identities or monogamous same-sex relationships. Reciprocally, many proponents of sexual and gender liberation do not identify as gay or lesbian.

Because the gay and lesbian movement has often been at the forefront in discussions of sex and sexuality, many people seem to label all matters relating to sex and sexuality as "gay" issues. Similarly, issues related to reproduction and raising children are generally designated as "straight" concerns, although people of all sexualities have a legitimate interest in bringing up the next generation. Clearly most issues of sex, sexuality, gender, and relationships rightfully concern people of *all* orientations. While people in some groups are typically hurt more than others by the constraints imposed by traditional roles and institutions, such constraints limit the full human potential of everyone. This is not, however, to argue that everyone *should* be bisexual, androgynous, polyamorous, or whatever. Making choices based on personal preferences is very different from having them imposed by external forces. We can all demand universal reproductive freedom (both the right to have and the right not to have children), and can reject the concept of "illegitimacy" whereby children of nontraditional relationships have less social and legal standing. People of all sexualities have a reason to challenge our society's erotophobia and its belief that sex is sinful and the body is shameful. We can promote education about sexuality and show that there is a wide range of acceptable and worthwhile sexual and gender identities, manners of sexual expression, and models of healthy and loving relationships.

MOVING BEYOND IDENTITY POLITICS

Bisexuals who base their attractions on individual characteristics other than sex/gender may feel that the sex/gender of one's desired partner(s) is a bizarre foundation upon which to build an identity, a community, or a movement. For some bisexuals, the real goal is to move beyond dichotomies such as gay/straight and male/female, not simply to add a third box labelled "bisexual" or to re-label one box as "LesBiGay(Trans)." This rejection of the dichotomy between sexualities and genders is the most radical potential of bisexuality.

Many bisexuals object in principle to the gay and lesbian movement's "us" versus "them" paradigm. How can it be true that people are inherently and fundamentally different depending on whether they are attracted to the same sex or the other sex when some people are attracted to both? Perhaps more than gay men, lesbians, or heterosexuals, bisexuals tend to experience an evolution of their sexuality over time. The idea that sexuality is inherent, fixed, or unchangeable strikes many of us as false. Many bisexuals do not want to be forced to make a choice about which "side" they are on; they are unwilling to denounce heterosexuality per se, and are certainly disinclined to regard their heterosexual lovers as the "enemy." Bisexuals do not appreciate implications by gay men, lesbians, and gay/lesbian-identified bisexuals that their other-sex attractions and relationships are less valid than their same-sex attractions and relationships (for example the assumption that bisexuals choose other-sex partners to gain mainstream acceptance or social privilege, not out of genuine love or erotic desire). Many bisexuals are wary of politics based on identity: they may see identity politics as a flawed but temporarily useful transitional strategy or as a fundamentally misguided means that is not consistent with the desired ends.

There is no need for bisexual people to reach consensus on the best way to organize and build community. To achieve both useful short-term reforms and far-reaching long-term social change, we can benefit from all the various strategies: alliance with the gay and lesbian movement, an independent bi-focused movement, a broad sexual and gender liberation movement, and a push to de-emphasize identity politics and re-define binary conceptions of sexuality and gender. Bisexual people have different values and different goals (ranging from increased acceptance of same-sex relationships to a change in the very way our society thinks about sexuality and gender), and thus will align with different communities and adopt different strategies.

Some gay, lesbian, bisexual, and transgendered people have sought to promote the notion that they are "just like everyone else." At the same time, others have promoted the opposite idea, claiming that sexual and gender minorities are inherently and immutably different. Bisexuals, gay men, lesbians, transgendered people, and other sexual minorities really *are* just like traditionally-gendered heterosexuals: our similarity is that we are so diverse. People of all sexualities and genders may be radical, liberal, middle-of-the-road, conservative, or reactionary; partnered or single; parents or child-free; monogamous, polyamorous, or promiscuous; vanilla or kinky.

Instead of trying to make sexual and gender minorities more "straight" (as the establishment gay and lesbian movement has tended to do), perhaps we should aim to make the mainstream more "queer." When all the different factors are taken into account, what is traditionally thought of as "the norm" is actually a minority. All of us who fall outside "the norm" in some way constitute a large and potentially powerful movement. We could all benefit from a society that respects difference, encourages healthy consensual sexuality, promotes social equality, and celebrates diversity.

NOTES

1. I use the term "sex" to refer to reproductive and genital anatomy (male and female) and "gender" to refer to internal identity (man and woman), outward expression, and social role (masculine and feminine); these do not always coincide. Because these concepts overlap, I often use the term "sex/gender." Sex/gender is a complex matrix, not a simple dichotomy. I use the term "other sex" because, while there are differences on average between men and women as groups, there are many similarities as well and they are not *opposites* of one another. "The other sex" (like "the opposite sex") tends to imply that there are only two, but this seems impossible to avoid when discussing a system of sexuality and gender that is based on dichotomies.

2. On the early sex radicals see, for example, Blatt (1989) and Goldman (1969).

3. The community of transsexuals, transvestites, and other transgendered people seems to prefer the term "gender community." The term "trans community" and terms like "LesBiGayTrans" seem to be used primarily by gay and bisexual people who want to include transgendered people. I prefer "gender" rather than "trans" because "gender community" can encompass all who fall outside traditional gender boundaries (including those who identify as neither or both genders), not only those who wish to cross over from one traditionally-defined gender to the other.

Open Letter to a Former Bisexual (or, Do I Hear "Post-Bisexual"?)

Indigo Chih-Lien Som

The original version of this letter was written in response to a bisexual movement leader coming out as gay, not bisexual. He feared that the bisexual community would take his decision the wrong way, that we would question his motives, accuse him of abandonment. Although I barely know this activist, his announcement of this decision affected my consciousness about my own bisexual identity.

I had been going around town idly saying, *"bisexual* is tired." Then I got your letter. It didn't change my mind, but it did make me think.

Reading of your decision to identify as gay, not bisexual, I was moved for the first time in months to write about bisexual politics and identity. I was reminded of what I feel should be the fundamental principles of our movement, the basic things that I always fight for in my struggle for bi visibility and everything else that I want. For me it all comes down to choice. Ultimately, "after the revolution" if you will, what we should all have is choice. Among other things, the choice to fuck whomever, love whomever and however. And call it whatever you want (or call it nothing at all), even if someone else wants to call it something else.

Your coming out as gay actually (for me) affirms the principles and purposes of the bisexual movement, quite the opposite of harming it or undermining it in any way. I/we have been struggling so that you could do this if you needed to. The whole point is that you should be able to do this without fear. Remember? Sexuality and sexual identity are fluid and change over time. People need to be able to call themselves whatever they need to in order to let themselves do what they need to. Sometimes those empowering, useful labels can just hang us up like so much big furniture.

For several months before I read your letter, I had felt distanced from the bisexual movement, at times even apathetic, but was unsure why. When I first experienced this feeling, I thought it was my internalized biphobia that made me not want to claim the label *bisexual.* In my conversations with other women who felt the same way, I began to figure out that it was something different. Although your process (a change in orientation, prompting a change in label/ identity) was very different from mine (a questioning of label/ identity, without any change in orientation), your letter pushed me to understand and clarify some of the reasons for this shift in my bisexual identity.

The more I think about it, the more dissatisfied I am with the word *bisexual.* Because it's not about being bi, whatever that means. It's about being yourself, having the freedom to transcend sexual labels. This is why I am tired—the bored kind of tired—of labelling myself bi if I don't have to. I am tired of worrying about it, and it hardly ever seems worth the trouble. I am with a woman right now, monogamously and hopefully for life. I still scope out both genders on the street; I get crushes; I write poems. My sexual feelings and behavior have not changed; what has changed is how I think about sexual identity and labels. I don't feel *bisexual*; I feel like this is my life.

For such a specific-sounding word, *bisexual* encompasses way too much. It's vague; it hardly communicates or explains anything about me. Almost anyone could say they're bisexual and it could mean almost anything. Lesbians who sleep with men, bi women who only sleep with women, straight men who swing . . . Spare me! Is there a word that describes a sexual orientation toward creative, radical people of color? Why not? I would rather claim that label, and the political connotations that come with it. I admit I have an English-teacher-within who scribbles in the margins of my mind with red pen, demanding word choice specificity and accuracy. At the logical extreme, I suppose I could label myself *donnasexual,* since I'm with Donna.

Once I was hanging out with some queer sisters, mostly lesbians, and the conversation turned to throwing around butch and femme subcategories and identities. My girlfriend joked, "Well, I'm a squishy butch." (And I'm a butchy squish?) Finally one woman who had been quiet said, "You all have more names for gay people!" I told her, "Well, we figure if we keep coming up with more and more labels, pretty soon we won't need any at all."

This is why I have always liked the word *queer* so much. Some bisexuals feel that its blanket vagueness reinforces bi invisibility, but I disagree. I'm not hiding behind *queer*, I just *am* queer. There's a lot of room to move inside *queer* without having to say, now I'm over here, oh now I'm going over there, and now I'm gonna take two baby steps to the left. And I recognize the luxury I have to be able to feel this way. People have "bled and died" (and still do, in some places) so I could say, "*bisexual* is tired." For them it wasn't tired, it was life and death. I am grateful to Lani and all our brave bisexual foremothers (and forefathers, I guess—I don't think/know about them very much).

Some people may say it's a strange way to show gratitude, that I am invisiblizing all that they/we have fought for. It's not like that. It's not about complacency. I come out and say, "I am bisexual" when someone needs to hear it. If I am in a homophobic or biphobic situation, I'll be the first to go off about bisexual this and queer that. I still send out bitchy bi-inclusion letters with my submissions to lesbian publications. But I don't want to come out to every fucking person and declare, "I am Bisexual." I much prefer to just be myself, to spend my conversations talking about bizarre bookbinding structures, Chitra Divakaruni or Dwight Okita, or funny-angry slogans to put on my sign for the *Rising Sun* protest. If it keeps people wondering "Well so what *is* she anyway? Is she a dyke or what?"—so what? If someone finds it confusing that I talk about my girlfriend and then later on say "Wow, look at that fine man!" then that's their problem. The confusion I cause them may very well get them thinking about (my) sexuality more the way I want them to than if I give them a word to slap on me.

Same thing with your transition from bi to gay. It got me thinking, thinking more the way I want to, about sexual identity. To me, you are not outside, it's not like you opened some door and walked out of this home we call bi. You're not selling out, leaving us, deserting. Although I might feel different if you weren't a European-American—or, in shorthand, "white"—man. Experience leads me to mistrust bi white men more than gay white men, at least at first. Because unlike gay white men, bi white men seem to act just like straight white guys; they still hit on me in that slimy, straight-white-guy way, and then they think it's okay because we're both bi. Like hell, whiteboy! So many bi white men seem so dishonest about their place of privilege in the world, when their behavior and attitude toward me show that they aren't that different from straight white men—in some ways, even worse. At least straight white men can't (ab)use their sexual identity to escape from the responsibility that comes along with their privilege and power to oppress as white men.

This is not to say that I prioritize race and gender over homo/biphobic oppression, or anything so oversimplified. I am reluctant to express my priorities in theoretical terms, though, because for the moment, this year, this decade maybe, I *am* more pissed (and scared) about anti-Asian hatred and violence than I am about almost anything else. Later, though, after Asians and other people of color take over the world like haoles[1] are so scared we're going to, maybe then I will become a full-time bisexual activist. Who knows? Maybe if I were white I wouldn't think bi is tired. Maybe it's because I don't feel a part of that vague white monolith, "The Bisexual Movement/ Community." There is this tiny part of me that thinks all these white bisexuals are being really trivial in choosing bisexuality as their focus. Often I feel like biphobia exists only in white lesbians, and why should I care about them? But then I am always reminded. There *are* some colored girlz who don't get it, who say *lesbian lesbian lesbian,* never *lesbian and bisexual women.* So I remind them. Educate, educate, explain. Insert "and bisexual, get used to it." But those reminders have gotten so easy, just part of my life. Other things are so much harder, require more energy.

And that's thanks again to the people who fought to make it easier for me. So now I can go to my writing group full of lesbians (including one former bisexual) and joke, "Okay, look out, I have a boy poem this week!" Now I and all these other young queer colored girlz can nod at each other and agree, *"bisexual* is tired." Such ungrateful children! But isn't that the way it is? Children look to the future; they take your shoulders for granted. I don't take anything for granted, but I may seem to act like I do, because that's how I—and hopefully all of us—move forward.

As an artist and writer, I have often heard that the role of creative people in our society is to push boundaries, put forth our visions—in short, look ahead and move everyone forward. I don't know if I want that role; I would rather see everyone take that responsibility, regardless of creative identity. Is it cutting-edge to say *"bisexual is tired"*? When I read of your fears and your guilt in your bi-to-gay transition, is it visionary of me to yell, "no way, honey, are you missing the point or what!?" I don't want to see anyone trying to live up to pretense, or false ideals. We can't live *bisexual*; we have to live our lives. I say get on with it.

NOTE

1. Haole: Hawaiian term for European/white people, literally meaning "outsider" or "without land." This term seems to be gradually coming into common use among mainland Asian Americans.

Bisexual *Women, Feminist* Politics

Tamara Bower

A major thrust of the bisexual movement has been the demand to include bisexuals in the lesbian/gay movement as it now stands, and the insertion of the word "bisexual" into the title of every lesbian/ gay organization. This is inadequate, especially for women.

I argue that the overwhelming oppression faced by women, including bisexual and lesbian women, is male supremacy; that the oppression of women is a fundamental oppression; and that heterosexist oppression is dependent upon the oppression of women. Before we jump into the lesbian and gay movement, shouting "we're queer too!" bisexual women (and all women) have to look critically at the existing movement. We cannot let our movement be dominated by the perceived interests of gay and bisexual men, who are often indifferent or hostile to feminism.

There is a direct link between the oppression of women and sexual repression, but there are serious differences between them as well. Men exploit women for specific material services such as sex, housework, and childbearing. This is parallel to how white people have exploited African Americans in slavery, and as expendable labor under capitalism. But sexual repression does not involve one group exploiting another group for services. Heterosexuals do not specifically exploit homosexuals for labor. Rather, the homophobe is repressing the homosexual potential in him/herself, and punishing homosexuals who act on that potential.[1]

The oppression of women has been fairly constant throughout recorded history. Women's sexuality has been repressed as an out-

Special thanks to Brooke, Ann Schneider, Jennifer Siegel, Brad Robinson, and to the editors, Naomi Tucker and Rebecca Kaplan, for their suggestions and criticisms.

come of men's ownership of women. Men have always had more sexual freedom than women, and the repression of men's sexuality has varied according to the interests of a particular ruling class. An example is the acceptance of male homosexuality in ancient Greece and Rome—patriarchal, imperialist slave-states. These societies justified male homosexuality on the grounds of a male citizen's right to use his inferiors—boys, slaves, and women—for his own pleasure. Even when both people were male, sex was still an expression of dominance (Foucault, 1984). Today in our society, gay men are oppressed not only because of sexual repression, but also because they are seen as threats to men's dominance over women. Men's sexuality is restricted according to what is perceived to keep men in power over women.

Bisexuals are often accused of exercising heterosexual privilege. There is no question that with our opposite sex lovers we have access to "privileges" such as legal marriage, and the safety to express affection in public. But for women particularly, this "privilege" becomes a more complicated matter. Heterosexism is a problem *not only* because it limits our sexuality, but also because it bolsters male dominance and power. Heterosexual privilege cannot be divorced from male privilege, and male privilege never benefits women unambiguously.

For women, heterosexual privilege is a double-edged sword. The cost of the privileges that a woman receives for heterosexuality often involves putting herself under the control of a man. It is a means to make women dependent on men. Men have more power and wealth than women in this society. Heterosexuality gives women rewards, like financial security and respectability, through being tied to a man—with his wealth and his respectability.

While feminists may struggle in our lives and with our male partners for a relationship based on equality and mutual respect—and may sometimes achieve this—we must base our analysis on the actual conditions of the majority of women. What is the condition of most women in heterosexual relationships? The majority of women are heterosexually married and have children (U.S. Bureau of the Census, 1990). Many unmarried women live with their male lovers. Whether married or not, whether housewives or working at an outside job, full- or part-time, the majority of women:

- Have primary or sole responsibility for housework and the raising of children (Hochschild, 1989).
- Are partially or totally financially dependent on their husbands or lovers. (Women as a whole earn 70 cents for every dollar men earn. Working, married women earn 33 cents for every dollar their husbands earn.)
- Are under pressure to keep themselves physically attractive in men's terms.
- And 50 percent of women are raped or battered by their husbands or lovers (Walker, 1979).

These are some costs of "heterosexual privilege." To what extent does "heterosexual privilege" apply to women who live alone, who are single mothers, or who are old or otherwise unattractive to most men? These women often live below the poverty line.

Lesbian-feminists have brought up selected aspects of these facts to argue that heterosexual women "collaborate with the oppressor"—the conclusion being that they should become lesbian (Brown, 1976, pp. 109-117). But I am bringing up these points to demonstrate how contradictory the term "privilege" is when applied here. Heterosexual privilege is different in kind, for example, from white skin privilege. Heterosexual privilege is given only to women who behave in certain ways, and simultaneously puts women under the control of a man.

Take for example street harassment. If two women walk down the street being openly affectionate with each other—kissing, holding hands—they are sure to be verbally harassed and likely to be physically threatened as well. If two women walk down the street together, not touching, they will also be harassed, possibly threatened. A woman walking alone will also be harassed and threatened. The only thing that will stop the harassment is if she walks with a man. He doesn't even have to be her lover for the harassment to stop (she could even be a lesbian walking with a gay man, if they aren't too queer looking). Of course most of us continue to walk down streets by ourselves, at least during daylight hours. But the crude remarks and phony sweet talk constantly remind us that to be without a man makes us a target. The collective effects of this harassment are to curb women's independence and to keep us tied to men. Are we bickering over bad and worse? My point is that all women are oppressed whatever their sexual orientation. We are damned if we are with men and damned if we are without them.

Lesbians *are* hit harder in certain ways. Lesbians suffer from the social stigma of being "unnatural," and from pressure to keep a major part of their emotional lives a secret. They share this with gay men, bisexuals, and other sexual minorities. But lesbians are not only attacked as homosexuals—they are attacked specifically as women. Lesbianism is particularly threatening to men, and is specifically and violently targeted. Women are attacked as lesbians when:

- We are known to be lesbians.
- We support lesbians.
- We don't "put out" sexually for men.
- We are feminists.
- We are critical of men.
- We are independent of men, or not accompanied by men.
- We are out of our feminine role: when we dress butch, are good at sports, drive a motorcycle.

Women don't have to be lesbians to be attacked as lesbians. Women just have to be out of line.

Men who challenge masculine gender roles are targeted in a similar way. Men get attacked as "fags" not only for having male lovers, but also for being sensitive, nonviolent, nonsexist, or otherwise failing to perpetuate male dominance and power.

Yet while gay men break down sex roles, they still benefit as men in a sexist society. While a gay man may not benefit from the exploitation of a female partner, he benefits from institutionalized sexism in the workplace and the world at large.

All feminists want independence from men. We do not want to be dependent on men physically, emotionally, or financially. We want the freedom to go wherever and do whatever we want in safety and without harassment. For lesbians and bisexual women, this includes our demand for the freedom to love other women. Heterosexual and bisexual feminists also want the right to be involved with men on equal terms. We want men to love us and respect us and to share equally power and responsibility. These are basic feminist demands.

Lesbian separatism was attractive to many angry women in the late 1970s and early 1980s, particularly to women who had been hurt by men in heterosexual relationships. For women who had little experience in lesbian relationships, it was easy to idealize lesbianism, and exclusively female communities, as free of all the problems we have with men. However, experience taught us that women can be as abusive as men; and that heterosexual and bisexual women cannot will away our sexual desire for men. Many former separatists now identify as heterosexual or bisexual. Many lesbians also burned out on hating men, hatred being a rather draining emotion.

This shift has opened up valuable dialogue and exploration of women's sexuality—initiated by sex radicals and bisexuals. And it has made room for a bisexual community and movement to grow. Unfortunately, this shift has often involved a transition from a blanket hatred of men to little or no criticism of men at all. What we must learn to do instead is to make a distinction between hatred, and justified anger and criticism—which does not exclude our other feelings of caring and desire.

Though, of course, there continues to be separate lesbian organizing, over the past several years many lesbians have shifted from the women's movement to the newer queer youth movement—an integrated movement of gay men, lesbians, transsexuals, and bisexuals. The word "queer" is popular because it is inclusive, keeping us from bickering over who belongs. This is attractive to bisexual women for obvious reasons, having suffered from rejection in some lesbian communities. But by identifying primarily as "queer," lesbians and bisexual women are placing their solidarity and alliance to queer men over that of other women. Feminist newspapers, women's centers, and lesbian organizations are disappearing and are being replaced in popularity and support by mixed lesbian and gay male versions of these things. For example:

- In New York, when the lesbians who were running the Women's Liberation Center were forced to give up the building due to the city's financial policies, the lesbian groups meeting there moved to the new Lesbian and Gay Community Center. The Lesbian and Gay Community Center is more than three times the size of the women's center, and unlike the old center, has a paid full-time staff (gay men's greater wealth being a factor, no doubt).

• In the 1980s when I was organizing bisexual women, our most effective publicity was through the feminist newspaper. It was the major information source on lesbian community events. By 1991, our most effective publicity was through lesbian and gay publications. Many women had never even heard of *Womanews,* the New York feminist newspaper, which ceased publication recently.

• A queer Take Back the Night march took place in New York in the summer of 1990 protesting anti-gay violence—clearly modeled on feminist events of the same name to protest men's violence against women. Feminist protests have not been nearly as militant or popular lately as this queer one was.

When lesbians have organized separately, gay men have disrupted lesbian meetings by demanding inclusion. A gay male reporter demanded admission to the National Lesbian Conference. The lesbians recommended that his publication send a lesbian reporter. Another gay man demanded inclusion in a Lesbian Town Meeting recently in New York. When, after much argument, he was forced to leave, he returned with the police, further disrupting the meeting. Even social events like lesbian dances, which used to be advertised as "women only," are now more commonly advertised as "primarily for women—but all are welcome," perhaps because they take place in these mixed centers. And I see more men hanging out in lesbian bars nowadays than I ever saw ten years ago, with some bars going so far as to advertise for lesbians to "bring your favorite boys."

Two factors have been influencing this shift of emphasis from feminism to queer liberation, both in the context of an already weakened feminist movement: the sexuality debates and the AIDS crisis. The debilitating fights over lesbian "sexual purity," with which bisexual women are only too familiar, have weakened the feminist movement. Lesbian chauvinism and standards of "politically correct" dress codes and sexual conduct were unlivable, if not devastating, to many women. In reaction, some lesbians and bisexual women have looked to gay men as role models for sexual freedom, because of their greater experimentation with activities such as casual sex and S&M, and their (sometimes) greater tolerance of bisexuality. Sexual libertarians such as Pat Califia have been some of the strongest advocates for an integrated queer movement.

With the AIDS crisis and the violent backlash against gays, there has been an upsurge in the political militancy of gay men, as exemplified by mostly male groups like ACT UP and Queer Nation. In the absence of militant feminist leadership, many lesbians have been attracted to this new queer militancy (and have also acted out of solidarity and compassion for the many gay men who have suffered and died).

This trend toward an integrated queer movement has dangers for women. Gay men's leadership is defining the enemy as "heterosexism" instead of male supremacy. How convenient for gay men, and probably other men too. By combining their energies with gay men, lesbians are benefitting in ways similar to heterosexual women— and with the same male control. I am not opposed to women working with men on areas of common agreement, such as lesbian, gay, and bisexual rights. I am also inspired by the militancy of groups such as ACT UP and Queer Nation. These are healthy developments, and it makes good political sense for us to form alliances on these issues—that is, as long as we can do so without undermining our goals as feminists. If and when we form these alliances, we must be clear on our feminism, and keep in mind that men can often be expected to be foggy about the importance of feminist analysis at best, and actively hostile to feminism at worst. We cannot expect men to know what the needs of women are.

A blatant example of the insensitivity of gay men (and other men, and the women who work closely with them) to women's issues is the betrayal of women during the debates around the National Hate Crimes Act, passed in 1990. Briefly, the Act recognizes the existence of hate crimes against minorities, but leaves out hate crimes against women (de Santis, 1990). It was a product of a coalition of civil rights, religious, gay, and ethnic rights groups, spearheaded by the National Gay and Lesbian Task Force (NGLTF). In 1989, the National Organization for Women, the National Coalition Against

Domestic Violence, and the National Coalition Against Sexual Assault tried to negotiate with the coalition to include women as victims of hate crime. The participating organizations' representatives were polled, and agreed unanimously not to include women. The coalition then canceled all future meetings with the women's rights groups. Their excuses were pathetic: including women would have doomed the bill to failure; statistics are already being collected on the gender of victims of crime. An appalling argument was that crimes against women are so pervasive, so overwhelming in numbers, and so culturally acceptable that they could not be included in the Act! It's true—crimes against women are pervasive, overwhelming, and culturally acceptable—and the sheer number of cases of rape, harassment, attack, domestic violence, and murders of women would dwarf the numbers of crimes against gay men and other oppressed groups. This alone points up the urgency of feminist demands.

A bisexual contingent was active at the 1991 NGLTF conference, pushing for bisexual inclusion. But how involved do we want to be in a group that is insensitive to women and our issues?

Gay and bisexual men ask us to drop our concerns as women and to work for our rights as "queers" instead. But we cannot divide ourselves up that way. Are we going to be the ladies' auxiliary to the gay and bisexual men's rights movement, or are we going to fight for ourselves? We want gay and bisexual men as our allies— but on our own terms, without undercutting our commitment to feminism, to ourselves as women. To do this we need an independent women's movement, and we need to stand up to men's sexism, especially that of the men we work with.

The loss of so many women's institutions has put many lesbians on the defensive. Lesbians are already in a hard place in this society, not only as queers but as women who dare to live independently of men. Much of the strongest opposition to bisexual inclusion has come from lesbians with such accusations as "bisexuals are taking over the community," "bisexuals make lesbians invisible." Bisexual women are sometimes perceived as being in league with queer men to destroy lesbian space. Yet it is far easier for lesbians to scapegoat bisexual women than it is for them to confront the gay men who are dominating the queer movement.

Bisexual women are unanimously bitter about lesbian rejection. And we have found more acceptance in the integrated queer movement than among most lesbians. How can bisexual women be expected to support women-only space when that is the place where lesbian chauvinism runs rampant, the place where we have most often been rejected? Yet most of us support women's space.

These conflicts are not insurmountable, but can be resolved by examining our situation as women in a sexist society: we have a common interest in ending male domination. To say "we're all queer" is not enough. Lesbians and bisexual women desperately need a feminist perspective. We are oppressed not solely as queers, but specifically as women. We have a vital interest in overcoming our differences and building an autonomous feminist movement— one which would include women's demands for men to love us and respect us, as well as our demands for independence from men, and the freedom to love other women.

The split between lesbian and heterosexual feminists was one major factor in the breakdown of the Women's Liberation Movement. It is crucial to the success of women's liberation from male supremacy that we heal this split. Pressuring women to identify as bisexual is not the point. A new bisexual chauvinism would be no better than any other chauvinism. But it is my hope that bisexual women, as "bridge-builders," can help lead the way to a new unity in the feminist movement, across sexual preference lines. We live the experiences of both lesbian and heterosexual women, and as feminists, we fight both battles. We are in a unique position to understand the differences and commonalities among us. It is our task to bridge this gap.

NOTE

1. My assumption here is that everyone has an innate potential for all sexual expressions, and that sexual orientation is not predetermined by hormones or brain cells. I will not take the space to argue this fully here—the main point being that repression against homosexuality is of a different power dynamic than that of exploiting labor.

Go Ahead:
Make My Movement

Laura M. Perez

In April 1991, i made my public debut as an out bisexual at a booksigning of *Bi Any Other Name* (Hutchins and Ka'ahumanu, 1991). I had never before entered a gay and lesbian bookstore and i wasn't sure what to expect. I knew i needed to attend this event, despite my fears. That fateful day i willingly crossed the invisible threshold from my straight-appearing life into a world of new possibilities, challenges, and friends. I hoped that community would welcome this Latina woman with open arms.

I now find myself digging deeper to discover who i truly am. As a bisexual Latina, my gender, ethnicity, and sexual orientation are three aspects that i cherish, love, and so project out into the world. Through my activism and participation in several bi and queer events and conferences, i have gained a better understanding of who i am, what i want for myself as an individual, and what i want for *my* bisexual community.

Two significant experiences in 1992 helped me to clarify my own personal goals and also to question the goals of the broader bisexual community. To compare and contrast the "Embracing Diversity" conference in Washington, DC, and the third national meeting of BiNet USA in Minneapolis, MN, reveals the struggles of the bisexual movement in the early 1990s and unmasks threads of racism that our movement has yet to confront head-on.

"Embracing Diversity" was organized by AMBi (Alliance of Multicultural Bisexuals) as a multicultural and anti-oppression two-day meeting/workshop. At the time, AMBi was a group of bisexuals of various races, ethnicities, classes, and genders. When i got word of a conference that was "for Lesbian, Bisexual, Gay, Transsexual and Queer-Positive Activists on multiculturalism and sexual diversity,"[1] directly addressing our community's needs through anti-oppression trainings, i *had* to be there.

This conference was a life-changing experience for me. Being surrounded by people from so many different backgrounds and places reaffirmed my positive beliefs and disproved my fears that "this bi community is just another white middle-class trip." "Embracing Diversity" was my first exposure to powerful bi activists of color whom i've since taken on as mentors. Elias Farajajé-Jones conducted the opening ritual and Lani Ka'ahumanu delivered the keynote address.

The next day was long and intense, filled with hard spiritual and emotional work kept within a tightly structured agenda. The highlight was a series of exercises designed to help us understand the networks of oppression and how each of us is privileged and oppressed in some way.

This exercise opened my eyes. What struck me the most were my misinformed assumptions and unexamined attitudes about Jewish people. Having been raised Catholic i believed that "we were the one true faith." I believed that Catholics and Christians were "normal," and that Jewish people were "different" and would not be saved unless they changed their ways. It was easy to dismiss Jews because they were so different from me. The fact that Christmas and Easter are national celebrations confirmed my beliefs. Since the conference i have begun the long process of educating myself about Jewish people, religion, and culture. I don't assume. I listen and learn from their experiences. I am very aware of the visible and privileged place from where i came.

The dynamics of oppression involve the many variables of our lives, some of which are: gender, race, class, age, abilities, and sexual orientation. We are systematically given or denied privileges by governmental, religous, medical, and corporate institutions (to name a few). These institutions set us up as the "haves" and the "have nots," perpetuating the fear of human difference. When we have privilege we don't notice it, because it is the "norm."

In the afternoon we attended workshops on subjects ranging from biphobia, direct action, HIV and health concerns, to organizing for a multicultural movement, alternative relationships, and spirituality. The day was not without its problems, but overall we created a sense of community. We were in it, whatever *it* was: the struggle, the movement, the day. We were in it all together—making mistakes, taking risks, learning, sharing, and somehow making *it* all work.

By contrast, just two months later, the Minneapolis BiNet meeting was far from a nurturing experience. This two-day working weekend was a long and difficult process, fraught with political and philosophical dissension. When i arrived i read "MultiKulti feminist bis no more?", an essay written by Elias Farajajé-Jones for this event and later published in *Anything That Moves* (Farajajé-Jones, 1993). In his essay he was protesting the organization's name change at the second national meeting from the "North American Multicultural Bisexual Network" to "The Bisexual Network of the USA" or "BiNet USA." The name change was an ongoing subject of much discussion and disagreement in terms of its implications for the organization, for our movement, and for the work to be done that weekend.

Members at the previous BiNet meeting in Seattle, WA (1991) had determined that BiNet's purpose was to "collect and distribute information regarding Bisexuality to facilitate the development of Bisexual community and visibility; work for the equal rights and liberation of Bisexuals and all oppressed peoples; and work to eradicate all forms of oppression inside and outside the Bisexual community."[2] The intent of the Minneapolis meeting was to develop a structure to implement these overall goals of the organization. The goals were based in pro-liberation and anti-oppression philosophies; however, the omission of any *dialogue* on liberation and networks of oppression, including racism, cut to the core of the issues facing BiNet.

The meeting was not representative of the larger bi community. Out of approximately 50 participants, only three were self-identified people of color. To my knowledge i was the only Latina and the only woman of color. I was isolated and, as the weekend went on, i felt very unsupported.

The discussion about putting "multicultural" back in the name of the organization was particularly disturbing. I strongly suspect that one reason there was so much opposition to "multicultural" was the composition of the group itself. Instead of viewing multiculturalism, as Elias Farajajé-Jones' (1993) essay argues, as a reflection of the multitude of aspects that make up a bisexual individual (and community) such as gender, class, HIV status, ability, age, race, or religion, the term was understood only as applying to race. Since bisexuality was our common denominator, people believed we should leave all other aspects of ourselves (our differences) at the door. Yet even the predominantly white attendees still had gender identities, class backgrounds, religions, and ethnic backgrounds that figured into the discussion.

The majority of those present failed to acknowledge their own diversity as a component of multiculturalism and did not understand that these very differences inform our lives and our movement. To be an out bisexual in a monosexually-defined society is to embrace the complexities of the middle ground and this, in my mind, goes hand in hand with multiculturalism. Breaking down dualistic assumptions and appreciating the many facets of all of our lives can only bring us closer to the freedom we seek.

BiNet could embrace multiculturalism as a reflection of the different cultures that comprise our bisexual community. Understanding this definition and changing the name would give people the opportunity to identify with their own unique experience. People of the dominant culture would no longer be able to complacently consider their own backgrounds as neutral. Each of us would be challenged to examine the places in our lives where we are given more privilege/credence and begin to do the work for "equal rights and liberation of Bisexuals and all oppressed peoples" as BiNet's purpose states.

Unfortunately, the people at the BiNet meeting bought into the fear and lies and were hard pressed to support each other. If someone had objections to the term "multicultural," they did not want to be accused of being racist, or not inclusive of everyone, or goddess forbid, not Politically Correct! So the reasons for not including the "m" word ranged from "people are going to think we don't have our act together because we keep changing our name," to "why are we prioritizing racism if we are bisexuals (first)," and "we don't have to put it in the *top* line in the name of the group, so why don't we put it as a subheading to the organization's name—that's a good compromise, isn't it?" In these responses i sensed a great deal of fear: fear of how others perceive us, fear of confronting racism within ourselves, and fear of committing to anything more than the common denominator of bisexuality.

The sole structure set up to talk about racism was a Multiculturalism Task Force, one of several different groups at the meeting. However, that task force fell into the trap of using unity language to avoid uncovering the realities of the privilege in our midst. The lack of people of color at the meeting, and the fact that racism was not dealt with head-on, were set-ups for failure. If what we do is more important than what we name ourselves, as the BiNet attendees stated, why wasn't pro-active, anti-oppression work begun at this meeting?

After the "multicultural in the title group" failed to reach consensus on alternative name proposals, i left this meeting emotionally drained and disillusioned. Most painful for me was that the two men of color were the loudest advocates for keeping the name "BiNet USA." I was dumbfounded; i didn't understand. How could the people i would naturally turn to be the ones i have to convince? Without their support i felt i had nowhere to go. All the sterotypical racist messages about being a Latina that i fight every day of my life took over. I felt like i was being "too loud, too pushy, too emotional, and asking for too much" when in fact i was not. I did not know either of these men very well at the time, but i could only guess that they were reacting to the situation with their own internalized messages. Racism (and every other form of oppression) is about power/entitlement and silence/silencing. When those not in the societal norm speak up they are "asking too much" or "being difficult." How many times have organizers of events grumbled about wheelchair access, interpreters, or sliding scale fees? When we have the comfort of power we do not give it up easily. When we find ourselves in a situation of privilege, we must pay attention and listen to the other voices. I stepped over an invisible line. I did not remain silent, and i stated my truths. The majority of the people there failed to listen, and were completely unaware of the power dynamic in the room.

Where had my community gone? Was the BiNet meeting a reflection of the order of things on a national scale? I wanted my home again, my safe space to say "i don't understand white people, i don't understand why you don't trust me." I could safely say those things during the "Embracing Diversity" conference, but not at the BiNet meeting.

BiNet and our movement as a whole must implement its anti-oppression goals. One way to begin to accomplish that would be to include "multicultural" in the title, thereby acknowledging and welcoming diversity. Another would be to offer ongoing anti-oppression trainings and materials at all annual meetings and regional gatherings, as well as articles in the BiNet newsletter.

I know that i must embrace the quintessential queer in me, or an integral part of me dies. And once i have completely accepted this part of me, i must let it go, because it is not all that i am. Yes i am queer; i am bisexual. And i am also Latina; i am survivor of many abuses; i am a butch-identified dyke who sometimes wants to be a boy; i am a femme-identified drag-queen wannabe. I want bisexual organizations and communities to honor and respect all of my diversity, and to incorporate all cultures as part of the broader agenda—not just in their mission statement. As activists we must be willing to confront oppression wherever and whenever we can. It will be a joyous time when single-issue politics embraces human liberation politics. I challenge all of us as a bisexual people to make that time now.

NOTES

1. "Embracing Diversity" conference brochure.
2. From the by-laws of the National Bisexual Network, aka BiNet USA.

To Give or Not to Give

Sharon Gonsalves

I was a regular blood donor until I became involved with a bisexual man in 1986. I stopped giving blood because I wasn't sure about my potential for HIV infection. Then I educated myself about HIV transmission routes, tested negative for HIV, practiced safer sex only, and did not put myself at risk. Three years later I started giving blood again with a clear conscience. At a blood drive sponsored by my employer I was deferred indefinitely because I had been sexually involved with a bisexual man. Though I insisted that my sexual activity had not put me at risk, Red Cross personnel could not hear me past the point of my being sexually involved with a bisexual man. They handed me a pre-signed deferment letter and told me to leave. I fought my deferment by sending the Red Cross the following letter, which I offer as an example of bisexual AIDS activism. The letter was also printed in *Gay Community News*.

July 5, 1991

Robert Hoff, MD
Assistant Medical Director
American Red Cross Regional Headquarters
180 Rustcraft Road
Dedham, MA 02026

Dear Dr. Hoff,

According to your letter which I received on June 28, 1991, my name, social security number and other identifying informa-tion have been placed in your register of deferred donors. The federal guidelines concerning blood donation require that I be indefinitely disqualified from donating blood for transfusion because I answered "yes" to question 5.6 a) Have you had sex with a man who has had sex with another man since 1977?

I understand that the new federal guidelines have been instituted in an effort to stop the spread of HIV, the virus which is believed to cause AIDS. However, by disqualifying me as a donor based solely on my answer to this question the Red Cross is conceding to the irrational fears of the uneducated general public and thus doing a grave disservice to the people of the United States.

The American Red Cross has the unique opportunity to educate millions of people from all sectors of the population about how to protect themselves from HIV infection. Instead it is scapegoating those of us who have taken the time to educate ourselves regarding HIV transmission and who are taking the necessary precautions to prevent infection.

A heterosexual woman who has unprotected intercourse with a man whose sexual history she does not know could easily have exposed herself to HIV and answered "no" to the above question. If she has not yet seroconverted to HIV positive, then her blood would pass the ELISA test and be transfused, thus potentially infecting someone. I, on the other hand, know my partner's sexual history, have been HIV tested, have not exchanged bodily fluids other than saliva with him, and do not engage in activities that might put me at risk including heterosexual intercourse with or without a condom. Maybe you don't want my blood anyway, but by not asking more specific questions you're not effectively screening the blood supply or making donors more aware of how to protect themselves from HIV infection. At the same time the general public is allowed to maintain a false sense of security believing that "As long as I don't associate with the wrong people I don't have to worry." This ignorance is highly insulting and will not help end the AIDS crisis.

I suggest that if the Red Cross really wants to do something to stop the spread of AIDS it should concentrate on education and start with its employees. Gay and bisexual men are not the problem. Attitudes like the ones perpetuated by the American Red Cross are.

With the utmost concern,
Sharon M. Gonsalves

I recommend that we begin challenging the Red Cross at blood drives whenever possible. Most gay and bisexual men removed themselves from the pool of blood donors in the early stages of the AIDS epidemic because of the blatant discrimination the Red Cross perpetuates against them. Many heterosexuals do not see themselves as "at risk" and are allowed to think that as long as they don't associate with the "wrong people" they have nothing to worry about. Women who are exclusively lesbian never had any reason to stop donating blood due to Red Cross-defined sexual practices.

Therefore, politically active lesbians, bisexual women, and our heterosexual allies are in a unique position to help educate Red Cross workers since we can get through more layers of the screening process than our male friends and lovers. Ask to have the word "sex" defined the next time you give blood. If you are practicing safer sex, the Red Cross does not see this as sex since their definition includes an exchange of body fluids. Let them know you are safer-sex educated. The more they come in contact with us, the sooner the discrimination will end.

I also recommend that the Red Cross stop asking about the sexual orientation of donors and their sexual partners, focusing instead on specific sexual practices. Screening should focus solely on sexual behavior, not sexual identity. With recent statistics showing one in 100 men and one in 700 women as HIV infected, the general population is definitely at risk. Transmission via unsafe heterosex (vaginal intercourse without a condom) is now the major cause of new cases.

Our actions can make a difference. My name was removed from the deferred donor list, but that is not enough. Bisexual individuals and the bisexual community must continue to visibly challenge the scapegoating of bisexual men, and promote AIDS/HIV/safer sex education. We cannot wait for our government to decide it's okay to teach safer sex. We all have to educate ourselves first, practice safer sex and then educate others around us. It's the only way to stop AIDS from spreading further.

Fluid Desire:
Race, HIV/AIDS,
and Bisexual Politics

Elias Farajajé-Jones
aka Manuel Kalidas Congo

Your silence will not protect you . . . the transformation of silence into language and action is an act of self-revelation, and that always seems fraught with danger.

—Audre Lorde (1980, pp. 20-21)

With a profound awareness of Audre Lorde's words, I am writing this essay to break silence and inspire action.

The articulation of a politics of bisexuality necessitates an understanding of how bisexuality and HIV/AIDS interrelate: how the pandemic exacerbates erotophobia and biphobia, how erotophobia and biphobia prevent education and outreach, how the struggles against HIV/AIDS and against bisexual oppression can parallel one another. In this essay I focus particularly on the African American experience, and though I do speak of black lesbian and bisexual women, I am dealing primarily with black gay and bisexual men, for that is my context.

BIPHOBIA AND MONOSEXISM

Within most HIV/AIDS organizing, bisexuals remain totally invisible, except when mentioned in passing or portrayed as blithe

---

In memory of Zawadi-Lazarus Garrett (October 3, 1960-January 10, 1992), my partner, and of Craig Gerard Joachim Harris (April 8, 1958-November 26, 1991), my best friend: Freedom-fighters in the struggle against AIDS.

transmitters of HIV. The dominant discourse constructs "bisexual" to mean promiscuous, pathological killer (witness the film *Basic Instinct*). Lesbians accuse bisexuals of contaminating their community; heterosexuals blame us for putting them at risk. In the face of such negative constructions of bisexual identity, what does it mean that bi men are made into objects of blame, yet not given information for structuring our survival? Our category of identity has become a category of epidemiology. But the very politics of bisexuality show that we can no longer separate humankind into neat little categories. From this we can learn not to separate people into those who need HIV/AIDS education and those who do not.

Bisexuals are included in name but not in reality. There is no material that addresses men who have sex with men and women.

In the current discourse on HIV/AIDS, whether in the dominant culture or within queerworld, bisexuals are perceived as being more dangerous, more the incarnation of evil than are lesbians and gay men. Bisexuality is seen as extremely dangerous by a sex-negative, erotophobic society. It brings homosexualities much too close to home in the dominant culture; it is frightening because the ultimate Other is no longer so *other*. There is something too transgressive about blurring boundaries between worlds that are never supposed to meet.

The real challenge to bisexuality comes as it struggles to name itself, yet at the same time seeks to subvert the either/or monosexual paradigm, which would have us believe that people are either lesbian/gay or heterosexual. People often ask, "What exactly are bisexual rights?" For me, as an anarcha-womanist, Two Spirit, queer-identified bi man of colour, the underlying right for which I struggle in the context of bisexuality is to NOT have to accept the monosexist paradigm, which seeks to define me and remove all possibility of self-determination from my life.

The monosexist paradigm is particularly harmful in the age of HIV/AIDS. Ironically, while the monosexist paradigm perpetuates a deep fear of those who do not fit that paradigm, such as bisexual and transgendered people, it also prevents the distribution of relevant information to these people. Thus, bisexuals are blamed for the spread of HIV/AIDS, bearing the brunt of societal HIV/AIDSphobia, but are not included in real ways in research, prevention, or education efforts. The word "bisexual" might appear, but there is no authentic inclusion of bisexual realities; i.e., prevention models for men who have sex with both women and men.

PARTNERS IN POLITICS

The links between bisexual politics and HIV/AIDS activism suggest that each must have a consciousness of the other in order to survive. On a theoretical level, both address similar oppressions head-on; both propose new models for the construction of identity and mandate the breakdown of barriers that divide people into us/them groups. In practice, HIV/AIDS activism and bisexual activism share common tactics and visions. The ways in which society associates HIV/AIDS with bisexual women and men, the particular HIV issues that bisexual people face, and the notable absence of bi awareness in HIV prevention/education, all point to the need for greater unity among our movements.

DEFINITIONS

In 1988, one of my cousins died of AIDS-related complications. I vowed on his grave that I would not let his death be in vain, that I would dedicate my life and energy to fighting HIV/AIDS, to tearing down the walls of silence, ignorance, and fear that are the true agents of death in our community. In the courses I teach at Howard University School of Divinity, I use the tools of sociologies of cultures and knowledges to articulate an African-centered, womanist, in-the-life theology of liberation.

The reflections in this essay are not merely the result of speculation on my part. They grow out of years of listening to the pains and joys of my sisters and brothers, of living and working with people with HIV/AIDS, of losing companions, friends, and relatives to the pandemic, of burying a partner and 12 close friends in six months, of accompanying people as they struggle to liberate themselves from the bondage of internalized homohatred/bi-hatred. The things of which I speak in this essay are realities that I must face every day of my existence. I am weary of watching my sisters and brothers in-the-life eat the bread of multiple forms of oppression daily. I am tired of observing so much silent suffering.

In talking about the African American community, I am constantly reminded that we have a much more fluid spectrum of sexualities than the white community does. Categories such as homosexual or bisexual might not necessarily have the same meaning for people of African descent as they do for white people. I use a variety of terms: lesbian/gay/bisexual/transgender; queer; in-the-life.

Whereas bisexuals were once assumed to have no politics, there is now a growing multicultural feminist bisexual movement in the United States. That is why I also sometimes speak of homosexuali*ties* and bisexuali*ties,* and homosensualities (physical contact, or the exchange of physical affection, such as holding hands or kissing, between people of the same gender which is non-genitocentric and non-orgasmocentric). I do not seek to impose any one term, realizing, for example, that for many people the term queer (which I myself prefer) is highly controversial.

The term "queer," by the way, is being adopted by people who feel that, by reclaiming a term that has been used in a derogatory way, they are participating in their own liberation. Much as the term "black" was once an insult or had negative connotations but is now a source of strength and pride, so the use of the term "queer" can be empowering. It refers to a radical tendency in our community to seek liberation and self-determination, not assimilation into the white, male-dominated, heterosexual culture. "Queer" is inclusive of lesbians, gay men, bisexual women and men, and transgender people. I also feel strongly about the term "in-the-life." For generations in African American tradition, "in-the-life" has denoted a broad spectrum of identities and behaviors, similar to those encompassed by "queer": we can all be included in-the-life. The word "life" carries rich spiritual connotations, especially for a people continually confronted with suffering and death. "In-the-life" understands our struggle for liberation as being directly tied to those of oppressed peoples throughout the world, fighting against white supremacy, classism, imperialism, sexism, ableism, and all other forms of oppression (Harris, 1986, p. 66).

In addition to homohatred, bisexuals are often exposed to biphobia/bi-hatred.[1] Bisexuals are perceived as being too transgressive, perhaps because we blur what people consider to be the very clear lines separating THEM from US. This is where new understandings of gender will have a very important role to play.

Compulsory heterosexuality (Rich, 1980) is a power inextricably bound up with the capitalist class structure and fed by racism, classism, sexism, and homohatred/bi-hatred. Heterosexism is profoundly rooted in a primal need to preserve these social structures and strictures. How could one speak of the oppression of black lesbian/gay/bisexual/transgender people and not speak of white supremacy? What about the fact that those of us women and men of African descent who are in-the-life live at a place of intersection of several different forms of oppression? In our experience of *Otherness,* we are doubly or triply **the ultimate Other, the Different One.** *As a black queer man, I am oppressed as a man of African descent, I am oppressed as a queer, and I am oppressed as a queer of African descent.* My oppression comes not only from the dominating culture, but also from within my own communities: In the black community, I am oppressed for being queer; in the queer community, I am oppressed because I am a man of colour.

THEOLOGY AND GENDER

Is it not part of being African-centered to examine our roots and see how they apply today? As we deal with HIV/AIDS, it becomes absolutely necessary to understand bisexualities in the African American community, and to search for responses to homohatred and the HIV/AIDS pandemic from within our cultural traditions. This leads us to look for models that are sex-positive, that are not women-hating, and that offer new visions of gender.

For example, Two Spirit people in certain Native American cultures represent other gender categories which transcend the female/male binary unit. Known by different names in different indigenous languages (such as *nadle* in Navajo or *winkte* in Lakota), Two Spirit people are often those who mediate between the visible and the invisible worlds and who have gifts of healing, vision, and prophecy (Williams, 1986, pp. 41-43). Two Spirit people play a special role in their cultures; although they represent a totally different construction of sexualities and genders, they would usually be defined as lesbian/gay/bisexual/transgender people in the dominating culture. Part of the transgressivity of bisexuality is that it says love knows no gender. Such gender subversion is something many people find threatening about bisexuality (Butler, 1990, pp. 35-78).

Furthermore, the rising visibility of the transgender community, which is not negligible in the black community, calls us to further grapple with the relationship between sexualities and spiritualities. In African religious traditions such as *vodun* (Afro-Haitian religion) or those based in the Yoruba tradition, there is a *theology of gender* that is very different from that to which most people in African American religious communities are accustomed. For example, in the Yoruba religion there are manifestations of the divine *(orisha)* that are bi-gendered. Furthermore, a female *orisha* can manifest through a man, just as a male *orisha* can manifest through a woman. Whatever the gender of the orisha or the initiate, the newborn initiate who is attached to a particular orisha is considered to be the *iyawo* or the bride of that orisha (Murphy, 1988, pp. 89-91). The body is not only the temple, but it is also the place where the Spirit manifests (as when people "get happy" or "shout" ecstatic religious experiences which might include trance, in some African American worship traditions). If sexuality can be perceived as a gift, then the body is to be celebrated. Unfortunately, because of the power of erotophobia we place too much emphasis on what is not to be done, leading to sexual repression, denial of critical information, and ultimately, to death.

THE EVIL OTHER

We are witnessing now the rise of a wave of pronounced biphobia. Various sources portray black bisexual men as the OTHER, as THE transmitter of HIV/AIDS in the African American community. This combination of biphobia and HIV/AIDSphobia is being used to discredit and destroy our community. Bisexual women and men are constantly portrayed as knowing and intentional transmitters of HIV/AIDS. Instead of turning collective queer rage against the government which does not provide explicit HIV/AIDS education or give enough money for research, some people now use bisexuals as their scapegoat. In an era of ever-increasing erotophobia, as this construction of the bisexual as *evil other* intensifies, it will become more and more difficult for bisexual women and men of African descent to come out.

This is a particularly vicious form of oppression for us: we are just beginning to organize our communities, to address the issues surrounding the diversity of bisexualities that exist in our worlds. However, there are still very few visible "out" black bisexual activists. So-called authorities on HIV/AIDS and human sexuality feel free to say that bisexuals are cowards, that there is no such thing as a black bisexual activist, and that we are consciously spreading HIV/AIDS.

Homohatred and bi-hatred have already significantly damaged the life of the African American community. They continue their destructive work by creating an atmosphere for HIV/AIDSphobia, the fear of HIV/AIDS and of people living with HIV/AIDS, and aparthAIDS, the systematic discrimination against and separating out of people living with HIV/AIDS.

HIV/AIDS/AIDSphobia/aparthAIDS

Almost any issue that concerns African Americans somehow points to HIV/AIDS, and almost any "HIV/AIDS issue" has disproportionate impact on African American communities. The following points underscore and explain this interconnectedness:

(a) Lack of a universal health care plan. How do we realistically talk about HIV/AIDS treatments when most of us people of colour cannot afford and do not have access to health care?

(b) The prison system. When 25% of the African American male population between ages 15 and 35 is imprisoned, and when most prisons do not allow HIV/AIDS education, condom/dental dam distribution (because this would imply that there is same-gender sexual activity taking place in the prisons), or needle exchange, is it not reasonable to conclude that a high percentage of African American men would have come into contact with HIV and gone on to become HIV+? What does it mean that these men might later have unprotected sex with both women and men?

Here one must also raise the issues of incarcerated lesbians and bisexual women of colour who are living with HIV. What structures are put in place to support them? Their situation is further complicated by the fact that institutions do not consider lesbians as being at risk; furthermore, the sexualities of lesbians and bisexual women are considered to be unimportant and nonexistant. This is rooted in erotophobia, which condemns women, women's bodies, and women's lives.

(c) Teen pregnancies. Wherever there is a teen pregnancy there is unprotected sex and the possibility of transmitting HIV.

(d) Mandatory testing. As important as testing might be in HIV/AIDS prevention, *mandatory* testing is not the answer, and in fact has dire consequences for people of colour, because test results can and will be used against us.

(e) Unemployment. When people cannot work/do not have jobs, they don't have access to health care or job-related health plans.

(f) Affordable housing. The right to housing is an AIDS-related issue for people of colour. What good does it do to have AZT, DDI, homeopathic, or Chinese herbal treatments if you don't have running water with which to take them, or a house in which to sleep and eat?

(g) Social services. People of colour are often denied access to social services, preventive care, and early treatment because of economic barriers and discriminatory practices. Furthermore, funding cuts are drastically reducing social services. As the face of HIV/AIDS becomes increasingly one of people of colour, of women and children, and of poor people in general, who will be there to take care of us?

(h) Black women's health issues. Women of colour with HIV/AIDS constitute 73% of women with HIV/AIDS. Since the CDC definition of HIV/AIDS was developed from observations of men, women will often die of an opportunistic infection before they are diagnosed with AIDS or given treatment. Not only are their health needs not studied, but they are not eligible for health benefits, child care, trial tests of experimental medications, rent subsidies, or other support services for people living with HIV. They are not provided with information on how to take care of themselves and how to

protect the people with whom they share needles or have sexual relations.

Furthermore, under the pretense of the best interest of future children, the medical establishment pressures HIV+ women, who are predominantly women of colour, to have abortions or to be sterilized. Such forced sterilization is genocide. As Sunny Rumsey Ahmed, an African Caribbean Muslim sister and HIV/AIDS terrorist says:

> Why should these women be treated any differently from white women with a family history of cancer, genetically transferable disease, chronic fatigue, multiple sclerosis, or a variety of potentially deforming disabilities? Many diseases are transferred *in utero,* and the law strongly protects the rights of women with these diseases. To advocate for sterilization and abortion because of a disease that affects primarily women of color looks like racism. (Ahmed, 1990, p. 104)

(i) Education. We are squeamish about sex education in this country, but it is now a matter of life and death. While we are processing, people are dying. When we become locked into endless debates about whether we can distribute condoms to our young people and encourage them to use them, we must remember that *THERE ARE OVER 1 MILLION HIV+ PEOPLE IN THE UNITED STATES* and that *EVERY SEVEN MINUTES THERE IS AN AIDS-RELATED DEATH* (Mann et al., 1992).

HIV/AIDS education is still grossly inadequate for bisexuals and for communities of colour. It is often not accessible in languages or terms that we understand; many of our people do not read.

It is of crucial importance that HIV/AIDS educational materials address people who are sexually active with people of all genders. Materials must discuss bisexuality and HIV/AIDS in a direct and open fashion, not in ways that ridicule the life experiences of bisexual women and men. Further, most materials have focused exclusively on men to the total detriment of women. Very little attention has been paid to lesbian sexuality, bisexual women's sexuality, and HIV/AIDS. As Alexis Danzig says in her excellent essay entitled "Bisexual Women and AIDS" (1990):

Because of heterosexism, bisexual women are at risk for HIV transmission as well as for the increased violence against people perceived as sexually different. It is important that lesbians who sleep with men, straight women who sleep with women, and self-identified bisexual women begin creating awareness of our sexualities, of our experiences with safer sex and HIV transmission with each other and with our mono-sexual sisters. . . . As women who are sexual with both men and women, reclaiming our bisexualities can empower us against disinformation and allow us to redefine for ourselves what "being bisexual" can mean about taking responsibility for ourselves and those we love in the AIDS crisis.

(j) Substance abuse. Here we are faced with several issues that have devastating consequences for the spread of HIV among people of colour: HIV transmission through the sharing of works for the use of heroin; the spread of crack like wildfire throughout all levels of black communities; and the fact that people perform sexual acts in return for crack. Cocaine, which does not grow in the United States, has been placed in our communities to accelerate the process of extermination. Consider the fact that in the 1960s, when the Black Power movement was at its zenith, heroin became widely available (as it is again now) and played a great role in dismantling our movement for self-determination (Banzhaf, 1990, p. 82).

(k) Media. The treatment of people of colour in the mass media has always been a crucial issue for us, but it becomes even more critical in an era in which the press, reflecting the dominant mentality, is busily assigning responsibility to various groups for the transmission of HIV. First the media tried to pin HIV on Haiti and Africa; then on gay and bisexual men. INNOCENT = white middle-class heterosexual women with HIV, and GUILTY/DESERVING-TO-BE-PUNISHED = queers, poor people, injection drug users, prisoners, and people of colour with HIV (bearing in mind that many people are in more than one of these categories at a time). The so-called "innocent" can offer preposterous hypotheses for the spread of HIV/AIDS, but when we speak of CONSPIRACY and GENOCIDE, then we are considered wildly paranoid and irrational. Yet history and our experience speak loudly for themselves.

Is it not genocide when one does things to remove the possibility of life from a people? Why is it so strange to imagine that this has not been carefully thought out? Is this not perhaps a plan that went awry, or is it going according to plan? Given the policies of genocide enacted on people of colour on this continent over the last 500 years, why consider what I say to be wild and careless? We have only to look at the Tuskegee Syphilis Experiment in which from 1932 to 1972, more than 400 African sharecroppers and day labourers in Alabama were subjects in a government study designed to determine the effects of untreated syphilis (Jones, 1981). This example tells us that the scientific community is willing to use African Americans as guinea pigs.

(l) International community of people of African descent/people of colour. HIV/AIDS is an issue for all peoples of African descent and all people of colour. We have only to look at the devastation HIV/AIDS is visiting on particular African countries which will have severe consequences on Africa and her participation in the international economy. Certain world powers would be only too happy to step in and take over the natural resources of African nations, given that they have destroyed their own. HIV/AIDS is spreading so rapidly in Africa that the worst-affected areas will show a net population loss within a few decades. AIDS is already the leading cause of death for adults in some African cities and one of the main causes of infant mortality. According to Uganda's large-scale, population-based national HIV seroprevalence survey, approximatly 800,000 adult Ugandans (out of a total population of 16.2 million) were HIV-infected (Mann et al, 1992, pp. 40-47).

CONCLUSIONS

In an era of violent homohatred, bi-hatred, erotophobia, and aparthAIDS, if we do not successfully subvert the monosexist paradigm, that paradigm might very well kill us. The rise of HIV/AIDS has meant that our invisibility—as bisexuals, as people of African descent—is now nothing short of a death sentence.

We also have to look at cultural diversity in the expressions of forms of bisexuality. Bisexuals, particularly bisexuals of colour, must remain in the forefront of the struggle against HIV/AIDS and

HIV/AIDSphobia, remembering that we have a very special role to play. As Alexis Danzig said, the HIV/AIDS pandemic calls us to empower ourselves. We cannot wait for others to address our issues; we must take responsibility for our own lives and health. We need bisexual HIV/AIDS activists who are vocal and constantly present to advocate for our issues. We will have to do much of the prevention/education work directed to our community for ourselves, developing networks of resources and information by and for bisexuals. How can we not develop a body of bi HIV/AIDS educators and activists if we are truly committed to struggling against oppression in all of its forms? It is becoming ever-more clear that rigidly defined, identity category-based HIV/AIDS prevention/education strategies are not working. Contrary to what the monosexist paradigm would have us believe, we do live in a world of fluid constructions of desires, genders, and sexualities. There are many who choose to have sex with all genders in varying relational configurations and who do not necessarily identify with any labels. Therefore, truly innovative HIV/AIDS prevention/ education strategies that target all women who have sex with women and men, and all men who have sex with women and men, might indeed be the key to prevention for the entire population.

We must take the very struggle for survival into our own hands. We must challenge our elected officials and our government to be accountable to us, because our lives depend on it now. And when they fail us, we must take to the streets and bear our demands—our rich, chanting voices—to the very doors of power. Our oppression is so patently connected to other forms of heteropatriarchal hegemony such as the war on the environment, and all the isms, that I cannot help but envision us queer-bi HIV/AIDS activists as freedom fighters and healers. Our bodies do matter.

NOTE

1. Biphobia/bi-hatred says that there are no such things as bisexuals; that bisexuals don't know what we want; that we are fence-sitters or whiners; that we have no politics or community; that we are confused; that this is just a phase; and that we are promiscuous transmitters of HIV.

Our Leaders, Our Selves

Loraine Hutchins

Since sexuality is such a tense topic these days, we bisexuals who come out publicly have no choice but to take ourselves seriously as leaders and role models. We need to know how to educate others about bisexuality, how to learn and teach leadership skills, and how to hold each other accountable as we work in coalitions. We must question authority while becoming conscious of how empowerment works. Valuing consensus and de-emphasizing hierarchies is important, but an unexamined distaste for leadership can hold us and the movement back.

This essay discusses what I've learned as an out bisexual leader for the last two decades—both in progressive social change movements and as an elected coordinator of BiNet: the bisexual network of the USA. I examine common organizing barriers bisexual activists face—class, race, gender, strategic, generational, and other cultural differences—and then discuss ways to address these differences positively. I focus on leadership development because of my belief that the unity and skills of ALL of us are needed—both to defend our freedom against those who would hate and misunderstand us, and to create the world where we long to be.

WHAT U.S. BI ACTIVISTS HAVE BUILT SO FAR

Starting with a loose friendship network woven between people in several midwestern and east/west coast cities during the late 1970s and early 1980s, we have shared knowledge of each others' activist efforts through newsletters, phone calls, occasional conferences, and visits. Since the mid-1980s we have grown into a political movement embracing hundreds of social and support groups, political action groups, and a national organization (BiNet USA) whose decentralized functions have rotated, by members' design, between Boston, San Francisco, Seattle, Minneapolis/St. Paul, Washington, DC, Miami, Chicago, and Portland, Oregon.

We've become organizers while facing AIDS, a public health crisis that has taken some of our best leaders. Bisexuals have helped create some of the first safer sex curricula and AIDS care systems, demanding that these services address bisexuals even as both the public health system and our own gay brothers and sisters sometimes continue to ignore us. We still have a long way to go in articulating a bi response to AIDS and a comprehensive bi health care platform, but we have begun.

We have also created a mixed gender movement with strong women leaders, something many progressive groups are still trying to accomplish.

We have made bisexuals visible, from bi magazines and newsletters to bi-produced videos and books, bi direct action groups, bi computer networks, bis on talk shows, bi caucuses in professional and political organizations, and bis included in the organizational titles and programming of everything from Pride committees to college courses. The 1995 *Bisexual Resource Guide* lists organizations in 48 U.S. States and 18 countries. In 1993 our new movement won public recognition as thousands of bisexuals marched in Washington with our name in the title of a national march for the first time in history.

Who are our leaders? Our leaders are the coordinators of local bi groups, those who serve as contact people and are willing to be quoted in the press. Our leaders are also our BiNet USA elected regional representatives and the six elected national coordinators. People who write and publish about bisexuality and the bisexual movement are also often looked upon as leaders. Lastly, there are people with no formal roles or titles who do the work of running bi groups, putting out newsletters, and organizing events. Though our movement is still small, we are big enough that organizers no longer all know each other face to face. This is both a measure of our success and a cause to re-evaluate.

Is it our goal to organize all bisexuals in the U.S. or in the world into one organization, under one political platform? To open a national office in Washington, DC? To have offices in each state? Do we focus on organizing for bisexual rights and understanding in the many other gay, straight, and mixed institutions to which we belong? Is organizing for liberation of all oppressed groups, including bisexuals, the best approach? As we become aware of where our movement is going and where we want to be, we discuss these questions on national and local levels.

We are learning by speaking out publicly on bisexuality, by facing the AIDS crisis, by responding to right-wing hate initiatives, and by helping mobilize national marches and lobbying efforts. But we seldom take the time to evaluate and document what we've done, much less pass it on to others in regular training formats.

The past few years have brought many more people into the organized bi movement. Some have just passed through. Some have become involved with social/support groups or specific events and then become committed to a larger vision of educational and political activism. Some have created new groups on their own. Organizing every bisexual into the same group is not necessary or feasible, but being conscious of different kinds of bi organizing and what bis want our movement's goals to be, is important.

Taking ourselves seriously means studying movement-building and organizational development before our bi support groups or other organizing efforts run into problems. Disagreement about priorities, exhaustion, even dissolution of some groups take their toll, but sometimes it is a comfort to remember that these stages are common to all organizing. While we can not avoid the problems, we *can* use them as stepping stones.

BARRIERS AS STEPPING STONES

Class Barriers on and off the Information Highway

The tremendous success of the April 1993 National Conference Celebrating Bisexuality was due partly to the miracle of the Internet.[1,2] Conference coordinators in Washington, DC linked up via computer with activists in other cities to coordinate logistics, produce a program booklet, and plan workshops and plenaries for over 600 participants. But what about those of us not yet "on-line," or who may never be, for reasons of access and class?

Telecommunications is rapidly changing our world. It equalizes by enabling more people (especially youth, since many students have computer access) to have input into decisions and discussions without traveling great distances to meet. When you are known only through your words on a screen, many of society's usual categories—race, gender, age, sexual orientation—can be obscured, fluid, or rendered irrelevant if you want them to be. People "come out" on Internet, receive their first baby bi pats of encouragement, are crisis-counseled into recovery, learn about organizing resources, make "virtual" friendships (that are sometimes consummated in the flesh), and mobilize lobbying efforts when human rights emergencies are at hand. The Internet facilitates quicker group-editing and approval of press releases and has made our media appearances more representative, opening up talk show opportunities and speaking engagements to a greater variety of bisexuals. Internet also exacerbates our differences. People connected to government, universities, and corporations are more likely to have access. It favors speed readers, fast typists, and the verbally agile.

Not many people talk comfortably about class differences, with respect to computers or not. While the gap between rich and poor widens, outside the U.S. as well as within it, it has become almost taboo to mention class differences. There are many aspects of class in need of further discussion, such as what it means to be working poor and bisexual, how unsupportive and inaccessible many of our movement events are to single parents, and how one's ability to be an out bisexual activist is related to one's employment and economic status. BiNet USA has tried to help equalize access by having sliding scale dues and holding elections for national coordinators by mail ballot rather than at annual meetings (members who can't always travel aren't prevented from running or voting). If nothing else, as activists we can initiate discussions about class and economics in our own organizations and among our friends, families, co-workers, neighbors, and associates.

Race and Other Cultural Barriers

It's hard to see privilege when one has it. Able-bodied people usually don't consider how many ways their lives would change if they were only able to conduct them in wheelchairs, yet those who use chairs face architectural and social barriers each day. So it is with white supremacy and other forms of oppression. As long as bis of color are not represented in proportion to the population, in politics and programming for bis, our efforts will not adequately reflect the richness and variety of everyone. Whites who are the majority in most bisexual organizations have choices as to how we challenge racism. We can remain overwhelmed and complain: "They don't come to us. We do outreach. We don't know why they don't stay." Or we can make a commitment to listen and educate ourselves about the issues of people of color, especially as they relate to bisexuality, and learn how better to support people of color in everything we do.

BiNet USA is organized for as close to 50% gender/racial balance[3] on national and regional levels as possible. However we are new at this and have made mistakes, focusing on symbolism (naming) rather than root causes (how we act). For example, because we have not adequately addressed racism among us, the tension plays out in ongoing debate over our name—whether it should include multi-cultural and feminist in its title or not, and whether multicultural is a term inclusive enough of everyone.

At this point many have said that our name is irrelevant; creating a diverse multicultural movement for social/sexual justice is the key issue. However, because racial discrimination and sexual and economic differences divide us, and because the movement for lesbian, gay, bisexual, and transgender rights is being called "the civil rights movement of the 90s" (as if there were no civil rights for people of color left to win), and because the Right continues to pit people of color against queers, what we say and do on racial justice issues and how we relate this work to sexual and economic issues is key.

Sometimes we can also over-attribute group tension to gender, class, or racial differences when the power dynamics between newer and older members are *also* key. When we were all new to bi organizing nothing was institutionalized. Now new people see something established they did not have a hand in creating. It is important to make sure everyone has an equal voice. Not all of us are equally talented or have the same skills or time to devote to organizing, but valuing the leadership in all of us serves a corrective and richly diversifying function. When people feel their own strength they hold whoever speaks for them more accountable. They make sure they control statements and directions of the group and take themselves seriously by pacing their organizing for long-term change, not just crisis-response.

If we get weary of endless "Bi 101" presentations and coming out counseling sessions, why not organize others to do speakers' bureaus and training workshops, rather than try to do it all ourselves? As one activist said, "At the 1990 conference I sat quiet while people debated initiating a national bi mailing list. I didn't speak up to let people know there'd been one in operation for three years, that it lived in my computer. I didn't want to appear controlling, but it was also that I didn't know how to pass on information, didn't feel comfortable as a leader." Does this sound familiar? I've heard many similar stories.

Gender Barriers

What unites bisexual women and men is often a shared sense of alienation from our own gender in the outside world. Bi women have felt ostracized by both lesbians and heterosexual women. Bi men have felt unaccepted in both gay and mainstream environments. Some bi women and men embrace feminism and understand that gender roles based in sexism have limited us all. Along with this often comes an understanding that homophobia is rooted in sexism and that we all have internalized it and reproduce it among each other. But not all bis identify with feminism, or understand it in the same ways, so there are tensions and disagreements among us. While bisexual feminists form the bulk of BiNet USA's current membership, the organization has yet to reach consensus on how or whether reproductive rights relates to bisexual rights, for instance.

Seattle and Boston have strong traditions of separate bi women's groups. However most areas of the country have only mixed-gender groups. Few mixed-gender bi support groups also meet *separately*, to gain the insights that only same-gender caucusing brings. On the other hand, if we primarily meet only with our own gender this can sometimes restrain important mixed gender interactions too.

Also, not everyone identifies as either male or female for their entire lives. An increasing number of transgendered people identify as bi, but many bisexuals still do not understand transgender issues or how or why they are related to bisexual rights. If we don't talk about gender and learn about it, we will never tap the potential power of our connected movements. Just because bisexals love more than one gender doesn't mean we know all there is to know about gender relations and identities.

Strategic Differences

Many bisexuals do not identify with queer culture or issues. They may not feel they belong in the lesbian or gay communities, nor are they always welcomed there. Yet in many ways the *national* bi movement was born out of the second national March on Washington for Lesbian/Gay Rights (1987), where we had the first ever national bisexual contingent. Lesbian and gay groups enjoyed growth after that march as well. Many of this new political organizing expressed an expanded bi-inclusive sense of sexuality, more embraced by the word "queer" than "gay." A few short years ago who could have imagined gay people creating slogans such as Queer Nation's: "Women loving women loving men loving men loving women . . . "? Identity definitions blur and change. There is even debate about getting beyond "identity politics" altogether, so as to move beyond the special interest group lines that divide us.

This state of flux about identities and social change was illustrated vividly in the naming of "The 1993 March on Washington for Lesbian, Gay, and Bi Equal Rights and Liberation." The discussions preceding this compromise title expressed a desire for both strategies to gain legislative "rights" AND for ongoing "liberation" of people's beliefs about sexuality. One effect this inclusiveness discussion had on the more conservative reformist gay movement was to re-evoke gay liberation (as opposed to "rights"), to begin to reframe the debate from one of "we just want to live like you do" to a larger national conversation about sexuality, expanding gender roles, relationship modes and ways of loving for all.

Such liberation potentially involves many more people than the 10 percent usually touted as being gay.

Sometimes our strategic differences play out around deciding whether to prioritize organizing social/support groups versus engaging in educational and political organizing around bisexuality. However, people need social events, support groups, workshops, marches, and speakers' bureaus. More to the point is to examine the assumptions behind any organizing. Is our goal to appeal to all bisexuals? Does our group study how existing discriminatory policies impact all kinds of bisexuals and how to change those policies in society and amongst ourselves?

Organizing on bi issues doesn't only happen in lesbian/bi/gay or transgender groups. It can mean anything from raising bi issues at a rural church group to organizing for sex workers' rights in the inner city or working on AIDS issues in a suburban political party. There are out bis raising consciousness about bisexuality in many places. The public interest/consumer/citizen action movements, the AIDS and health reform movements, the Latin American Solidarity movement, the anarchist movement, the socialist movement, the libertarian movement, the polyamory[4] movement, the transgender or gender identity movement, the leather/sm movement, the women's movement, the men's movement, the environmental movement, and various movements for people of color rights all have visible, out bisexuals in their midst. In workplaces, many bisexuals are beginning to come out in the computer industry and in the teaching and helping professions. Go to any neo-pagan gathering, punk music concert, or science fiction convention, and you will find a prevalence of bi beings. Of course, if we don't network to remain aware of what each other is doing, we have no movement. But if we do, sparks of connection and joint actions can fly.

Educating people about bisexuality may succeed best within multiple movements—not only because there is no one way to be bi, but also because the nature of an identity that situates itself between gays and heterosexuals has shown us how important it is to network AMONG groups, as much as to create one's own. As one bi activist who came from the environmental movement and is taking an anti-racism class said, "I find common cause with queer straights [his term for progressives who understand sexual politics].

I don't have much in common with straight queers [including straight-identified bis who have only an interest in assimilationist identity politics]."

While we build bi social/support groups we must also build larger efforts to change society into a more human welcoming support group for us all.

Generations of Leaders

During the organizing of the April 1993 National Conference Celebrating Bisexuality, a debate erupted on the Internet. The debate involved local activists who had joined together to work on the national conference, and centered on national-versus-local organizing priorities. In hindsight, I think the debate was also about different generations of leaders—newer leaders challenging older leaders, asking for more space and more power. Some questioned whether the growth of a national movement would deplete local resources and leadership. They also felt they weren't being heard by those recognized as national leaders. Some of the leaders who had been carrying the weight of national organizing had a hard time listening to the feedback; they didn't feel heard either. The discussion focused on the nature of leadership, how to hold leaders accountable, how to craft a shared political vision. A newer generation of leaders is beginning to share power with people who've founded the movement. At turning points like this, either we strengthen our bonds or we grow apart.

A number of bi groups have organized anarchistically on consensus principles drawn from the feminist and peace movements. But these principles are not always clearly taught. Without this teaching they can end up working *against* inclusion of new people, not welcoming them. "Newcomers are dissatisfied with the lack of structure in our group which older leaders take as a badge of pride," said one newer activist. "These older organizers took initiative, started the first groups. But when you're new and there IS a group and you can't figure out how to get into its inner circle or change it, that's a problem."

Despite the fact that many people first realize they're bi in their teenage years, few of us network with youth groups. Nor do we often seek out the individual bi youth who most need information and support in foster homes, juvenile detention centers, isolated rural areas, or on city streets. A lot of bi energy first emerges on college campuses, but many bi groups apart from universities are not aware of bi events on campuses near them, nor are we establishing mentoring relationships with these organizers who will succeed us. Most of us probably long for bi elders as mentors too, no matter what our age.

Bisexual events draw people who have no other activism experience *and* those who have been organizing in the queer, progressive, and women's communities for years. Some of us came out in the 1970s when gender roles and boundaries were being challenged. Some of us came out in the Reagan/Bush AIDS era when society became much more polarized. Whether youth, seniors, or in-between, and no matter how our religion, ethnicity, or other factors shaped our sexuality, we all share the experience of bisexuality and have something unique to contribute.

SURVIVAL CONCLUSIONS

Suppose you know all this and still feel stuck. Without clear guidelines and structures that we develop and regularly reaffirm, we may feel inhibited, unable to directly address our concerns with others, and/or isolated as leaders ourselves.

We need to study models from past and present, compare our vision to what exists, and brainstorm what we want. Organizing and leadership development are learnable skills, but we have to acknowledge how we each possess them and develop the leadership potential in each of us if we want bisexual liberation to continue.

Whatever groups we work in—be they social/support or political action, be they bi groups or groups within other movements—we need to have regular training in grassroots organizing skills such as fundraising, meeting facilitation, crisis-counseling, public speaking, media strategies, political lobbying, direct action, and coalition-building. We also need to teach and practice the arts of criticism/self-criticism, respectful listening, workshop planning, conflict resolution, and cooperative decision making. And we must spend regular time reflecting on and sharing our histories together, evaluating what we have learned.

Together we have created a movement for bisexual rights and liberation. I have outlined some of our strengths, problems, and choices. At this writing we as local, regional, and national activists have just begun discussing where we want to go as a movement, and where we want BiNet USA to go as a membership organization in coalition with other organizations and movements. BiNet USA's dues-paying membership has not yet reached the one thousand mark. Our treasury has never had more than $1,000 at any one time, which always gets quickly spent on newsletters, conferences, and postage. Still we are beginning to wrestle with how best to build membership and how to raise and allocate money. More regional clusters of groups are holding conferences than ever before—in the Southeast, the Southwest, the Pacific and Northwest states, the Midwest, and the Northeast. We have empowered BiNet USA to take affirmative stands on the sexual orientation civil rights bill and sodomy reform, and against hate crimes. BiNet USA members decided in April 1993 to defer lobbying on military issues, abortion, and gender roles until we have more dialogue on these topics. The group also has a national structure of issue-oriented task forces (currently on Sex Positivism, AIDS and Health Care, Multiculturalism, and Working Against Anti-Semitism), in addition to our geographical regions.

I am less concerned with who our leaders are than whether our grassroots energy is organized and impassioned enough to give any leader clear direction and hold them accountable. The goals and actions of our leadership must come from broad-based articulated priorities, not from any small group or individual.

Of course we'll disagree. Have no illusions that we're one big happy family or will ever be. Understand that movements and coalitions are always built by people with differences, united only by common vision, persistence, and hope. The bi movement is nothing more, and nothing less, than what each of us cherishes and makes real each day of our lives.

* * *

Some of my favorite training resources are: *Homophobia: How We All Pay the Price* (Blumenfeld, 1992); *On Conflict and Consensus: A Handbook on Formal Consensus Decisionmaking* (Butler and Rothstein, 1991); *Resisting Racism: An Action Guide* (Mallon, 1991); *Breaking Old Patterns, Weaving New Ties* (Adair and Howell, 1990); *Calling Home: An Anthology* (Zandy, 1990), stories and poems of working class women; and *Dreaming the Dark: Magic, Sex, and Politics* (Starhawk, 1982).

NOTES

1. The term "Information Highway" refers to the telecommunications revolution that will soon link telephones, computers, and televisions into one big interactive system: provided we can afford to access it. Who will control this system: private industries or the public? Will the information be available to all, even if only through public libraries, or will it be just another example of survival of the richest?

2. Originally developed by the Defense Department, the Internet is a global network linking computers via phone lines. Internet includes interest groups on every topic imaginable, including discussion lists on bi identity, theory, and activism, bi women's issues, and multiple relationships.

3. Why 50% people of color balance? (white) people often ask. The U.S. population is swiftly becoming more racially diverse. It is estimated that, if present trends continue, 50% of the population will be non-white by the year 2000. Why not prepare? Also, it works better psychologically when we come to the table as peers. With less than equal balance the effect is more of tokenism, tending to discourage people of color's participation, not encourage it.

4. "Polyamory" means multiple committed/loving relationships.

Connections

Can We Work

Together?

OVERVIEW

Rebecca Kaplan

If you are comfortable in your coalition, it's not broad enough.

—Bernice Johnson Reagon, 1983

From the earliest bisexual organizing several decades ago, our activism has involved connections with many communities—gays, lesbians, sex radicals, Quakers, anarchists, and feminists, to note a few. Bisexuals have always played key roles in those movements, but did not often feel safe to come out as such. So it is a natural progression for bisexuals to want recognition in those communities where we have always been. As a result, bisexuals are also likely to understand the broader political imperatives of working together. At the same time, just like any marginalized group, bisexuals sometimes need our own separate spaces as well. Finding that balance between when to organize separately and when to work in coalition is paramount to all successful activism.

What ties together the following essays in Section II, *Connections,* is a desire to work both within and alongside other movements for liberation, and to embrace the diversity of bisexual people. The section begins with essays that focus particularly on sexual diversity. Each *biSEXuality* essay tells us something about bi communities and about the links we have with other groups. *Coalition-Building* expands upon those themes, with essays that argue for connections with many other communities.

It is an act of empowerment to reclaim and celebrate the "sex" in bisexual. Yet this is no easy task for a group that is constantly subject to sex-related slurs and popularly perceived to be inordinately sexual, promiscuous, vectors of disease, and uninterested in emotion or politics. The need to combat such sexual stereotypes pressures many bisexuals into defensive posturing, denying and disassociating from any sexual "deviance." Thus we hear: "We are NOT swingers/kinky/nonmonogamous," responses which reinforce the sex-negativity and erotophobia of our culture and alienate those bisexuals who do happen to fit one of those categories.

Nonetheless, the organized bisexual community has been more successful than many others in standing up for the rights of people who are marginalized for their sexuality. Many bisexuals are reclaiming the positive value of sex and challenging erotophobia. Addressing the crucial issue of bisexual responses to erotophobic slurs and the need to take liberatory rather than defensive stances, Carol Queen calls upon us to make the bisexual community a comfortable place for all kinds of "perverts." She demands that we not seek acceptance for bisexuals at the expense of other sexual minorities in our communities.

How does bisexual identity affect one's sexual experiences? How do our sexual desires and choices inform and define our politics? Marginalized sexual desires—for various genders and/or forms of erotic play—may catalyze exploration of new political ground, as well as new ways of being. Being sexual with both women and men can create a sexuality different from that of monosexuals, as Greta Christina explains. Cecilia Tan makes a similar point about discovering a "bi/switch" view from the middle, through sexual experiences that include both women and men as well as top and bottom roles in S/M. Writer and pornographer Mark Pritchard presents another example, arguing for the liberatory powers of erotic images.

Bisexuality challenges many of society's assumptions about the relationship between gender role and sexual orientation. Robin Sweeney untangles some common misperceptions, such as the presumption that anyone who fits the visual stereotype of a butch dyke or a queeny fag must be exclusively lesbian or gay. Gender identity is no predictor of sexual behavior.

Understanding the interplay between sexual minority communities highlights the importance of building strong coalitions. As

Brenda Blasingame notes, coalition work is a multi-level process for bisexuals, since we must build alliances in several directions. We need to cultivate allies among lesbians and gay men, as well as among heterosexuals. We also have to build strong bonds across the many differences that exist within our own bisexual communities. *Coalition-Building and Other Queer Stories* focuses on questions of community boundaries, of inclusion and exclusion. As Dajenya pointedly states, we cannot separate ourselves into different categories of identity, and then choose one as the sole basis for our community or action. Dajenya's essay demands that we challenge all forms of oppression if we want to achieve true liberation.

Many essays in this section take up questions of who gets to belong, what makes up a community, what makes up a coalition, and when coalitions are appropriate. Some writers share specific coalition-building strategies: Longtime activist Robyn Ochs has developed a framework of "bisexual etiquette" for those working with lesbians and gay men. Kory Martin-Damon explains how bisexuals can become more aware of transgender issues and calls for unity among bisexual and transgendered people. As people who are marginalized for violating gender roles, transsexuals should be natural allies with bisexuals, who are marginalized for challenging the necessity of basing sexual orientation on gender divisions.

Importantly, many contributors acknowledge that power relations are critical to understanding questions of insider and outsider status. This is particularly relevant to the painful "bisexuality debates" in the lesbian community. To understand the responses that lesbians may have to bisexuality requires an analysis of male dominance in Western culture. Elizabeth Armstrong accounts for the different responses that lesbians and gay men have had to bisexuals as a product of the intersection of misogyny and heterosexism.

Tension between lesbian and bisexual women has been a source of anguish, particularly for bi women who identified as lesbian before coming out as bisexual. Women in these situations have often felt banished from communities that they had called home, and are strongly invested in creating a positive lesbian-bi coalition.

Nishanga Bliss demands that lesbian/gay groups recognize bisexuals by name, and explains why the naming of our presence is so important. But some efforts for name-inclusion in lesbian/gay events have met with passionate opposition. One such example is the controversy over adding "bisexual" to the title of the Northampton, Massachusetts Pride March. Stacey Young uses that example to analyze the arguments in these "bisexuality debates." Though divisive and painful for many women, the highly vocal anti-bisexual sentiments in some lesbian communities have ironically led to increased bisexual visibility. The ensuing dialogue has in many instances promoted greater understanding.

Another barrier to effective alliance-building between bisexuals and lesbians/gays is the argument that bisexuals benefit from "heterosexual privilege." As Orna Izakson points out, this is similar to the accusation that Jews systematically benefit from white-skin privilege. Orna and Brenda Blasingame deconstruct "privilege" as relative and contextual; bisexuals can be simultaneously marginalized and privileged. It is incumbent upon us to use whatever privilege we do have to fight heterosexism and other oppressions.

Though many people argue in favor of coalition-building, it is not always clear with whom the coalitions should be. Is an alliance of lesbians, gays, and bisexuals the most logical and productive grouping? What about transsexuals, and/or SM-ers, and/or other sex radicals? Or should we form alliances of gender or ethnicity—such as women or people of color of all sexual orientations—and deal with issues of sexuality later? Perhaps the coalition we would want is an alliance of everyone who has been excluded from power to fight all oppression simultaneously. The voices on the following pages offer a variety of views on what constitutes an effective coalition.

Part A

biSEXuality

An erotic politics cannot be based on hierarchical struc-
tures. . . . A movement of small groups is strengthened by an
underlying network of human connections, a weaving of close
relationships that bind it like warp and weft. Community is
inherently erotic.

—Starhawk, 1982

Sexual Diversity and Bisexual Identity

Carol Queen

In the 20 years since I first began to identify as bisexual, I have heard us described in a number of different ways. We are really homosexual, but closeted. We are really heterosexual, but kinky. We are fence-sitters. We are vectors of disease to our straight wives or lesbian lovers. We are swingers. We are nonmonogamous, polyfidelitous, or promiscuous. We are prostitutes who are really lesbian, but have sex with men for money. We make love to the person, not the body. We are sexually adventurous, even sexually elite. We are openminded. We will fuck anything that moves.

In some respects the contemporary bisexual movement organized in response to these beliefs; we constantly refer to them. Like the lesbian and gay movements before us, we begin by asserting, "We are not!" to cultural images we take as myth or half-truth: *not* swingers, *not* promiscuous, *not* kinky.[1] And yet of course many of us are these things, just as some of us are shy and celibate, and some are monogamously coupled and intend to stay that way. But because we have been defined not culturally, nor even emotionally, but sexually—particularly in the absence of a viable bisexual movement to emphasize all the other issues of importance to us—our sexual otherness has been the only thing observed and remarked upon. It stands to reason that we would feel the need to stand up and articulate all the other things we are. Even those who are wildly and diversely sexual feel the limits of being recognized for that alone. Hence we embrace "anything that moves [us] . . . beyond the myths of bisexuality," to quote our magazine;[2] we develop social support networks, political action committees, and theoretical frameworks. We protest homophobia, "heterophobia,"[3] and biphobia, and we scrutinize history for role models. We struggle to place ourselves in a social context: are we a third sexual orientation? Are we queer?

Can the lesbian and gay community be made to embrace us, the heterosexual community to accept us? With the creation of the bisexual community comes much cultural work, and questions of identity are central.

And all the while, busy bisexuals are having sex: with women, with men, with both at once; with partners whose gender is unclear, fluid, or mixed; in and out of committed relationships; a lot or a little; in groups and alone; for love, for fun, and for money; safely and unsafely; drunk and sober; in every possible combination, location, and variation. It is sex, after all—fleshly or fantasied—that leads us to a bisexual identity, whether we embrace it ourselves or are labeled by others. But too many of us, when faced with a sexual stereotype we cannot relate to, would like to vociferously deny that "they" (the swingers, the transgenderists, the closeted husbands) are part of our community.

It is time for the bisexual community to face this ambivalence about sexual variation. We tackle issues of gender and racial difference, difference of physical ability/wellness, cultural differences of many kinds: how diverse are we willing to be? We choose to make our meeting spaces and conference halls wheelchair accessible; will we also choose to make a safe space for those who fall at all points on the sexual spectrum?

We can make a brief survey of some sexual variations within the bisexual community and see that any single one introduces complex questions about bisexual identity—enough to write an entire piece about it alone.

First and perhaps most central is Kinsey's heterosexual/homosexual continuum.[4] We can identify as bisexual even if we are almost-homosexual or not-quite-heterosexual; in fact, in one of the great mysteries of identity formation/choice, some of us who are behaviorally bisexual do not identify as such, while others who are Kinsey Zeroes and Sixes do. We are challenged to develop a politic within which the issues of same-sex as well as other-sex[5] coupling are equally relevant. To make this dilemma more difficult (and perhaps more fruitful to examine), look at the expanded possibilities in Fritz Klein's (1985) update of the Kinsey Scale,[6] which has us take into account not only behavior, but also sex history, dream and fantasy, friendship networks, romantic attachments, and other variables when we determine whether we are a Zero, a Six, or somewhere in between. Perhaps the complexity of feeling and experience the Klein Scale seeks to quantify is one reason some have trouble selecting (or accepting) a label, whether homo, hetero, or bi.

Another source of confusion is the notion that a person attracted sexually to more than one gender must be incapable of sustaining a monogamous relationship (since obviously there are too few hermaphrodites to go around, the only source in one partner of the male and female genitals or qualities we supposedly "need" to be satisfied). Bi people, then, must live somewhere on the nether side of monogamy, or so the mythos goes. We must, at least, seek triadic relationships in which we have one partner of each gender, or perhaps we are out-and-out sluts—promiscuous people who do fuck anything that moves. But the strategies developed by bisexuals in real life make both others' assumptions of our promiscuity and our defensive response to them ("We can too be monogamous!") seem simplistic. The monogamy/nonmonogamy question can be complicated, and not just for bisexuals. Many bisexuals do eschew monogamy, preferring a variety of sexual friendships of varying degrees of emotional intimacy. Some prefer serial monogamy, and some choose partners of different genders at different times. Some seek (and a few find) the ongoing more-than-twosome of our dreams, making polyfidelitous commitments to two or three (or more) lovers. Some, while monogamous, derive our bisexual identification from acknowledging fantasies. And there are some bisexuals who do prefer hermaphrodites, or would if we could find them—there is a distinct subset of the bi community which experiences bisexuality as a lived protest against gender categories, whose members appreciate cross-gendered and genderbending partners not only for fine gender-neutral qualities but precisely because with them we can have "maleness" and "femaleness" in the same person.

Certainly the bi community has its share of people who ourselves play with gender-erotics: crossdressers, people with an other-sex persona or two, those who, through hormones, have become physically transgendered, and transsexuals who, through surgery, come to embody the other sex.[7] The gender players tend to see gender roles and identities as fluid vs. immutable, transgressable through sexual play even if oppressive in daily life. Perhaps the potential fluidity of sexual desire inherent in a bisexual orientation makes bi people more likely than others to eroticize and experiment with gender play, and perhaps not. Gender-bending, especially in its playful, eroticized aspects, is little-understood (except perhaps by the people who do it) and much under-studied. In any case alternate gender identities raise still more questions relative to bisexual identification: if a man has sex with other men only when he is crossdressed and in a female persona, is that sex to be understood as homo, hetero, or bi? If he has sex with women only when he is crossdressed, is their sex lesbian? In the fanciful realm of genderplay a bisexual couple, one woman and one man, could have "heterosexual" sex one day and adopt the personae and sexstyles of gay men the next, of lesbians the day after that, and switch roles altogether and have a gender-switched version of heterosexual sex the next day. ("Girls will be boys and boys will be girls,"— the Kinks' "Lola" wasn't a popular song just for its melody.)[8] A person with an alternate-gender persona might think of her/himself as bisexual even in a monogamous relationship; perhaps, depending on which gendered persona she/he assumes, a given sexual episode with the same partner might feel homosexual or heterosexual. (These are "what-ifs" not addressed even by the Klein Scale.)[9]

A desire for gender-play with a partner (whether or not either partner is bisexual) is only one example of what I call a "sub-sexual preference." I define this as any erotic element of sufficient importance to a person that they recognize and pursue it. "Sexual preference" has become a synonym for "sexual orientation" and refers to the gender/s of desired sexual partner/s, but there is a great deal more to sexual desire than gender, a fact bisexuals probably know better than anyone.

Another of these preferences has to do with a dynamic of control, power, and trust. Bisexuals attracted to sadomasochistic and/or dominant/submissive play[10] might discover in such play an additional wrinkle of sexual orientation: a preference for switching top or bottom role according to the gender of their partner. Another complication of identity: Is it "bisexual" to do s/m with both genders but genital sex with only one? Variations that share the s/m subculture but that need entail no power exchange are fetish play (eroticization of materials like leather, rubber, or fur, or objects like shoes, or physical attributes like long hair) and fantasy roleplay (of which genderplay is one category; other modalities are age play and play involving a setting or an era—a boys' school, ancient Lesbos). Eroticizing race or culture is another little-addressed variation. I have heard this discussed most interestingly by bisexual people who themselves are mixed-race, whose sense of erotic potential may have been influenced by a sense of belonging culturally to more than one world. (This is different from, though perhaps related to, race-fetish, which I think has to do with eroticizing perceived Otherness.)

And of course many bisexual people either work in or patronize the sex industry—as consumers of or producers/subjects of pornography, as paying voyeur/voyeuses or paid exhibitionists, as clients or prostitutes. Some bisexuals seek out gratifying erotic images and experiences through the arena of commodified sex; some people's only other- or same-sex experiences are through the medium of pornography or paid sexual entertainment. Some bisexuals have our first (or only) same- or other-sex experiences in front of a camera, in a peep show, or with a client. And some people separate the sex they have for money from the sex in their private lives and do not identify as bisexual on the basis of their sex-work experiences— though perhaps under other circumstances they would.

Even such a cursory sexual anthropology raises questions, the most basic and probably least answerable of which is "What is sex?" (Christina, 1992). Is s/m sex? Is sex for money different from sex done with other motivations? Is erotic transgenderism sex while transsexualism—which seeks to correct a "problem" of gender identity—is not? Another question, relevant to my overview of sexual variations among bisexuals, is: Who is the bisexual community? Now that we have begun to organize and create culture, developing our identity politics beyond a simplistic "kinky and promiscuous/NOT," who are we? Who identifies as bisexual now—and whom do we embrace?

The psychological puzzle of identity formation is another topic too large to tackle in its entirety here, but we can look at several factors. What is to be gained by embracing a bisexual self-identification? Bisexuals today can look to their community-in-formation for peer acceptance and a source of self-understanding and analysis, among other things. What, then, stands in the way? Some factors are internalized bi-, homo-, or "heterophobia"; a mistaken understanding of what it means to be bisexual; and a fear that support will not be forthcoming, or will be insufficient to counterweigh the risks associated with coming out.

Still, many people who are sexual with both men and women, yet not bi-identified, do not seem to be plagued with internalized biphobia or an unsupportive environment. Some prefer to call themselves "queer" rather than "bisexual"; others, when asked, may say something like, "I don't like labels," or "I'm just sexual."

Do some people not identify as bisexual because they feel "beyond bi," perceiving their sexuality as not embraced by the bisexual community's evolving standard of correctness or "normalcy"? I'm not sure we have such a thing, but I am equally unsure we have done enough to acknowledge our commitment to diverse bisexual modalities. I know that in my own post-lesbian struggle with identifying as bisexual I worried about affiliating with yet another community where I would risk doing it the "wrong" way; I had heard the bi community protest, "We are not!"—but hadn't received such a clear or positive message about what we are. When we register a protest to all the ideas about bisexuality harbored by the biphobic (or simply uninformed) straight and gay/lesbian worlds, are we capable of acknowledging also that, for some of us, the "myths" are true? How diverse are we willing to be?

As a community whose standards and politics have not yet had a chance to rigidify into one or another notion of "political correctness," we have the opportunity to influence the ideals of our members toward a politics of inclusion, and we also have the opportunity to look at the example set by other sexual minority communities when confronted by the question of erotic diversity. The gay and lesbian communities (particularly the latter) have been fractionalized by disagreements about s/m, genderplay, pornography, and sex work. Unless we explicitly agree that we want our community to welcome bisexuals from all walks of erotic life, and that our discussions ought to have as their aim understanding, not pathologizing or condemning, sexual diversity, we will find ourselves repeating an unfortunate historical mistake.

We are already influenced in this direction by the biases of our communities of origin. Heterosexual hegemony is oppressive to nonheterosexuals, but ironically, heterosexuals are not given much more sex-positive societal support than we are. Many of us bear the influences of conservatively religious or simply puritanical and erotophobic families or peers, most of them straight. So, of course, do many gays and lesbians, who have the additional influence of a sexual politics that evaluates behavior and identity in a sometimes extremely judgmental way. Lesbian feminists have been criticized by some bisexual women for exhibiting this tendency, but the lesbian "sex wars" actually brought under scrutiny (and sometimes fire) women of diverse sexualities—the more diverse, it seemed, the less right a woman was said to have to embrace the identity "feminist" or even "lesbian." Our understandable outrage at this politically motivated (or couched) judgment should never obscure the fact that many feminist lesbians are bi-positive and that no one owns the term "feminist"—bisexual and heterosexual women, sex workers, s/m players, and many others are also fiercely feminist, and many are insistent that the intersection of feminism and sexuality concerns a woman's right to make her *own* erotic choices, with support and without either coercion or censure.

Since the new bisexual community is strongly influenced by feminist politics, the contribution of "sex-positive" feminists is particularly important. While it continues to be crucial to analyze our experience for instances of gender-based inequality wherever it appears, including the realm of the sexual/erotic, it is equally critical to insist upon our capacity to be sexually empowered. Many of the highly vocal feminist voices in this discussion belong to bisexuals, hopefully ensuring that bisexual feminism will not be tempted to analyze sex in a simplistic, oppression-oriented way. This may open new doors to feminism in our community, attracting both the bisexual women for whom a lesbian-feminist-inspired critique of male sexual expression has never seemed very relevant and also bisexual men (and other male partners of bisexual women). A bisexual feminism in which erotic and emotional openness to men is a given may speak very persuasively to men who also experience as oppressive heterosexist gender role expectations.

We already know that a bisexual identity is not sufficient to ensure agreement or conformity—we are too diverse in every way.

Let us make that a strength, not a failing, of our movement. If we begin to reify "bisexual" (as if in saying the word we agree to the specifics of its meaning—already a mistake, in my opinion, and not yet possible at this stage of our community development) we may be tempted to leave out the wonderful, difficult complexity of acknowledging the diverse spectrum our community holds. I would prefer us to mindfully write it in—we may not fuck anything that moves, but, in our rainbow of difference, we are practically everything that moves, and if we welcome each other in these differences as well as in our similarities we will weave community of a strong cloth indeed.

I consider this an evolutionary opportunity. No other community has tried, as part of its basic philosophy, to commit itself to a policy of sexual acknowledgement and inclusion[11]—certainly none with the potential size and influence of a truly organized international bisexual community. Bisexuals, with our dual experiences of rejection and inclusion in monosexual[12] communities, may be better prepared than they have been to embrace our sexually variant peers; we have been the variants in both heterosexual families of origin and queer communities of choice. Perhaps in learning to come to terms with bisexuality's duality of desire we become more ready to explore other erotic variation, or at least to accept it.

And of course we mirror the heterosexual world (with all its buried homosexual practice and desire) and the homosexual one (how few queers there are without heterosexual experience, and how silent we are expected to be if we actually liked it). Communities based on, or grounded in, any sort of common sexual identity are full of people with secrets. Many heterosexuals and homosexuals also play with gender, with eroticized power, with fetish and fantasy; consume and produce pornography, buy and sell sex, and conduct some variant of monogamous or nonmonogamous lives. Just as we bisexuals must learn to bridge the Kinsey Scale in our loves and lusts, potentially being able to help gay and straight monosexuals think of themselves as something other than opposites, so, if we embrace a politic of sexual inclusivity, may we be able to nudge everyone else in the same direction. It is, after all, the same sex-negative cultural history that makes everything but monogamously-married kink-free heterosexuality stigmatized, the "norm" against which all these "variants" are measured. If we do not agree on a new, sex-positive sexual morality we will find ourselves in the end acting out of the same learned bigotry that labels as perverts all of us who do not fit that restrictive mold. For now many of us are glad to embrace the label "pervert" the way we embrace "queer"—taking back the power to name from those who would use it against us—but wouldn't it be nice to do away with the word, with the entire idea, altogether?

To welcome and acknowledge our own community's queers will enrich us. It will not lead to a tyranny of kink, in which only the people who play hard and wild are cool, if we can agree that our politics of inclusion is for everyone—a polyfidelitous harem is no more nor less honored than a monogamous union, a swinger is no more nor less honored than a virgin or a celibate, a Kinsey Three is no more nor less honored than a One or a Five, a Zero or a Six. I want to argue for a sexual standard no more restrictive than "Is it consensual?" and a community that considers it good to empower people, lovingly, to make their own sexual choices. Would that not make it easier to affirmatively answer the question "Am I bisexual?"

NOTES

1. As Loraine Hutchins has noted in her essay "Love That Kink" (Hutchins and Ka'ahumanu, 1991), "kinky" may be a synonym for "sexually deviant or Other" because such sexual behavior has traditionally been attributed to ethnic minorities, particularly blacks. I use the word mindfully, both to conjure up the labeling process oppressed, non-normative people undergo, and to emphasize that we bisexuals have undergone naming from without and in some cases impose naming on others.

2. *Anything That Moves . . . Beyond the Myths of Bisexuality* is the bisexual community's quarterly magazine, established in 1990 and published by the Bay Area Bisexual Network, 2404 California St., #24, SF, CA 94115.

3. I set off "heterophobia" in quotes particularly to distinguish it from homophobia, the fear and hatred of homosexuals and/or of one's own homosexual component, which has far more vicious and socially sanctioned consequences than anyone's fear and hatred of heterosexuals (which is not to say that such fear and hatred does not exist or has no repercussions on individuals' lives).

4. Alfred C. Kinsey's groundbreaking mid-century research (1948, 1952) uncovered the incidence of homosexual and heterosexual behavior in American society. His conceptual tool, known as the Kinsey Scale, puts sexual behavior on a

line graph numbered Zero through Six; Zero is completely heterosexual, One is primarily heterosexual with incidental homosexual activity, and so on through Six, exclusively homosexual. Kinsey intended his scale to describe behavior, not identity, so when I say that someone decides on a Kinsey rating I am departing greatly from the way Kinsey thought of sexual orientation.

5. I prefer the usage "other-sex" to "opposite-sex" because I do not consider the sexes (nor, for that matter, the genders) opposite. This usage also opens the possibility that there are more than two sexes/genders.

6. Sexual orientation scales are discussed critically by Amanda Udis-Kessler in an appendix to *Closer to Home* (Weise, 1992).

7. Transsexualism is not a sexual preference, but an issue of gender identity (a sense that one was born with a body inconsistent with one's self-perceived gender). However, a transsexual might be someone's preferred object choice. Transgenderism is less easily definable; a person who is transgendered might only crossdress, might do some body modification short of full surgical reassignment (a transgender male might get breast implants and live as a "shemale," for example), and/or might think of her/himself as neither male nor female, or both at once. And some transgendered people might experience their gender issues as intersecting with their sexuality: as one transgenderist said to me, "Some people want to [change their gender or experience it as fluid], some need to; some find it a turn-on, some don't."

8. The Kinks were a British band particularly popular in the late 1960s and early 1970s whose most famous hit, "Lola," tells the story of a boy who goes to the big city and gets bowled over by a transvestite—perhaps ushering in the era of genderbend politics: "Well, I'm not the world's most masculine man, but I know what I am, what I am, I'm a man, and so's Lola . . . Girls will be boys and boys will be girls, it's a mixed up, muddled up, shook up world, except for Lola."

9. I am indebted to William Henkin and Sybil Holiday and their work on alternate personae, and to the insights and experiences of several of my friends who are so genderbent that even gender support communities seem to them too rigid.

10. Sadomasochism is the eroticization of giving or receiving (or both) intense sensation or pain. Dominance/submission is the eroticization of dominant and/or submissive role-playing. Both have in common the element of erotic power exchange. (See Califia, 1981; Califia, 1993; Thompson, 1991; Queen, 1992b.)

11. One exception is San Francisco Sex Information and a few other similar sex education organizations which function as inclusive communities where all forms of consensual, nonexploitive sexuality are honored. They strive to provide information and resources for all sex-types. SFSI can be contacted at (415) 621-7300.

12. The term "monosexual" is used by some bisexuals to describe individuals whose sexual desire or behavior is directed toward members of only one sex—that is, heterosexuals and homosexuals.

Bi Sexuality

Greta Christina

So. When you have sex with men, you are straight, and when you have sex with women, you are a lesbian. As a bisexual woman, this is what I hear; again and again, this is what I hear. Your sexuality comes in compartments, like Tupperware; your heart has two chambers and you cannot feel with both; your soul is like Berlin before the wall came down.

And the truth of my experience is this: my sexuality is whole. I am not straight with men and lesbian with women; I am bisexual with both. Enjoying sex with both women and men is no more an inherently schizophrenic form of sexuality than enjoying both intercourse and oral sex. Bisexuality is a unified and unique sexual identity, an entirely different way of being, unlike either hetero- or homo- sexuality.

You see, being bisexual isn't just a matter of being sexual with women and with men. The experiences influence each other; there's cross-pollination and there's overlap. The experience of being sexual with both affects what sex is like with each. And the experience of being sexual with both affects my entire thinking about sexuality and sexual politics.

So I want to talk about the sexuality of bisexuality, and the sexual politics of bisexual politics.

SEX

First off, I'd like to discuss how having sex with women has affected the way I'm sexual with men. The main difference is that I place less emphasis on the erection than I once did. I've learned from women that there doesn't have to be a hard dick present in

161

order for it to be hot sex. So when I'm with a man, and he doesn't get a hard-on, or he comes and gets soft before we're done feeling sexual, I don't feel inadequate or get angry or even think that there's any reason to stop. God knows I used to, and I know a lot of straight couples do feel that way. Straight sex is so often about the man's hard dick: it starts when he gets hard, it's over when he comes, and if he never gets hard or comes it wasn't really sex. Since I started having sex with women, I don't feel that way about men anymore. The stuff that the straight world traditionally calls "foreplay," lesbians call "sex." And that's what I've learned to call it, whether I'm with a woman or a man.

Naturally, this kind of influence works both ways. So how has being sexual with men affected my sexuality with women? I think the most important area is sexual assertiveness. I have learned from men that it's a turn-on to be passionately desired; that as long as you are willing to take no for an answer, being honest and brazen about your desires can be very hot stuff. Sexual timidity is almost a cliché among lesbians; all those sexy women lusting after each other and never telling, none of them wanting to risk rejection by making the first move. When I'm with women and find myself stuck in that trap, it's often helpful to remember how good it felt when some guy I had the hots for made his indecent intentions known. Now, assertiveness and initiative are very different from aggression and invasiveness (another distinction I learned—rather unpleasantly—from my dealings with men). Obnoxious assholes harassing women on the street are certainly no model of sexual interaction. But having been pleasurably courted, pursued, and seduced by men has certainly taught me a thing or two about the pleasurable courtship, pursuit, and seduction of other women.

At this point, the lesbian feminist part of my political conscience is insisting on a clarification. Whenever I talk about the things I've learned from sex with men, she reminds me that I could have learned the same things from women. Therefore, I would like to make it clear that I'm describing my own experience of being bisexual and how this experience has shaped my own sexual perceptions. I am most emphatically *not* arguing that lesbian sexuality is somehow incomplete and needs some good old-fashioned hard dick energy to really round it off. When I say I learned some specific thing from having sex with men, it means that's the way I learned it—not that it's impossible for other women to learn it in other ways.

Clear? Good. Let's get back to the topic at hand: learning about sex from both women and men. I could probably go on about this subject for hours. I could talk about how sex with women has made me more relaxed and less goal-oriented about sex; or how sex with men has made me appreciate sexual differentness and contrast. But the unique sexual nature of bisexuality is not simply a case of both sides learning from each other. Being bisexual is more than just having two facets to your sexuality where most people have only one; it's more than the ways those two facets interact. It is a unique and integrated sexuality, with profound differences in degree and kind from hetero- and homosexual forms of monosexuality.

Now, I'm *not* going to pull out the old conventional wisdom/bisexual public relations line about bisexuals being different because we're gender blind. You've probably heard it before: "As a bisexual, I'm just not concerned about the gender of a person. I'm interested in what they're like as an individual. I'm attracted to certain qualities in people, regardless of whether I find them in a man or a woman." Yes, it's a very nice thought, very progressive. Makes the straight people feel ever so much safer, as if bisexuality were simply a kind of equal-rights feminist politics or another version of we're-all-really-the-same-under-the-skin-so-why-can't-we-live-together-in-peace-and-harmony middle-class white liberalism. In my experience, though, it's bullshit. I'm sure a lot of bisexuals do get turned on by (for instance) intelligence and assertiveness and big dark brown eyes, regardless of whether they find those qualities in women or men. But I'm beginning to smell the presence of a party line, and I don't like it. I see men and women as being pretty goddamn different. If anything, being bi has made me hyper-aware of the sexual differences between them. And I *still* get hot for both.

But I do experience something that is similar to gender blindness. It's this: being bisexual means that I could potentially find myself sexually attracted to anybody. Therefore, as a bisexual, I don't make the distinction that monosexuals do between the gender you fuck and the gender you don't. And it seems—from the outside, anyway—that this distinction is pretty central to monosexual life. In hetero society, it's most obvious when you look at the difference between same-sex friendships and opposite-sex friendships. Certainly, much of that difference has to do with sexism, power dynamics, the differences between male and female culture and language, and so on. But I also see a core difference in the way monosexual people feel about friends that they might possibly want to fuck versus friends that they never will. I've seen it among lesbians and gay men as well: there's a certain relaxation with friends of the opposite sex, and a certain tension with friends of the same. I've seen the sharp intake of breath that says, "Oh, goodie, I wonder if . . . " and the sigh of relief that says, "Oh, good, I don't have to wonder." Because I'm bisexual, that cadence, that back-and-forth rhythm, doesn't exist for me. I'm not saying that I see the entire human race as one giant singles bar. There are certainly people I don't want to have sex with, and people who don't want to have sex with me. But that distinction is not based on who's male and who's female. The "maybe/possibly" list and the "probably not/no way" list does not split along gender lines.

And this, I believe, makes for a fundamental difference in the way that, as a bisexual, I see those gender lines. It's not that I see less difference between the genders than monosexuals (although some bisexuals do). It's not that I don't prefer one gender over another (although some bisexuals don't). And it's not that I'm attracted to people regardless of their gender (although some bisexuals are). It's that not making the distinction between the gender you fuck and the gender you don't makes you see the other differences between the genders in a radically different way. And for that matter, it makes you see the similarities in a radically different way. I think bisexuals have a unique sense—a sense that comes from first-hand experience—of which sexual tendencies are common to the culture, which ones are idiosyncratic to the individual, and which ones tend to break down along gender lines. And I think this way of seeing extends beyond the sexual realm.

But enough about sex. Let's talk politics.

POLITICS

Bisexuals are perceived by both gays and straights as more sexual than others, the same way that gay men were (and often still are) seen by straight society. The perception works like this: Straight society defines us solely by our sexuality, therefore sees nothing but our sexuality, therefore sees us as hyper-sexual, therefore trivializes and condemns us for being driven exclusively by our sexuality, therefore continues to define us solely by our sexuality . . . and merrily around the circle we go. This makes for an unpleasant connection between sex-negativity and biphobia. Because we are feared and scorned, we are marked with the stigma of being "too sexual." Then, because we have been marked in this way, we are feared and scorned even more. The society that hates and fears sex naturally condemns those it perceives as being more-than-acceptably sexual. The sex-negative stigma becomes its own justification.

Furthermore, since many of the common myths about bisexuals target our supposedly excessive sexuality—we're naturally promiscuous, we can't be monogamous, we have to have both men and women sexually at all times in our lives, we like three-ways or group sex the best, we have no political or cultural commitment to the queer community and are only in it for the sex and so on—we often wind up defending ourselves by downplaying our sexuality and buying into the sex-negativity of the dominant straight culture. Many of the bisexual party lines negate or trivialize sex, emphasizing love and relationships instead: "We're not promiscuous! We can be monogamous! We like queer culture just as much as queer sex! Maybe even more! Let's call ourselves bi-sensual, bi-relational, or just plain bi; keep sex out of our name! This isn't about sex, honest!" The very word "bisexual" is seen by many in the community as being too much about sex and not enough about love or politics; thus, after much debate, we were represented in the 1993 March on Washington, not as bisexual, but as "bi." The San Francisco bisexual community, perceived as sexually radical by many other bi communities, is often taken less seriously as a result of this perception. *Anything That Moves: Beyond the Myths of Bisexuality*, a national bisexual magazine published in the San Francisco Bay Area, receives constant criticism within the bi community for the too-sexual nature of its name.

I see this as a dangerous trend. It's a way of selling out, trying to buy approval from the straight community at the expense of our own sexuality. It's important to remember, in the midst of our myth-bashing, that while the myths and stereotypes don't describe all or even most bisexuals, there are those of us who *are* promiscuous, *are* nonmonogamous, *do* like to have both male and female lovers at once, *do* like three-ways and four-ways and six-ways and fifty-seven-ways more than any other way, *are* more interested in sex than in politics . . . *and that this is okay.*

Look at the way lesbians and gay men have stopped defending homosexuality and are now attacking homophobia. They have begun to turn the debate around, away from "There's nothing wrong with us, please accept us" to, "What's wrong with you that you don't accept us?" Bisexuals must learn to do this, not only about our sexual orientation, but about our sexuality itself. We all know what it is to have the sex fears of mainstream straight culture projected onto us. But we cannot defend ourselves by embracing their fears as our own. We must confront sexual stereotyping—not timidly, not defensively, but with honesty, chutzpah, and pride. We have to stop saying, "No, we're not that nasty bad sexual way at all," and begin saying instead, "Some of us are like that, and some of us are not, and we think that's just fine—why do you have a problem with it?"

Bisexuality and S/M:
The Bi Switch Revolution

Cecilia Tan

I am part of what has been called "the bi switch revolution" (Wiseman, 1992) within the S/M community, which refers to the emergence of a large population among S/M players, who interact with both women and men ("bi") and enjoy both the top and bottom roles in S/M play ("switch"). As a bisexual in the S/M community, I feel an important part of my emerging role is to act as a link between the bisexual community and the S/M community, an alliance that could prove important in the political realm.

CULTURAL DEFINITIONS

I must begin by making some definitions of my own. I define bisexuality as the aspect of sexuality that allows a person to have erotic interest in both men and women (whether simultaneously or serially). S/M is the aspect of sexuality that allows a person to have an erotic interest in the broad range of activities that involve consensual exchange of power, including bondage, whipping, role-playing, and much more. Within S/M, players are typically divided into two roles, Top and Bottom. These general terms encompass the various types of opposites, dominant and submissive, sadist and masochist, giver and receiver. An individual who enjoys being on both sides is known as a "switch."

Switches and bisexuals both occupy a middle ground between extremes. On any spectrum, it is the individuals at each pole that make the strongest cultural definitions, who set the most easily identifiable archetypes and exemplary role models. As such, even if they are in the majority, those in the middle are defined as outside the norm, a threat to the status quo. For many years, the S/M community was locked into strict roles of Top and Bottom. Tops were distinguished from Bottoms by distinctive modes of dress and visual signals accepted throughout the community as norms. For example, Tops wore their keys on the left beltloop, Bottoms on the right. There was also the infamous hanky code, in which bandanas of different colors hung from the back pocket of someone's jeans signified what kind of S/M the wearer was into, red meaning fist-fucking, gray meaning bondage, and so on. Tops wore their hankies in the left pocket, bottoms on the right. Many people today still enjoy Top or Bottom roles and visual cues, but their use is less prevalent, more playful, and more of a choice than a mandate.

Previously, when a person entered the world of S/M for the first time, he or she was taught these rules, and was unable to participate without choosing one role or the other. This stricture on role choice reminds me of my own experience as a young college woman: when I felt various erotic urges toward women, I joined the campus lesbian and gay students organization and was told that I had to accept that I was fully a lesbian, or I didn't belong there. The artificial division of people into either/or roles does not leave room for those who are in the middle or who enjoy traveling from one end to the other at will. The division is also exactly that: a splitting of what should be a unified group. Switches and bisexuals both have a need to claim the middle ground.

EXPLORING THE MIDDLE GROUND

Many bisexuals, myself included, feel we are attracted to people for qualities other than biological equipment. So, as a bisexual, when I am considering someone a possible partner for erotic inter-action, their gender is not necessarily first priority. Adding S/M into the equation ups the qualities beyond gender to consider. Because S/M play eroticizes more than just the genitals, there are many additional attributes that make a partner desirable. Both women and men have arms and legs that may be bound, backsides that may be paddled, and minds and hearts which can fully participate in an S/M interaction ("scene").

In my case, one might wonder if my de-emphasis on gender for

S/M play is because I identify so strongly as bisexual. Many S/M players are monosexual, and seek out partners of a particular gender as a matter of course. But a good number have come to realize their own bisexuality as a result of casual S/M play with both men and women. By my definitions of bisexuality and S/M, people who play with partners of both genders are behaviorally bisexual. Some of these players will eventually come to identify as bi as a result, while others will not. The range of activities in S/M that are not gender-specific allows for erotic interactions to take place between otherwise exclusive groups. I recently witnessed a self-avowed woman-identified lesbian flogging a "Kinsey Six" homosexual man. Scenes like this are not uncommon and tend to be free of political repercussions. Is S/M one of the few arenas where dykes and fags can interact erotically? Is S/M an arena where people of any gender or orientation can safely experiment with bisexuality? In my experience, the answer is yes to both questions.

In the political arena, it seems logical that various sexual minorities would ally with one another. But the lesbian, gay, S/M, transgendered, and bisexual communities are still mostly isolated and alienated from one another. Breaking that isolation between groups is a key to sexual liberation for all. If a unified movement toward freedom of sexual expression is ever to come about, the bisexual community is one place we can see it happen; S/M is one of the tools that can make it happen; and now the time is ripe for it to happen.

People are coming out as bisexual and as S/M players all across the United States. The reasons are myriad and numerous enough to fill their own book. Between a rising interest in sexuality in the general populace, the rebellion against the Sex=Death 80s (for example, the explosion in popularity for mainstream literary erotica, the rise in sales for mail order sex toys), the pop culture influence of S/M chic (Madonna), and the return of bisexual chic (Suede, Sandra Bernhard, and others who have revealed their bisexuality to gain popularity, notice, or panache), many people are coming to the ideas of S/M and bisexuality without the indoctrination of the past, or are more easily able to overcome that indoctrination. Enticed by the chic images of the mass media, the new (but not necessarily young) explorer may venture into bisexuality or S/M, two communities which maintain a sex-positive attitude.

The rapid growth of the bisexual and S/M communities has contributed to the lessening of strict roles and polarization. When a community grows slowly, it is possible to indoctrinate every member of the tribe. But this is not so in a mass culture. People can read books, watch videos, mail order, fantasize at home, interact through computer bulletin boards, and formulate their own modes of interaction and identities before they meet another player or potential partner face to face at a convention, rally, brunch, seminar, encounter group, or bar. Gay bars and leather clubs are no longer the secret societies they once were, nor are they the sole entrance into participation in those communities.

And here we have the bi switch revolution. People are coming to discover their sexuality with the freedom to experiment more. Experimenting across power-exchange lines is not so different from experimenting across gender lines. Within the S/M community then, we find people who would have been straight tops, playing with both men and women, and enjoying being on the receiving end as well. Many switches claim their experiences on one end heighten their appreciation and help refine their technique on the other end. The old guard is not wholly comfortable with this new attitude, but it is beyond their control now. The new face of the community is not locked into one or two strict roles. Switches are living in that in-between space, and uniting people heretofore divided into tops and bottoms. Bisexual S/M players are uniting the gay and lesbian leather communities. Now imagine a "bisexual revolution" outside the S/M world. Bisexuals could play the same role of unifying factor among other isolated sexual groups: gay, straight, lesbian, transgendered.

In a perfect world, for me, no human would be locked into one predetermined role, whether gender-based, orientation-based, power-based, or otherwise. This kind of world would be free of stereotypes, sexism, ageism, racism. . . . Bisexuals and S/M switches have a necessary advantage in our ability to envision such a world, for we are already living it. Those of us in the middle ground must work together to spread the word, to continue to show new generations that there is something other than life at the extremes. The view from the middle is great; come on over!

Liberating Pornography

Mark Pritchard

I am a pornographer.

I write sex stories and publish them, as well as stories and articles by others, in a magazine I put out with my domestic partner, Cris Gutierrez. The magazine, called *Frighten the Horses,* has been around for three years at this writing. It is one of dozens of small queer publications produced by individuals and small groups who are queer (as opposed to corporate products like *Spin* or investor-funded publications like the *Advocate)*. In it we publish essays, opinion, and news about abortion, queer rights, and freedom of expression, as well as three or four pieces of fiction about the dirtiest, most realistic, most transgressive sex people can have.

Even before I became a pornographer, I was interested in issues of gender politics and feminism. Now I cannot separate the two realms. My sex writing and my erotic vision inform my politics, and my politics inform my pornography. I have a broad definition of "queer"; I define it as practically anything that goes against the grain of straight American society. This wide approach, ironically, means that *FTH* is not queer enough for some, too transgressive for others. I think the magazine, as a whole, comes out to be exactly as queer as I am—bisexual and sort of butch, except when I'm being nelly. It also keeps me involved in the question of how my bisexuality in particular, and transgressive sexuality in general, subvert the status quo as represented by *Cosmopolitan, Playboy,* and *Vogue.*

Straights see sex as the defining characteristic of queers; we are queer, in their view, precisely because we have sex "unnaturally." Rather than reject this view as limiting, I embrace it and use the sexual power they have abdicated out of fear as a source of strength, identity, and inspiration.

In December of 1988, I came back to San Francisco after teaching English in Japan for two years. While I was away, I missed San Francisco's diversity and the way nonconformity can be not only tolerated, but celebrated. I realized that living in San Francisco provides, for many, the opportunity to be themselves, and even to re-create themselves.

So when I returned, I swore I would use my freedom and never suppress my identity or my vision. I came out as bisexual. I did some writing and performing. I got involved with organizations working for social and sexual justice. I got the idea for *Frighten the Horses,* which I subtitled "a document of the sexual revolution."

I deliberately chose the phrase "sexual revolution" in order to reclaim it. I knew that the original "Sexual Revolution" was little more than media hype of the 1960s—rather than changing gender roles to a revolutionary degree, all it really amounted to was an improvement in contraception so men could fuck without having to worry about the "girl" becoming pregnant—a sexual atmosphere of impunity that lasted until the herpes and AIDS epidemics in the early 1980s.

After two years away, I looked at San Francisco with new eyes. I saw a genuine sexual revolution: people fucking, talking, making art, making politics about sex. This was not the 1960s myth of sexual abundance at the expense of women. This was dykes, fags, drag queens, radical faeries, sadomasochists, bisexuals, and sex workers, all of them horny and doing it and willing to talk about it and form a community because of what they have in common: a taste for the liberating effects of pleasure, a deep mistrust of straight society, and a realization that they must stick together.

Joining with the feminist movement, queers contribute to a change much more profound than that of the 1960s. Attitudes about women and sexual minorities are genuinely changing, not because of "the Pill," but because women and queers are taking to the streets, the airwaves, and the printing presses, asserting their presence and expecting their rights. Formerly, it was enough of a challenge—both to queers and to others—for queers to simply exist. Being queer, or playing with gender or power roles behind closed doors, was its own reward. Today, people who fuck with gender aren't just being weird in somebody's underground movie; they're marching in the streets, lobbying in the legislature, and infiltrating corporate offices. The rewards—changed attitudes about sex and gender, legal rights, safety in public—are much greater.

That is what fundamentalists are afraid of when they interpret gay rights as threatening "traditional values." Sex and cultural diversity *are* threatening to the fundamentalist vision of the world, because they expose the myth that there is only one way to be saved. If you start allowing people to make decisions about their own pleasure, you lose control of them. Women and queers in daily life threaten the status quo; they make it less possible for straight men to run everything.

To reverse this trend, fundamentalists have tried to reimpose conformity. Conformity means hiding your difference before you are punished for it. Young people feel this pressure and, without role models to show how to be queer and proud, deny their own desires, even their individuality. Their connection with their own selves is severed. This self-censorship is the first line of defense for authoritarians, and it is insidious, because they get us to do it to ourselves. Their second line of defense is less subtle: police and legal harassment, discrimination, queer bashing.

Both these systems, the one that shoves us down and the one where we do it to ourselves, provide good reasons for us to be afraid and to conform. But that's not what I'm doing. Instead of knocking me down, the pressure to conform simply reemphasizes my difference and reminds me of who I am. It creates in me a stubborn urge to resist the message that there is something wrong with me. It made me decide to come out, when before I passed as straight. People yelling "faggot" now strengthen my resolve to defend anyone who gets called a faggot.

The decision to claim the word faggot for myself began about six months after my return to the States. A national conference of anarchists was being held at a junior high school in my neighborhood, and I stumbled upon it one morning and walked in to investigate. As I was standing around listening to boring announcements and wondering what I was doing there, a large contingent of queers came dancing out of a side door onto the platform and took over the microphone. They complained about incidents of homophobia at the convention, announced they would resist, and asked all gay people to stand up, come forward, and join them.

I was afraid to. This was before I was familiar with the concept of "queer" as a claimable identity, and I wasn't sure I qualified. So I stood there while several more people spoke. But then a woman took the microphone. She declared that sometimes she loved men and sometimes women, and that she wasn't sure whether that made her gay enough, but she knew one thing: that anytime, anywhere, somebody got called a faggot, then she was a faggot too, and would stand up to defend them.

A month later I was sitting in the bleachers at the Oakland Coliseum watching an A's game. Some white kid a few rows away started yelling "faggot" at the opposing team's right fielder. Remembering what the woman had said at the conference, I went over and not so politely demanded that the kid shut up. "What are you, a faggot too?" he sneered.

I wish I could simply have answered "You bet I am," but unaccustomed as I am to snappy dialogue, all I said—standing there in my leather jacket and "Silence Equals Death" button—was, "What's it look like?" At that point he shoved me, and a security guard separated us and threatened to throw the asshole out, so I did not have to have the first fight of my life.

But looking back on that moment, despite my inability to declare it on the spot, I now recognize that as the moment I became a faggot. Not when I sucked a cock for the first time, not when I was arrested at a Queer Nation demonstration, but when I stood up to a kid who reminded me of the bullies who harassed me when I was eight years old.

But why pornography? Why not just write a bunch of solid, well-researched pieces on abortion, Jesse Helms, and censorship? Why do I have to publish sexually explicit material? Why do I have to get an erection, indulge my fantasies, delve into the dirt, and encourage you to do the same?

Because it turns me on, and pleasure is my right. Because fighting for artistic expression is meaningless unless there's some art being made in the first place. Because there are already many people writing those solid, well-researched articles. But most of all, because sex writing turns me on.

Sex writing—pornography—has a bad reputation. Over the years, it has been suppressed, criminalized, blamed for corrupting readers and society, and trivialized as a genre that does not deserve serious consideration. When it was not being suppressed, producers of porn found that consumers were often undemanding, and emphasized quantity over quality, with the result that a lot of pornography was written to order by writers who were only in it for the money.

That is why the term "erotica" gained prominence in the 1970s: to distance work which might be more soft-core, more artful, or perhaps simply more vague—from the artless and usually politically incorrect one-handed porn of the era, which feminists criticized for its negative attitudes toward women. The 1970s were the era of Nancy Friday's books full of women's fantasies and of the mass marketing of Anaïs Nin's proto-feminist stories, with their poetic descriptions of liaisons among Parisian bohos. Americans were sold the following formula to justify buying sex writing: Pornography was low-class, violent, anti-woman, and tawdry; "erotica" was sex-positive, polite, middle-class, and feminist.

At the time, during my teens and twenties, feminism, not queerness, was the only alternative to the status quo that was visible to me. (I could read about feminism in *Ms.* magazine and in other national media, but my sexual identity was so unformed I would not have responded to news about early gay rights moves.) Feminism helped me justify my feelings of not fitting in. Because I was ostracized for being short, funny-looking, and nonathletic, I identified with women who wrote of being marginalized. It didn't matter that they were talking about a very different kind of powerlessness; all I knew was that I felt powerless. I also identified with the feminist vision of justice and gender equality; I knew it was preferable to the system of conformity and brutality I had chafed under as a kid, and to the idiotic male-female roles being acted out in high school.

For all it offered me, the 1970s feminism I soaked up was a little inflexible about sexual imagination. Many different kinds of sexual fantasies, not to mention activities, were suspect. Equality was the goal, and that meant any vestige of male dominance had to be eliminated. I remember trying to keep track, with my first lover, of the number of times I was on top and the number of times she was on top, so we could keep it equal.

If my sexual activity could be equalized, my sexual imagination proved harder to control. In order to be the kind of male that feminist writers were saying I should be, I tried to obey then-current dogma by keeping a tight rein on my fantasies. I believed the dictum that all men are rapists, and I thought I had to repress my imagination so all that hate and violence wouldn't come out. This made sense because it fit the Christian notion I had grown up with, that if you think about something, it's just as bad as actually doing it.

So I tried to eliminate all politically incorrect fantasies from my mind. And for a while I was successful. If anyone had told me that I would ever, for example, whip a woman, I would have been shocked to even think about such a misogynist deed. But one night my lover said to me, a little impatiently, "Mark, pull my hair." What happened after that was a revelation. I found out that force and love could coexist. I found out that I had been suppressing all images of strength for myself, not just the violent ones, and when I stopped doing that, I became stronger. I realized that there was power in my erotic longings—the power to become whole.

Sex writing is fantasy, and it contains that power. When you read something that turns you on, it connects to something that is already inside you. If a story is really powerful, it may become part of your erotic mythology, something you call on to help you back to the place where you are turned on, loving, lovable, and strong.

But the road is not always nice. In pornography, messy things happen. People fuck and get fucked, suck and get sucked, whack and get whacked. Some people find this disturbing, judging the porn as they would if it were actually happening, just as my teachers back at Trinity Lutheran School might have suggested. Nevertheless, pornography is fiction. The events are not really happening. The piece is a creation of the writer. If it turns you on, have fun. If it does not, turn the page. Only you, the reader, knows which is which.

Sometimes I get turned on imagining or reading about tenderness. Sometimes I get turned on imagining or reading about impolite, cruel, even violent acts. I'm not sure what my fantasies say about me, but I do know the difference between fantasy and reality. I know that imagining something is not the same thing as doing it, despite what my grade school teachers told me. I know how liberating it is to discover your desires, own them, come out about them; I also know that shame and repression are cold, hard weapons, worst when used on yourself. I believe we need a forum to share, discuss, debate our secrets; I believe writers need a reason to stop that insidious self-repression. Most of all, I want this society to be a place where I and others are turned on, liberated, and empowered by our pride in our erotic selves. More good pornography can do that.

Lately I've been thinking a lot about how important pleasure is to me. As I get older, I find that I am more impatient, intolerant, and crabby. I used to be willing to ride across town 45 minutes on the bus; now I drive, racing to cut people off, and if my search for parking takes more than three minutes, I start cursing. I have high blood pressure. I am less willing to give people the benefit of the doubt; I am more likely to lash out or put my foot in my mouth than I was ten years ago.

Yet, when I have sex, I turn into a human being. I am more generous, patient, and accepting of myself and others. I forget I'm getting fat; I forget to feel anxious; I feel beautiful and loved. I am liberated from the commerce and conformity of the world.

Pleasure does this. There must be a scientific explanation that involves endorphins, or a spiritual explanation that involves souls, but I'm willing to settle for a skin-deep observation that, when I'm getting pleasure, life is better and I am a better person. This notion has led me to the not very original conclusion that I ought to get more sex.

That may seem obvious, but it isn't to me. To my parents, pride was a sin and pleasure for its own sake was deeply suspect; if you were having all that much fun, you were probably not doing your job. If you had leisure, best to do it in an organized team setting, so that you could learn good sportsmanship and competitiveness and other allegedly character-building qualities. Later, in the "me decade," I was so disgusted by Reaganite excesses on the one hand, and the navel-gazing New Age movement on the other, that I thought the less energy I spent pursuing my own needs and desires, the better. In sex, I concentrated on my partners and got a charge out of being a good lover.

Only recently did I come to the conclusion that pleasure is its own reward, not merely a byproduct of a good sexual relationship or a payoff for a job well done. I don't really have any philosophical explanation of why this is; it is self-evident. People may have been trained to think something else, as I was, but if they're lucky, they'll get over it.

My luck is that I have a stable, open relationship. I have been with my lover for more than seven years; we are both bisexual, and neither of us believes in monogamy. We provide for each other the rewards of a stable relationship, including the kind of great sex you have with someone who knows everything about you. This means that whenever we date other people, it's entirely for fun. We aren't making up for what we don't get at home; we're looking for friendship and thrills. When I date someone else, it is because I want to get to know them, because they intrigue me, and mostly because I want pleasure.

Bisexuals are sometimes accused of being selfish, self-centered, hedonistic, or promiscuous because, like homosexuals, our whole world supposedly revolves around sex. In other words, we are sometimes accused of pursuing pleasure too seriously.

I'm not sure how to take such accusations. Using the Calvinistic criteria of my youth, I am a great sinner. I have rejected marriage and consumerism, and I revel in pleasure. I do drugs and publish pornography. And the more I do it, the less I feel like growing up and settling down. The politics of pleasure which has its fulfillment in my bisexuality subverts the status quo by offering an alternative to all the negative things the nuclear family represents economically, environmentally, and sexually. It is true that my life sometimes revolves around the pursuit of pleasure; what's wrong with that? I like to suck cock; I like to eat pussy; I like to fuck and get fucked. In those moments, when I am giving and receiving pleasure, I am most myself—at peace with myself, my partner, and the world. What's wrong with that? Pleasure is worth pursuing for its own sake.

This also means that pornography—my pornography, the kind I write and publish—is just a toy, a tool I use to get more pleasure. There is "bad" pornography too, "bad" in the sense that people get exploited in its manufacture, or "bad" in the sense of being poorly done. But I'm over the idea that there's something "bad," in a moral sense, about my pursuing pleasure, whether in the flesh or on the page. I discover and embrace my desires; I enrich eroticism for myself and my readers; I bring into being the realm of love.

Too Butch to Be Bi
(or You Can't Judge a Boy by Her Lover)

Robin Sweeney

I am flirting with a friend of mine. I've always wondered what might have happened if Lisa and I had gone beyond gossiping and flirting to actually have an affair. She is a cute femme. Lisa flatters me, letting me know she thinks I'm smart and an ideal butch.

"So, what are you doing this weekend?" she asks me, expecting to hear plans for misbehavior with the girls in town.

I am blushing even before I answer. I mutter something about going to visit Victor in Los Angeles.

"Who's Victor? A friend?"

"Well, no. Not exactly. He's someone I'm playing with."

"A boy? A real boy? Oh, really? You top him, right?"

"Actually, no." There is a long and extremely painful pause while Lisa processes this.

"Robin, I knew you played with boys, but having sex with one? You can't be bi—you're too butch."

It wasn't difficult for me to come out as a lesbian. In fact, most people I knew in high school assumed I was gay long before I started grappling with my own identity. I have, as one lover told me, "the face." When I asked her what she meant, she said that I just looked like a dyke. And it's true. Even in pictures of me at four or five, I look like a little dyke. No one has ever been surprised to find out I was queer.

I ran into pretty standard teenage homophobia—my own internalized version and from others—but I was fortunate to grow up in a Southern California town with a surprising number of openly gay and bisexual adults and teenagers. While Aaron Fricke was making headlines taking another boy to his prom, the administrator in charge of student social events at my high school made it quietly known that same-sex couples were allowed to attend the prom together.

Even though I fit the stereotypes and images of what a lesbian was supposed to be, it wasn't always a comfortable identity for me. I was sexual with men—and liked it—and that fact was a problem for a lot of women and men I met in the lesbian and gay community. It was a problem for me, too. I didn't know how to come to terms with being bisexual and still maintain my butch identity and connection to the gay community.

In college, I was very involved with the lesbian and gay community, and I rarely described myself as bisexual or talked about the relationships I had with men. "Real dykes" don't have sex with men, or if they do, they certainly don't mean it. It was accepted in most of the communities I've been a part of to get drunk and pick up an opposite-sex partner for a one-night stand, but not to have an affair with one. Sleeping with a man was sort of the lesbian equivalent of the frat boys getting drunk, sucking each other off, and blaming it all on being wasted the night before.

I loved being part of a lesbian and gay community and getting to be an activist. Meeting openly gay people was incredibly validating. But it was made clear to me that I was too butch and too "obvious." The women's community was small and closeted, and vicious to the women who didn't fit the rigid ideas of acceptable looks and behavior. The few women who publicly came out as bisexual were treated like pariahs. I was terrified of losing the little bit of a community I had found, and I didn't come out as bisexual.

I met more and more lesbian women and gay men who, in private conversation, talked about relationships, self-concepts, and plain old lust that didn't match up with the exclusively lesbian or gay identity most of us publicly presented. Some people spoke of former boyfriends or girlfriends they had loved before they came out, or members of the opposite sex on whom they had crushes. Several gay male friends have talked to me about becoming upset when they were attracted to a woman, after having been exclusively attracted to men. And I am not the only butch woman who has been startled to realize the hot thing in the rugby shirt and short haircut isn't a dyke after all, but a cute boy.

As a telephone crisis counselor, I heard a great deal of pain and grief from people who felt they didn't fit the standards of what a lesbian woman or gay man was supposed to be. I talked to them about the Kinsey scale[1] and the idea of sexuality taking place along a continuum. I was able to tell upset callers not to worry about the crush they had on their best friend, and that sexuality was not an either/or question. At the same time, I lied about how I felt and thought of myself, since hiding was easier than confronting people's assumptions about me.

> *A friend who is a mover and a shaker in our local bisexual community tells me that she mentioned my name at a meeting. Susan, a bi activist at the meeting who knew me through other circles, couldn't believe that I was bi.*
>
> *Susan is the butch lover of a butch ex-lover of mine, Bobbie. Bobbie and I have spent time talking about Susan's bisexuality, and I have told her how difficult it has been for me as a butch bisexual woman. What did Susan think I was talking about? Did she think I was just being supportive?*

Sexual minority communities do a lousy job of confronting our assumptions about ourselves and each other. We hold onto the same notions about difference that the dominant, heterosexist culture teaches us and apply these to our own queer[2] communities. Most of the time this doesn't work, and nowhere is this more true than in our assumptions about appearance, gender, and sexual identity.

I am a butch bisexual woman whose romantic and sexual partners are primarily other butch women, with some notable exceptions. Frequently, I like to appear as masculine as I can, often passing for male on the street. I like to keep my hair short. I'd rather wear jeans and boots than anything else. Sometimes I pack when I go out, putting my dildo in my pants and wearing my dick out of the house. (No, people don't really notice that often. And the ones who do notice are the ones I'm probably trying to attract.)

This doesn't necessarily mean I am a transsexual—someone who feels she was born into the wrong-gendered body—although there certainly are butch women who decide to go through gender reassignment to, as one of my female-to-male transsexual friends has put it, "make the outside match the inside."[3] Nor am I necessarily a transvestite—a person who desires to dress and appear as the oppo-

site gender, both for erotic purposes and because that person feels
more comfortable in the clothing usually assigned to the opposite
gender. I am a butch woman, and I like being a butch woman.

Even when I am not trying to appear particularly masculine,
people still often respond to me as male. I am frequently called
"Sir" by bank tellers and grocery clerks. I usually pitch my voice
as high as I am able and reply, "Thank you, ma'am," no matter
what gender they are.

The physical gender one is born with, the gender identity that one
feels the most comfortable being, the gender (or genders) of sexual
partners, and the sexual fantasies and desires one may have are all
different components that make up sexuality. There is a difference
between being born a male and feeling masculine, or between being
born a female and being feminine. And being feminine or being
masculine doesn't necessarily have anything to do with wanting to
"run the fuck" or be the top sexually. None of this has anything to
do with the gender to whom a person might be attracted. Unfortunately, we all often assume false connections between these different aspects of sexuality. (For example, ask yourself what those guys
mean in the "straight-acting, straight-appearing" personal ads, and
what this says about their assumptions about identity.)

Much of my butch identity and masculine role-play is connected
to having sex. One of my favorite sexual fantasies is being a younger boy having sex with a big, bad older man. I am fortunate enough
to explore this with my female lover, whom I often call my daddy.
My daddy also has 37 pairs of high heels, and then I am a slightly
older boy having sex with someone who is definitely not another
man. On occasion, I like to wear lingerie and feel like a pretty girl.
Being a butch with cleavage is a social category I enjoy, with all of
its challenges and opportunities for confusion. The butch fatale is
an under-celebrated figure in our sexual communities.

But being a butch woman who is also bisexual can be difficult. It
feels sometimes that the the idea is so challenging—since the assumptions in our communities are that all butch women are lesbian
women and all femme women are bisexual women—that often a
butch woman trying to come to terms with being bisexual is stuck.

One of the saddest conversations I ever had was with a butch
friend of mine, who called me full of news. She is a very cute, queer

woman, who had never slept with a man—nor, she told me, had she wanted to—until recently. She said that she finally figured it all out, the answer to why she was interested in men and what she was going to do about it. She triumphantly announced that she wanted to have sex with men and therefore must be gender dysphoric.[4] I asked her why she considered herself gender dysphoric. Did she feel like a man? Did she want to be a man? No, not really, she told me. She liked her butch boy look, but still thought of herself as a woman. She definitely was going to start sleeping with men, though. I asked why she wouldn't just consider herself bisexual. There was a long pause, and she said that she just wasn't bisexual. She was a butch; she couldn't be bisexual. She just wanted to sleep with men and women.

This may seem trivial. After all, what do my sexual history and fantasies really have to do with bisexual politics? Why worry about something like gender, appearance, or fantasy when there are other issues that may seem more important?

The questions of inclusion and acceptance are crucial to the bisexual community. Most people, if given a chance to explore the way they feel about themselves, and who and what they desire, have very complicated sexual identities. The bisexual community has a responsibility to be a place where the chance is given for this kind of exploration and truth-telling.

Some of this was complicated for me as I began coming out into S/M.[5] Figuring out I was into S/M was even more difficult than trying to be butch and bisexual. I always fantasized about rough sex and bondage, and once I met a woman who was willing to teach me what she knew about being kinky, I started exploring S/M.

There were practically no resources available to me at the time. The local gay phone line didn't know anything; there were no women's leather groups in the area and there were few books I could find. The only leather bar in Philadelphia was a men's bar not open to women. Most painful, though, was that when I tried to talk to my friends about S/M, most of them freaked out. It was a very isolating time for me.

Coming out as bisexual in the lesbian and gay community and coming out as a pervert were similar experiences for me. It often feels as though we are the secrets that the rest of the community wants to hide. Lesbians and gays may experiment with opposite-sex partners, but being openly bisexual is not acceptable. And even though many folks at one time or another play around with some sort of S/M or domination and submission, sadomasochist is an identity to which most people won't make a commitment.

Once I finally found the S/M community, some strange things happened. I found more people who were enthusiastic about my being butch, but there was not an overwhelming support for being bisexual. A number of lesbian women and gay men I met did S/M together, but did not consider themselves bisexual. They were simply doing what has come to be called "pansexual play." Sometimes this kind of play involves genital sex, but most of the time it does not. If you're just tying someone up and whipping them, and you both get excited and get off, but it isn't genital, is it sex? On the one hand, I really admire this sort of queer-on-queer sex. But on the other hand, it leaves me sort of puzzled. If having sex with both men and women isn't being bisexual, than what is it? And what is sex about, if it isn't having pleasure with another person?

Being a pervert in the bisexual community hasn't always been easy, either. There is a lot of fear in the bisexual community about sex, and especially about S/M. The bisexual community sometimes seems so wrapped up in our new ways of talking about and thinking about sex that we forget the fact that there are sexuality issues we may not know or understand. Bisexual people can be as uncomfortable about different sorts of sexuality as anybody else. We don't want to discuss the stuff about sex that makes us uncomfortable, and bisexual leatherpeople are often silenced in both their communities. We need to remember that being bisexual doesn't necessarily give one instant access to the world of sexual understanding.

> *The group house I'm living in is looking for a new member. We tell the prospective members about ourselves, including the fact that we are all bisexual women looking to create a household that will be positive about bisexuality.*
>
> *We interview one lesbian woman who is obviously uncomfortable with the idea of living with three bisexual women. We wrap up the interview as quickly as possible and I see her to the door.*
>
> *"Listen," she says to me once my housemates can't hear her, "as soon as the house turns all lesbian, give me a call."*

I am by turns angry and amused. I am the butchest of the three roommates; obviously she thought I was the most likely to get over my "bisexual phase." Ironically, when I return to my housemates and tell them this, we compare notes and discover I am the woman who has most recently had sex with a man.

Much of the politics of the bisexual community involves challenging the idea that sexuality is an either/or proposition. But the next step beyond this must be confronting the assumptions about gender identity and sexual orientation that exist in our own bisexual community and in the mainstream lesbian and gay community.

It is difficult enough to get past the message that we aren't supposed to be queer. The world we live in makes it pretty clear that anyone who is not exclusively heterosexual does not really exist. I think every lesbian, gay, and bisexual person knows someone who has killed themselves—either slowly with drugs and alcohol, or more quickly—because they couldn't imagine themselves finding any acceptance for wanting to be sexual and romantic with a same-sex partner.

But once we find a community that is accepting of our same-sex interests, we run into an entirely different series of messages. A number of these are about appearances and what they are supposed to say about who we are. The ideas about femmes (femme women aren't really interested in other women, and femme men aren't really interested in women at all) and butches (butches are always the aggressors in sex, whether they are men or women) permeate our queer culture. These ideas make it difficult for us to explore who we are and who we want to be. Many people feel too threatened to challenge the status quo of an already fringe community, for fear of being outcast from the one place where they have struggled to belong.

Just as the lesbian and gay community threatens the dominant culture, the mainstream gay and lesbian community reacts with a combination of fear, curiosity, and anger to those queer folks who are too different. Leatherpeople, transgendered folk, and bisexuals all make the mainstream lesbian and gay community uncomfortable. I think we threaten the long-held political idea in the gay community that "gay people" are just like heterosexuals.

We also threaten each other. More of the rotten responses I receive about being a bisexual butch woman come from other bisexuals, particularly men, who don't want to deal with any woman who is not some Barbie doll standard of femininity. (An ex-boyfriend told me his idea of bisexual women is "two beautiful feminine women together." I then asked him what I was, if a bisexual woman was, by definition, feminine. He said I was just a woman who has sex with both men and women. Gosh, isn't that bisexual?) The bisexual community has to start talking within itself and with other communities about gender issues.

I know that my life is different since I'm a bisexual, a butch, and a pervert. I grew up feeling like I was different from the rest of the kids; as I became an adult I figured out some of the reasons why. And even when I found a queer community, I discovered I was queerer than I thought. My life is also more difficult than it has to be, due to homophobia—both within and outside the lesbian and gay community—and the nasty habit we as queer folk have of always looking for someone else to pick on.

Until we figure out how to create a community that has more room for all of us who are lesbian, gay, bisexual, and just plain different because of our sexual identity, little of the way the outside treats us is going to change. Ideally, I want a sexual minority community that is just that—a community made up of lesbian women, gay men, bisexual and transgendered people who are educated about all of our issues. And I want a community that celebrates the fact that we are sexual in a sex-positive way, a community open to all of us getting to be who we truly want to be. I want a community that doesn't limit us by our sexual identities.

And then maybe I'll stop having to explain that I'm not too butch to be bi.

NOTES

1. The Kinsey scale was devised by pioneer sex researcher Alfred Kinsey (1948, 1952) to describe sexual behavior and orientation. The scale ranges from six to zero, with zero being exlusively heterosexual and six being exclusively homosexual, based on both psychological reactions and overt experience. Most people fall somewhere between one and five on the scale.

2. A brief word on words. Throughout this essay I refer to the lesbian and gay community, the gay community, the lesbian, gay, and bisexual community, and

the queer community all fairly interchangeably. All the terms loosely refer to the same group of people—people whose sexual orientation includes members of their own sex—albeit with slightly different emphasis. The language for who we are is remarkably frustrating.

3. I am grateful for the female-to-male transgendered people who have answered my questions, been my buddies, and put up with my weirdness for much of the background for both this essay and my own personal identity. One of the biggest support groups for FTMs in the United States can be reached at: FTM, c/o James, 5337 College Avenue #142, Oakland, CA 94618.

4. Gender dysphoria is the clinical term for individuals who feel their biological sex does not match their gender identity.

5. I use the terms S/M, sadomasochism, and leather to refer to the same thing, although there are certainly people who are into leather who do not do S/M and sadomasochists who are not into leather. I suggest *Leatherfolk* (Thompson, 1991) as a place to begin for more information on the leather community.

Politics of the Bisexual Deep Fry

Michèlle T. Clinton

i said
  my woman left me
    & i don't think i'll ever have another girlfriend

she said
  i must have my mouth on you

i said
  i'm not attracted to white women

she said
  i like the darkness of your nipples

i said
  it's not exactly because of inherent ugliness on white skin

  it's because white girls always think i'm a butch
  you're so strong they say
  & bat their eyelashes
  which makes me feel like feeding my cat to my dog
  you're so powerful which of course means male
  you're so tough inside that rough black skin they say
  black skin which means black attitude
  which of course means mannish

she said
  you're such a girl

i said
   plus lesbians hate bisexuals
   bisexuals are the nigger of the queer community

she said
   all my ex-lovers are bisexuals

i said
   even though my family kicked me out
   & black nationalists say my kind destroys the black family
   even though a queer is a queer is a queer
   to any christian homophobe
   i know you hate me

   i know you can't hear inside my private story
   you think my addiction is for dick
     & i want to hide behind the shadow of a man
   i don't want a bisexual movement
   i don't want a bisexual newsletter rap group parade
   i don't want to steal or pollute the purity of lesbian space

   i want you to care about me inside my private parts
   i want you to let me be the queer that i am
   & know i am not your enemy

   plus i'd like to get laid

she said
   maybe we can work something out

i said
   plus lesbians run out of energy so quick
   lesbian bed death

   i've heard stories of 3 & 4 year celibate relationships
   lovers who turn into sisters
   passion dies w/ time
   girls don't really have a sex drive
   drive as in driven as in need as in got to have some

i've seen those feminist videos
soft vanilla sex
nobody sweats
nobody fucks
nobody gets nasty
rumor has it
feminists don't like to fuck because it makes them too
vulnerable

beware the single-celled lesbian woman
who knows the body language of cats
who can take care of exactly herself
who knows exactly what her self
   alone in a room wants
who doesn't wanna be opened by fire
who doesn't wanna fuck or possess or control

her orgasms are the strokes of baby fingers
that aim to imitate masturbation

she will not give it up to you
she won't let herself want it

she said
   i got something for you
   this has no ego mode
   this has no sperm
   this is a toy for like-minded women
   who wanna take that plane of infinite pleasure

i said
   maybe we could work something out

Part B

Coalition-Building and Other Queer Stories

*If I am not for myself,
    who will be for me?*

*If only for myself,
    what am I?*

If not now, when?

—Rabbi Hillel (Mishnah, Pirkei Avot 1:14)

Bisexual Lesbian

Dajenya

I am not just bisexual
I am a lesbian
I am not just a lesbian
I am a bisexual lesbian.

Some say this is a contradiction
and I'm just trying to confuse terms.
Yes, these are confusing terms,
but no more confusing
than trying to hide half the truth.

Some say I'm trying
to make lesbians less visible.
Not so.
I'm trying to make myself
more visible.

I am a lesbian.
I love women.
I love womankind.
I am woman-identified.
I study our hidden past.
I struggle in the present.
I work hard for our future.

I have had love for a woman
deeper than for any man.
I desire a woman
to be my partner in life.
I love women.
I am a lesbian.

I am bisexual.
I was born that way.
I have loved girls and boys.
I have loved women and men.
I have sought love
where it offered itself.
I have paid the price
of both lifestyles.

I have been bashed
for loving women
and isolated
for loving men.
You speak of privilege—
let me tell you:
the isolation was much worse
than the bashing.

Now I make choices.
Am I finding myself
or has society beaten me down?
Today I choose to choose a woman.
I won't be shut out from my community
that I've worked with
ever since Stonewall.
I won't be told that I don't belong
in the only world I've ever belonged in.
I love women
and I am a lesbian.

and too
I am bisexual
in my history
in my capacity
in my fantasies
in my abilities
in my love for beautiful people
regardless of gender.

I have the right
to claim my lesbianism
And my bisexuality
even if it confuses you.
I am a lesbian.
I am bisexual.
I am a bisexual lesbian.
Deal with it.

November 1991

Traitors to the Cause?
Understanding the Lesbian/Gay
"Bisexuality Debates"

Elizabeth Armstrong

No bi woman I know has escaped the pain of being ostracized by some elements of the lesbian community. (bisexual woman)

I was in love with a woman. I was a lesbian. But reality broke through soon enough. There was the fact that I wasn't a "real" dyke, defined by Kate Clinton as "penis-pure and proud." Again, after the honeymoon of acceptance, everyone was waiting for me to renounce my feelings for men. (bisexual woman)

I bitterly resented the double standard which dictated that dykes should embrace a Virginia Woolf, an Eleanor Roosevelt, a Muriel Rukeyser as long-lost lesbian sisters given their sometime love for women, but would cast me into the outer darkness because of my refusal to pledge eternal allegiance to the cunt. (lesbian who got involved with a man)

No one in the gay bar would ever guess I had a girlfriend and the same went for my straight friends. Why did I keep my two worlds apart? For safety. In gay circles, it was a major faux pas to sleep with a "fish," while in the hetero world in which I was raised, to be a fag was an unpardonable offense. (bisexual man)

Claiming that lesbians sleep with men and calling themselves "bi-dykes" oppresses lesbians as surely as straight male por-

nography. . . . Armed with heterosexual privilege and statistical distortions, bi's try to redefine "lesbian" in their own image. Bi's are getting a lot of support for this—from straights who always believed that lesbians fuck men and from gay men who are more comfortable with women who fuck men. If it only weren't for those damned uncooperative lesbians. (lesbian)[1]

Bisexuality in lesbian and gay communities is currently a subject of heated debate, as the quotations above indicate. Bisexuals are pushing for inclusion and recognition in lesbian and gay communities, wanting their emerging identities as bisexual people and their sexual relationships with both genders to be fully acknowledged and respected. Lesbians and gays, however, are often reticent to embrace bisexuals as members of their communities. For in spite of the claims of self-identified bisexuals, lesbians and gays often do not believe that bisexuality is an authentic sexual identity. They view bisexuality as a transitional stage on the route to coming out as lesbian or gay, or to realizing that one is actually straight. Claiming to be bisexual when one is really lesbian or gay is seen as denial, while claiming to be bisexual when one is really straight is seen as kinky, and potentially exploitative of people who are lesbian or gay. Often when lesbians and gays acknowledge that some people do manage to sustain a bisexual identity, they do not think these people should be a part of the lesbian/gay community. Many feel that bisexuals maintain access to heterosexual privilege through their opposite-gender sexual relationships, and are likely to take advantage of it. They feel that bisexuals are less committed than gay men or lesbians to their same-gender partners and to the larger community.

While gays and lesbians share the above feelings, lesbians seem to hold these views more strongly and are more likely to express them. In a 1991 forum in *The San Francisco Bay Times* on bisexuality in the gay/lesbian community, all the letters were from women. The editor of the paper, Kim Corsaro (1991b, p. 6), noted this:

One particularly striking feature stands out about all of the letters that we have received this month: every single one of them has been from a woman (or women). Never before in the entire history of this paper has any issue which affects the entire community been addressed solely by one gender of our readership. It's not that gay men are immune to disliking bisexuals or don't care about the issue. I think it just simply isn't threatening to them in the same way.

This gender imbalance is represented in the quotations at the beginning of this paper, displaying the difference in intensity and amount of discussion of the issue of bisexuality in lesbian and gay communities. The difference in intensity in bisexual men's and bisexual women's experiences of rejection from gay and lesbian communities is also apparent in the qualitative difference between being "cast into the outer darkness" and committing a "major faux pas."

Lesbians may feel more more threatened by bisexuality than gay men and more justified in expressing their anti-bi attitudes because of their commitment to lesbian *feminism,* which provides ideological support for these attitudes. According to lesbian feminism, the central dynamic of male dominance involves "compulsory heterosexuality," or the coerced sexual availability of women to men (Rich, 1980). In a lesbian-feminist framework, a woman's commitment to feminism can be measured by the strength of her commitment to women, which is sometimes evaluated by how thoroughly she manages to exclude men from her life. Clearly, bisexuals cannot measure up to this standard. Bisexual women are viewed as more problematic than straight feminists because bisexual women make deliberate decisions to include men in their lives, while heterosexual feminists can at least argue that they cannot help being straight. And, to top it off, bisexual women are more likely than straight women to seek access, through their connections with women, to the sanctuary of the lesbian community. So, lesbians often view bisexuality as antifeminist, politically incorrect, and threatening to feminism and the lesbian community.

Many bisexual people, particularly women, find rejection from lesbian/gay communities extremely painful. What makes rejection harder is that their identification with the lesbian/gay community often leads them to internalize negative attitudes about bisexuality, and to question whether they really do belong in the community. Bisexuals have been slow to gather the strength to challenge the lesbian/gay community directly about the pain they have experienced. Gradually, during the 1980s, bisexuals began developing a collective understanding of the ways lesbian/gay attitudes about bisexuality are stereotyped and inaccurate. In spite of feelings of hurt and betrayal, many bisexuals are now committed to finding a place in the lesbian/gay community. Bi women also feel the need to push for inclusion in lesbian communities because of their desire to be part of the larger women's and feminist communities that overlap with lesbian communities.

Some bisexuals also recognize that lesbian and gay rejection of bisexuality does not come from a position of social power, but rather from fear and powerlessness. Realizing this, bisexual activists have chosen a strategy of attempting to alleviate the fears of gays and lesbians about the consequences of having bisexuals and bisexuality in their communities. Activists have developed written materials to dispel myths about bisexuality, particularly the beliefs that bisexuality does not really exist and that bisexuals are "traitors to the cause of lesbian/gay liberation."[2] But even if ambivalence and suspicion about bisexuality come from a position of disempowerment, they are still unacceptable prejudices. Bisexual activists point out the hypocrisy of rejecting people on the basis of loving the wrong gender in a community founded on the premise that people should be able to love whomever they choose. Using their own lives as examples, bisexual activists have attempted to convince gays and lesbians that the bisexual identity is a distinct, long-term sexual orientation, embraced by people with integrity committed to the lesbian/gay community. While bi activists acknowledge that not all bisexuals will treat gay men and lesbians with respect, or be loyal to gay and lesbian communities, they argue that bisexual people are no more or less likely to hurt individuals or betray the community than gay men or lesbians. Some bisexual activists also try to emphasize the alignment of bisexuals with gays and lesbians by emphasizing the vulnerability of bisexuals to homophobia and gay-bashing from straights, while acknowledging that bisexuals do have access to heterosexual privilege. But bi activists also point out that anybody, gay or straight, can choose to take advantage of heterosexual privilege, and that "passing" for straight is as painful and damaging for a bisexual as it is for a lesbian or gay man (see Blasingame, this volume).

While alleviating the fears of gays and lesbians by education and example is important, it will not entirely eliminate biphobia, particularly among lesbians. As we saw above, a certain amount of biphobia is fed by a feminist politic based on a specific analysis of the dynamics of gender relations in society. While I find the use of feminism to justify the exclusion of bisexuals disturbing and inappropriate, bisexuality *does* have a different meaning for lesbians than it does for gay men. Perhaps with a deeper understanding of the connections between male dominance and sexuality, it is possible to develop a politic that is loyal to feminist insights about the role of male dominant sexuality in women's subordination, but that is also supportive of the inclusion of bisexuals and bisexuality in lesbian and gay communities.

GENDER AND HETEROSEXUALITY

Phallocentrism: The Connecting Link Between Gender and Sexuality

Catherine MacKinnon (1982, p. 2) sees sexuality as the primary location of male power over women, and therefore sees sexuality as creating gender:

> the molding, direction, and expression of sexuality organizes society into two sexes—women and men—which division underlies the totality of social relations. Sexuality is that social process which creates, organizes, expresses, and directs desire, creating the social beings we know as women and men, as their relations create society.

Compulsory heterosexuality is an implied consequence. To MacKinnon, what makes a woman a woman is the way she exists sexually in relation to another group of social beings, men:

> Socially, femaleness means femininity, which means attractiveness to men, which means sexual attractiveness, which

means sexual availability on male terms. What defines woman as such is what turns men on. (MacKinnon, 1982, pp. 17-19)

Gender domination and sexual hierarchies overlap in a phallocentric view of sexuality. As a society, we tend to see sexuality as residing in the male, particularly in his penis.[3] Consequently, masculinity gets defined as the ownership of an active, penis-centered sexuality, while femininity gets defined as a passive, (also penis-centered) sexuality, owned by men, and only "activated" in the presence of a male penis. In this view, men generate desire, while women respond to men's desire. Sexuality becomes implicated in the perpetuation of male domination and gender categories themselves through our phallocentric notion of sexuality, which defines men and women as having different and interdependent sexual natures.

Phallocentric Heterosexuality and Gender Identities

Phallocentrism links gender and sexuality, with compulsory heterosexuality as the consequence. Heterosexuality is used to solidify men's and women's gender identities, and homosexuality is seen as attacking and undermining their gender identities. As one would expect, the way heterosexuality operates to solidify women's gender identities is quite different from how it operates to solidify men's gender identities.

For men, compulsory heterosexuality involves the requirement or expectation that in order to be a man they must have an insatiable, penis-centered, heterosexual sexuality. They must show continual proof of their heterosexual virility and conquests to other men (and women) to win and maintain access to the status of manhood and the privileges and power of masculinity. Compulsory heterosexuality puts a burden on men, which all men (gay, straight, or bi) must bear, but which different men respond to in various ways. Male sexual lore tends to focus around worries about sexual performance (i.e., impotence, premature ejaculation, and sexual stamina) and penis size. The bragging (and often lying) that men do about their sexual prowess expresses men's fears of being found wanting.

For men, it is crucial that women both be sexually available and sexually affirming. Men feel dependent on women because they believe women hold the power to destroy the feelings of virility upon which their fragile sense of masculinity rests. Women can expose their impotence or inadequate sexual performances. Even though women rarely do this, and in fact generally conspire to bolster men's fragile masculinity, men resent that the "objects" upon which they are supposed to prove their virility have the latent power to destroy their masculinity.

Compulsory heterosexuality for women complements men's compulsory heterosexuality. Women's compulsory heterosexuality involves the forced sexual availability of women to men (Rich, 1980). Women develop a reactive, responsive sexuality instead of an active, agentic, desiring sexuality. Even sexual pleasure itself is experienced vicariously, as Shere Hite (1976) illustrates in her examples of women who prefer men's orgasms to their own.

Because of the way women's sexuality is defined, it is less important, at least in terms of actual sexual practices, to women's gender identity than it is in the formation of men's gender identity. Ethel Spector Person (1980, p. 629) found that while "sexuality consolidates and confirms gender in men, it is a variable feature in women." Women's gender identity does not rely as heavily on sexual performance or sexual conquest. Women do not "perform" sexually: they are the site of men's performances. They do not make conquests; they are the prey. This relieves the pressure on women a little; women's gender identity is less fragile than men's in some ways because it does not require reaffirmation by sexual performance.

Gendered Homophobia

Due to the different ways that heterosexuality bolsters men's versus women's gender identities, phallocentrism and gendered compulsory heterosexuality lead to gendered homophobia. Straight men and women are threatened differently by lesbians than by gay men.[4]

One manifestation of homophobia specifically directed against lesbianism is lesbian invisibility. Straight people perpetually ask what it is that women *do* together; how can sex occur without a penis in the room? The horribly homophobic notion that "lesbians just need a good fuck" to "cure" them stems from the obviously phallocentric belief that all "good" or "real" sex involves a penis. Straight people are likely to dismiss even the most overt signs of lesbianism because of their inability to see women's sexuality other than as responsive to men. Lesbian invisibility is paradoxical, as on one hand it means that lesbians are often not as vulnerable to physical violence and homophobia as gay men, but on the other hand it means that lesbians find it harder to be taken seriously as self-defining sexual beings, and harder to achieve positive identity-affirming visibility. Society is not particularly threatened by the explicitly sexual aspect of lesbianism, because people just do not see it.

What is experienced as threatening is women's refusal to be sexually available to men on men's terms. Whenever any woman resists male power, regardless of her sexual interest in women, she is likely to be labeled a lesbian. The term lesbian is used as a stigmatizing label by men (and sometimes other women) to keep women in line; that is, to keep them sexually available to and affirming of men.

Understanding homophobia against lesbians through the lens of phallocentrism helps make sense of one of the perennial mysteries of homophobia in our society: the prevalence of "lesbianism" in straight male pornography. Showing women having sex with each other is absolutely central to straight pornography, and not seen as threatening. These women are not "coded" by the viewers as lesbian because the reason they are naked on the page is for male viewing pleasure. In the text, the women always reassure the viewers that while they enjoy their scenes with women, they prefer sex with men. The male viewers are intended to experience the lesbian scenes as evidence of the woman's "kinkiness" and her willingness to do anything. The women are supposedly preparing each other to be "fucked" by a man, *not* having a sexual experience that is complete and fulfilling in its own right.

It is taboo for two men to touch each other in straight pornography because of the fundamentally different way homophobia against gay men works in our society. Homophobia directed toward gay men tends to focus on sexual practices. In a phallocentric society, gay sex is undeniably sexual and highly visible as such. Even the slightest physical contact among men is often viewed as evidence of homosexuality (except for physical contact in highly ritualized, super-masculine, heterosexual settings, such as athletics). The reaction of straights to male homosexuality has much to do with the importance penetration has acquired in our phallocentric society. "Real" sex does not happen without penetration (and people think lesbians do not practice penetration). Homophobic jokes about gay men and gay men's sexual practices invariably focus on anal sex, although straight people engage in anal sex as well. Straights often have a visceral revulsion to gay male sexual practices, completely different than their response to lesbian sexual practices.

The stereotype of the effeminate gay man is a form of homophobia that is a direct consequence of male compulsory heterosexuality. Logically, if heterosexual conquests are what makes a man masculine, then failing to engage in these, and, in addition, becoming the object of other men's sexual conquests would be feminizing and emasculating. For men to allow themselves to be penetrated means emasculation, the voluntary acquisition of the low-status position of women, which threatens the whole conceptual scheme. To protect this scheme, the label gay, like the label lesbian, is used to frighten heterosexual men into more conscientious adherence to the "rules" of compulsory heterosexuality.

GENDER AND HOMOSEXUALITY

Men and women who resist compulsory heterosexuality in our society do so in the context of a sexual system that is deeply implicated in the maintenance of male dominance, as discussed above. This cannot help but shape the meanings that become embedded in gay and lesbian identities and communities. Gay and lesbian identities tend to solidify around what is most threatening to dominant society, often in a direct, confrontational, reactive way.

Exclusive Lesbian Identity and Inclusive Gay Identity

As I have argued above, what is most threatening to straight society about lesbianism is the possibility that women will no longer be sexually available to men. Building a lesbian identity around women's exclusive sexual interest in women challenges the notion that women need men to be sexual and challenges men's claim to ownership of women's sexuality. Asserting that lesbianism is not just about "liking women too" allows for a clear distinction between self-identified lesbians and the exoticized "lesbians" of straight male pornography. Drawing the boundaries clearly, and allowing no compromise, makes it more difficult for men to coopt and re-appropriate women's sexuality as "kinky," and "exotic," but still for men's pleasure. Lesbians often deliberately cultivate aesthetics that are not attractive to straight men, thereby communicating their unavailability and disinterest:

> I actively try to retain some item of apparel (like the motorcycle jacket) or retain some key piece of my appearance (like the short hair or weapons) that tells the straight boys the tits are not for them. (Anonymous, 1989, p. 42)

Contemporary politicized lesbian identity is forged not only out of a recognition of the preferred gender of one's sexual partners, but out of a commitment to gender exclusivity in one's partners. This insistence on exclusivity intensifies the meaning of the choice of sexual partners because of the clear message to men: "This is not for you." Lesbians are asserting ownership of their own sexuality, and promoting women's sexual agency.

As we saw above, what is most threatening to straights, particularly straight men, about male homosexuality is the threatened loss of masculinity and masculine privilege. Many straight men have a defensive hatred of homosexuality stemming from feelings of gender inadequacy. Gay men are quite conscious of the gender significance of homosexuality, and tend to use gender playfully, both in their campy appropriation of feminine styles and dress, and in their super-masculine styles that are perhaps even more threatening to straight men. Because all men are punished by straight men for exhibiting even the smallest sign of gayness, the gay community is fairly generous about allocating the benefits of membership:

> Gay men aren't real concerned about excluding people from this elite [that] we consider ourselves to be. I've never heard of anyone's credential being challenged, like "I'm not going to

believe you're gay until I fuck you." We give everyone the
benefit of the doubt. You wanna party with us? That's fine.
You don't have to make it with other men if you don't want to.
Your loss, if you don't, you know?[5]

Men have virtually nothing to gain from the larger society by identifying as gay, hence there is little reason to interrogate men's self-
identification, even if they also have connections to women.

In sum, lesbian identity tends to be defined more around gender
exclusivity than gay identity because gay men's and women's experiences of sexuality are quite different. Lesbians are less likely to
have their sexuality taken seriously, and are not as visible as gay
men. Lesbians will be subject to sexism regardless of their sexual
identity, although the sexism may be intensified when combined
with homophobia. Gay men are less likely to face the problem of
being eroticized and exoticized by straight women. Gay men, while
they retain a great deal of male privilege, lose gender-based privileges among men, as well as being subjected to homophobia.

Gay and lesbian feelings about bisexuality are consistent with
these identity constructions. Lesbians have problems with bisexuality, particularly women's bisexuality, because to them it seems to
undermine all the progress lesbians have made toward making it
difficult for men to reclaim and eroticize women's sexuality.

For gay men, bisexuality is a problem of an entirely different
order. Because gay identity is not as centrally organized around
NOT being with women, when gay men are with women it poses
less of an identity threat. Gay men are also less likely to be threatened by bisexuality among other gay men because their opposite-
gender sexual activity does not seem to undermine or negate the
meaning of their same-gender sexual activities in the same way.
Because gay sex is so much more visible than lesbian sex, if both a
self-identified gay man and a self-identified lesbian have sex with a
member of the opposite gender, the general culture is more likely to
point to his gay encounter and her straight encounter as most salient.

Lesbian and Gay Communities

> I think bisexual women can bring up our worst fears and insecurities, and that relates directly to the powerlessness we often feel as women and as lesbians, individually and as a community. Several years ago I was in a relationship with a bisexual woman. I was not very accepting of her sexual identity; in fact, I was enormously threatened by it. If we stayed together for a long time, why wouldn't she consider herself a lesbian? Did that mean that I was somehow lacking? What if he had tons (or just an average amount) of money? She could bring him home to her parents, she could be secure in many ways she could never be with me . . . and so on. I don't think my response was very different from what many of us feel when we imagine relating to bisexual women in the lesbian community. . . . The fact is, a woman's power in this culture has historically been defined vis-à-vis her relationship to a man. That is only beginning to change, but in the meantime, lesbians (sans men) are way on the outside, economically and culturally. . . . Because of our separation from men, we simply don't have the same access to power and privilege that everyone else has. (Corsaro, 1991a)

In the previous section I uncovered the logic behind gay men's and lesbians' different reactions to bisexuality. Here, I delve more deeply into the fears lesbians express about bisexuality, particularly issues of powerlessness, as raised by Kim Corsaro in this passage.

One of the biggest fears that lesbians have about being involved with bisexual women is that bisexual women will leave them for men. Implicit seems to be the assumption that given a "choice," bisexual women would always prefer a man. Why do lesbians think that bisexual women will always pick a man? They think so largely because lesbians have experienced life without the privileges and protections afforded to women through connections with men, and see that for many women, aligning themselves with men is not simply a mobility strategy but a survival strategy. It is difficult for lesbians to believe that given the possibility of forging such alliances with men, women would choose not to do so. In our society, it is not just sex that is defined as belonging to men, but economic, social, cultural, and political power as well. Lesbians may resent being put in a position of having to compete with men for the affection of women, viewing the competition as dreadfully unbalanced in a society where men monopolize many of the resources to which women need access in order to survive. In addition, thinking of what men have to offer their lovers tends to raise the fears that lesbians have about their cultural, political, and economic marginalization. These fears involve anxiety about the very survival of the community; and feelings that everyone else, including gay men and bisexuals, as well as straights, has access to benefits gleaned from connections with men. This feeling is supported by the comparisons lesbians make between their impoverished communities and the much more affluent and culturally powerful gay communities.

Sometimes lesbians fail to realize that while bisexual women raise these fears in lesbians, they are not the source of these fears. Bisexual women certainly are not the cause of the marginalization of lesbians, and do not inevitably end up with men. Bisexual women are not the only group of women who can "betray" lesbians by taking advantage of heterosexual privilege. For women, "heterosexual privilege" is the reward given for conforming to compulsory heterosexuality. All women, lesbian, bisexual, and straight, make choices between getting access to power vicariously through their alliances with men, and challenging male power through aligning with women. No woman will, or should be expected to, make perfect choices all the time. It is true, however, that lesbians are often more likely to be aware of the privileges that straight women unwittingly get through their connections with men, to reject those privileges, and to suffer the consequences. Lesbians, however, do not have a monopoly on the punishments meted out to those who resist compulsory heterosexuality. Heterosexual privileges are often withheld from straight and bisexual women, too, when they refuse to have sex with men on men's terms, when they refuse to make themselves "attractive," or when they refuse to marry.

Clearly, women's dependence on men for social and economic status has a significant impact on lesbian attitudes toward bisexuality. Because straight men have not depended (as heavily) on connections to women for their social and economic status, gay men do not suffer a loss of the same magnitude when they break off connections with women. While for women the goodies stemming from heterosexual privilege are heavily material, for men the rewards of heterosexual privilege fall in the realm of prestige, coming more from proof of his heterosexual virility than from the economic and social benefits of a connection with a particular woman. Even in marriage, the particular characteristics of the woman to whom a man is attached are not as important in defining his lifestyle as a man's characteristics are in defining a woman's lifestyle. Single men, including gay men, are often more financially secure than married men because they do not transfer income to women. Gay men do not have to worry about being able to provide for their lovers; two male incomes combined often provide for an affluent lifestyle. Correspondingly, in the gay world, little attention is paid to men's connections with women. The fears that lesbians have about being left for a member of the opposite gender are just not as relevant for gay men.

While lesbians' concerns about bisexuality are fed by women's feelings of societal powerlessness and insecurity, gay men's lack of concern about bisexuality may be fed by feelings of indifference and disdain for women. In the quotations at the beginning of this paper, Michael Brewer reports that gay men consider having sex with a woman to be a "major faux pas"; that is, something likely to be seen as "in bad taste." When he reveals that gay men sometimes refer to women as "fish," he shows that gay men's relative lack of concern with bisexuality can be a consequence of sexism. Gay men may not believe that women are valuable enough to threaten their relationships with men.

FEMINISM, SEXUALITY, AND BISEXUALITY

Understanding now that the reactions of lesbians and gay men to bisexuality are tied to the workings of male dominance in this society, here I argue that the feminist goal of severing the connection between male dominance and sexuality is better served by refusing to categorically exclude bisexuals from lesbian and feminist communities. While the lesbian response to bisexuality is generated through a reaction to oppression, this response is not necessarily the best way to undermine the sources of the oppression. A more subtle politic may generate a more fundamental challenge.

Most feminists would agree that the goals of feminist sexual politics are to both prevent men's control of women's sexuality, and to develop women's sexual agency. Using the terms popularized by the anthology *Pleasure and Danger: Exploring Female Sexuality* (Vance, 1984), in this section I will refer to men's appropriation of women's sexuality as the problem of danger, and the development of women's sexual agency as the problem of pleasure. Feminists differ in how they prioritize these two goals and in the strategies proposed for achieving these goals. These differences have tremendous consequences for the political assessment of bisexuality.

Some feminists, generally identified as radical feminists, following the reasoning of Catharine MacKinnon, place heavy emphasis on freeing women from sexual danger, viewing the complete and total sexual safety of all women as a necessary condition for women's sexual pleasure. Sexual pleasure is problematic until after the demise of patriarchy. In this view, lesbianism, bisexuality, and heterosexuality are (nearly) equally flawed options. MacKinnon (1982, p. 19) refuses to privilege lesbianism as a potential escape from the system: "If being *for* another is the whole of women's sexual construction, it can be no more escaped by separatism, men's temporary concrete absence, than eliminated or qualified by permissiveness." MacKinnon's view tends to be too pessimistic to feed liberatory politics on the day-to-day level. Understandably, her view has not been the primary one appropriated by lesbian feminist communities to make sense of their situation.

Adrienne Rich (1980) is much more optimistic about the possibilities of women's resistance to compulsory heterosexuality. Rich, and the lesbian feminism consistent with her perspective, sees lesbianism as the answer to both the problem of sexual danger and the problem of sexual pleasure. By separating from men, women remove themselves from the reach of sexual danger. Relationships with other women provide sexual pleasure. Like MacKinnon, Rich dismisses the possibility of a non-compulsory heterosexuality before the overthrow of patriarchy. In Rich's view, directing energy toward women and away from men is viewed as an assault on patriarchy. Lesbianism becomes a feminist political act. Heterosexuality becomes at best an inferior option, and at worst evidence of lack of commitment to feminism. Bisexuality is viewed as suspicious fence-sitting, demonstrating an unwillingness to relinquish heterosexual privilege to fully join the feminist struggle. Lesbian feminism both justifies pre-existing biphobia, and generates biphobia by providing a lens through which to understand experience.

Predictably, bisexuals and those supporting bisexuality have had problems with Rich's view. However, some of the harshest criticisms of Rich have come from lesbians, arguing that she sidesteps the whole issue of women's sexual desire, defining lesbianism and women's sexuality primarily in terms of politics. Cherríe Moraga argues that "Through this perspective, lesbianism has become an 'idea'—a political response to male sexual aggression, rather than a sexual response to a woman's desire for another woman" (1983, p. 129). She and Amber Hollibaugh feel that viewing lesbianism as a feminist political act allowed feminists to avoid discussing sexual desire. Hollibaugh and Moraga (1983, p. 401) feel uncomfortable in lesbian spaces that are simply places for women to get a reprieve from men and sexuality, and not places for women to be sexual with each other. They view lesbian feminist avoidance of desire as an acceptance of the dominant characterization of women's sexual nature as passive.

Out of their critiques of white lesbian feminism, Hollibaugh and Moraga developed the core of another feminist theory of sexuality, a theory that places more emphasis on women's sexual pleasure without ignoring the importance of freeing women from compulsory heterosexuality and sexual violence. In this perspective, women's sexual pleasure cannot wait. Rather, women's sexual agency is seen as tied up with women's agency in general. Our ability to fight against sexual violence is fed by our emerging clarity about who we are and what we want, sexually and in other ways. Developing sexual agency might be more unlikely in heterosexual relationships, but it is not impossible. Unlike Rich, Hollibaugh and Moraga feel that it is important and possible to distinguish between sexual practices and sexual systems. They can identify "heterosexuality outside of heterosexism" (p. 395), and attempt to understand heterosexuality at both of these levels. Sexual acts are better seen as influenced by and influencing politics, but not as political acts in and of themselves. This goes for lesbian sexuality as well. Lesbianism is not a political act, nor is it necessarily purely liberatory. Hollibaugh and Moraga reject the belief in lesbian purity. They feel lesbian feminists are mistaken when they assume that physically and socially separating from men would enable lesbians to rid themselves of heterosexual notions of sexuality. This view leads lesbians to believe that they "could magically leap over heterosexist conditioning into mutually orgasmic, struggle-free, trouble-free sex" (Hollibaugh and Moraga, p. 395). When it does not work that way in the real lives and relationships of lesbians, the lesbian purity view can leave lesbians feeling guilty and inadequate. Cherríe Moraga makes the point that, like it or not, we cannot start developing greater sexual agency from some imaginary vision of what a perfect sexuality would be like, but rather we must start from what we know about sexuality and desire, regardless of its contaminated or imperfect origins:

> But we can't ask a woman to forget everything she understands about sex in a heterosexual and culturally-specific context or tell her what she is allowed to think about it. Should she forget and not use what she knows sexually to untie the knot of her own desire, she may lose any chance of ever discovering her own sexual potential. (Moraga, 1983, p. 130)

When lesbianism stops being privileged as *the* answer, both politically and personally, and is seen more realistically as one, often very good, way of both increasing women's sexual agency and challenging male dominance in sexuality, then bisexuality suddenly seems less threatening to the feminist project. If lesbianism is not pure to start with, bringing in bisexuality is not going to contaminate it. Hollibaugh and Moraga's view is neither as totalizing and pessimistic as MacKinnon's, nor as naïve and utopian as Rich's. It is better suited to the political realities of a long-term struggle. Hollibaugh and Moraga's theory addresses the pleasure and danger aspects of sexuality better than the other approaches, while simultaneously providing a theory that supports the inclusion of bisexuality in lesbian communities.

Hollibaugh and Moraga's perspective has concrete implications for feminist sexual politics. First and foremost, it means acknowledging and respecting women's sexual pleasures and desires. No desire should be policed simply because it makes others feel uncomfortable. Terms such as "politically incorrect," "false consciousness," and "internalized oppression" should not be used when talking about desire. Women's self-identifications must be respected. No one can claim to know what another women "really" is. For bisexual women or lesbians who are involved with men, it is important to take seriously their personal assessment of the importance of their connections with men. Even in lesbian communities, women have still been defined on the basis of their relationships with men, in this case, whether they have them or not, regardless of their personal self-identifications.

Taking women's sexual desires seriously does not mean ceasing to make judgments. Rather, the basis of these judgments should be situational and not categorical. For example, instead of using "bisexuality" in straight male pornography to assess bisexuality in general, one could inquire more seriously into the conditions under which men are able to reappropriate and exoticize women's bisexuality and the conditions under which women are able to put forth their own active and desiring bisexuality.

The importance of the lesbian community for the development of women's sexual agency cannot be overestimated. The more viable lesbianism is as a sexual option for all women, the more likely that heterosexuality can be authentically seen and experienced as a choice, instead of as "compulsory." The ability to disengage socially and sexually from men allows women both a space somewhat safer from male violence, and a place to develop active, initiatory desire. This can be hard to do in a heterosexual context, as men are continually placing women in the role of the object of someone else's desire.

In spite of my efforts, many lesbians will not be convinced on theoretical grounds to include bisexuals in their communities. It is of course critical to take lesbian concerns seriously. I hope I have done so. There will need to be many more discussions between lesbian and bisexual women about these issues. This is simply another contribution to the discussion.

NOTES

1. The quotes are, in order: (1) Ann Schneider, "Guilt politics,"(Hutchins and Ka'ahumanu, p. 276); (2) Elizabeth Reba Weise, "Bisexuality, The Rocky Horror Picture Show, and me," *(Ibid.,* p. 137); (3) Jan Clausen, "My Interesting Condition," (Clausen, 1990, p. 13); (4) Michael Brewer, "Two-Way Closet," (Hutchins and Ka'ahumanu, 1991, p. 140); and (5) excerpt from a letter by the Revolting Lesbians of San Francisco in a forum on "bisexuality in the gay/lesbian community" in *The San Francisco Bay Times,* vol. 12, no. 8, May 1991, p. 6.

2. This phrase is taken from an unpublished handout on the "myths and realities of bisexuality" distributed on the U.C. Berkeley campus in the spring of 1991, which was "excerpted and altered from Sharon Sumpter's and Amanda Udis-Kessler's pieces on the myths and realities of bisexuality."

3. When I discuss men and women in this section, I am outlining an ideal type, an extreme case. I do not think all men or all women are like this, merely that these patterns have at least some impact on all of us.

4. There are also gender-neutral forms of homophobia directed against gay men and lesbians.

5. White gay man interviewed in San Francisco in the early 1980s, quotation excerpted from Murray, 1992, p. 117.

Bisexuality,
Lesbian and Gay Communities,
and the Limits of Identity Politics

Stacey Young

Bisexuality as a topic of some debate and a fair amount of con-
jecture has periodically surfaced and gone underground again in the
gay and lesbian and feminist communities and press over the past
several decades. Recently, it has reemerged in a new way, raising a
number of questions dealing with sex, identity, politics, and community. The character of these debates about bisexuality was reflected in the controversy surrounding the 1990 Lesbian and Gay
Pride March in Northampton, Massachusetts, and in the pages of
Gay Community News, which covered the events leading up to the
march. *GCN* printed many letters from lesbians and bisexual
women who addressed that controversy in particular, as well as
more general questions about bisexuals and our relation to lesbian
and gay communities. A close look at the Northampton controversy
and *GCN*'s coverage reveals a good deal about some of the different
ways that identity and community are conceptualized within lesbian
and gay politics; some people call for flexible, inclusive definitions,
and others urge caution, warning against indistinct definitions they
think could weaken lesbian and gay struggles against homophobia.

These notions of identity and community can be adequately understood only when located within the larger historical and political
context surrounding these events and distinguishing them from ear-

Earlier versions of this paper were presented at the National Women's Studies
Association Twelfth Annual Conference at the University of Akron, June 20-24,
1990; and Pleasure/Politics: 4th Annual Lesbian, Bisexual and Gay Studies Conference at Harvard University, October 26-28, 1990.

219

lier exchanges about bisexuality. The *GCN* exchange differs from previous exchanges[1] in two ways. First, the issues raised in this debate reflected the influence of the women's movement's emphasis over the last decade on difference, diversity, the instability of social categories, and the politics of exclusion. The debate about bisexuality owes a significant debt to these earlier discussions, initiated by feminists whose concerns with race, class, ethnicity, and sexuality (as well as gender) first challenged attempts to homogenize our communities rather than work within their very real heterogeneity.

The second factor that distinguishes the *GCN* exchange is that bisexual women's voices outnumbered those of non-bisexual participants. Also, this discussion was initiated by a bisexual woman, differentiating it from those in *Lesbian Connection* and *off our backs,* both of which were begun by lesbians who wrote in opposition to (former) lesbians sleeping with men. Moreover, the discussion in *GCN* surfaced as bisexuals were becoming more visible in the lesbian and gay movement and press. There are many more bisexual organizations now than there were five or ten years ago; many "lesbian and gay" entities are adding "bisexual" to their titles; more people seem to be coming out as bisexual in queer communities; and more people of all sexual orientations are referring to these communities as "lesbian, gay, and bisexual." Bisexuals, lesbians, and gay men are joining together to confront the AIDS crisis, and more is being published on bisexuality (see, for example, Christina, 1990; Geller, 1990; Hutchins and Ka'ahumanu, 1991; Weise, 1992). In the convergence of all of these factors, the climate for bisexual women is changing, as reflected in the *GCN* exchange.

This exchange was initiated in the February 18, 1990 issue of *GCN* with a letter from Micki Siegel of West Hatfield, Massachusetts. The Northampton Lesbian and Gay Pride March (formerly the Lesbian and Gay Liberation March[2]) had in 1989 included the word "Bisexual" in its title. In her letter, Siegel wrote that, for the first time in five years, she would not be working on the steering committee for the march because of organized—and successful—efforts by some lesbians in Northampton to remove "Bisexual" from the title of the march and bisexuals (including Siegel) from its steering committee.[3] Siegel reported that the lesbians who sought to remove

"Bisexual" from the march title and bisexuals from the steering committee claimed that the inclusion of "Bisexual" in the title of the event made lesbians invisible. Among the lesbians making this argument were Sarah Dreher and Lis Brook of Amherst, Massachusetts, who stated the reasons for their opposition to the more inclusive title in a letter published in the March 11, 1990 issue of *GCN*. They wrote:

> Last year, in addition to the inclusion of "Bisexual" in the march title (thereby diverting a political issue into a sexual one), there was no lesbian representation among the speakers at the rally. Nor were any lesbian (or women's) issues addressed. (Dreher and Brook, 1990, p. 4)

They went on to argue that bisexual issues are distinct from lesbian and gay concerns because bisexuals enjoy heterosexual privilege. Responding to Micki Siegel's letter (and referring to her throughout their own letter as "Mrs. Siegel"), Dreher and Brook concluded:

> For reasons we cannot comprehend, some bisexual women seem to feel they cannot create their own community, but must attach themselves to the lesbian community. For many of us, our lesbianism is a way of life, not just something we do in bed. If Mrs. Siegel and her ilk are so concerned with having their sexual minority status respected, why don't they march in the Lesbian/Gay Pride March as supporters, under their own banner? (Dreher and Brook, 1990, p. 4)

This exchange was followed in subsequent issues of *GCN* by five more letters, as well as two columns published in the "Speaking Out" and "Community Voices" sections of the paper, the last of which appeared in the May 27, 1990 issue. All of the letters and both columns were written by women, either bisexual or lesbian. Interestingly, none of these writers supported the position taken by Dreher and Brook: all of them argued for a connection between lesbians and bisexual women, though for different reasons. Although none of the letters that followed commented on Dreher's and Brook's assumption that the reason no lesbian or women's issues were addressed at the previous year's march was that "bisexual" was included in the title, several did address the irony in their insinuation that bisexuality is not a way of life but just something to do in bed. Several women who wrote in addressed that insinuation, along with Dreher's and Brook's assertion that the inclusion of "bisexual" in the march's title diverted a political issue (lesbianism and male homosexuality) into a sexual one (bisexuality). They pointed out that these were nothing more than recycled homophobic (not to mention anti-sex) slurs that lesbians themselves have fought and continue to fight when these slurs are directed at lesbians.

One of the main arguments made in this debate was that those who work to exclude bisexual women from lesbian communities engage in the same kind of oppressive exclusion they fight elsewhere. In her letter published in the May 6, 1990 issue, Kathy Morgan observed, "The last time I heard this debate the vote was to add 'lesbians' to the name of a gay organization." Here the discussion drew on previous challenges made by butch-femme and S/M lesbians who continue to struggle against the efforts of some lesbians to exclude them from lesbian community. As Bet Power, a lesbian from Northampton, Massachusetts, wrote in an April 8, 1990 *GCN* article to protest the exclusion of bisexuals:

> While we're moving toward self-definition, pride and "respectability," let's take all of us along! . . . Lesbians, Gay men, Bisexuals, S/Mers, TVs [transvestites] and TSs [transsexuals] have an enormously difficult life experience in common: persecution because who we love and sleep with or how we sleep with who we love (or ourselves) is different than conservative heterosexuality.

The arguments made in these letters raise questions of how and why we define queer communities. First, does it make sense to try to draw rigid boundaries around these communities? What is the nature of our desire to create community on the basis of identity? Do we continue to assume that shared identity reflects shared experience, or shared politics? Second, who draws those boundaries and on what basis? Are the categories "gay," "lesbian," and "bisexual" sufficiently definable and distinct to use them as a basis for conferring or withholding membership in our communities? Third, do we even want to and have the power to be gatekeepers?

I'll begin with the question of identity and the categories "lesbian" and "bisexual." How would we decide who belongs in which category? Some see a very clear line between bisexual women and lesbians, as well as a self-evident need to restrict community and movement to lesbians only—and to only certain lesbians at that. One proponent of such a view is Linda Strega from Oakland, California, who wrote the following in a letter to *Lesbian Connection* (1986):

> How many Lesbians are now unknowingly friends or lovers with a bisexual who is telling some man or men about her, about their sexual intimacies, divulging Lesbian personal and political information, maybe passing on VD or AIDS (which originate with men), and who cannot have respect for Lesbian lives or she wouldn't be fucking and lying to Lesbians? . . . How can Lesbians allow a woman who fucks with men to call herself a Lesbian? . . . *Lesbians* do not choose to get pregnant, any more than Lesbians fuck with men. When women who do these things call themselves Lesbians, they are trying to redefine Lesbianism in patriarchal terms. If patriarchy can't kill us, get us to kill ourselves, lock us up, persuade us to hide in our closets or get us to become het or bisexual, then they will try to define us out of existence. If *anyone* can call themselves a Lesbian, then what about those of us who are still Queer Dykes who love each other and love ourselves and don't want sperm anywhere near us? [emphasis in original] (p. 16)

Others see the categories as being much less clear. As Greta Christina puts it:

> Is a lesbian: a woman who only fucks other women? That would include bi women who're monogamously involved with other women? A woman who doesn't fuck men? That would include celibate straight women. A woman who would never get seriously involved with men? Rules out lesbians who've been married in the past. A woman who never has sexual thoughts about men? That excludes dykes who are into heavy and complex gender play, who get off on gay men's porn, or who are maybe just curious. Do you have to be 100% directed

at women and away from men in thought, feeling, word, and deed from birth to death to qualify as a "real" lesbian? That would rule out all but about two women on the planet. I hope they can find each other. (Christina, 1990, pp. 14-15)

Christina's questions are important. On some level, one is tempted to conclude that we should drop altogether the task of defining who belongs to queer communities, given the ambiguity of our categories (an ambiguity that becomes even more apparent where those of us who used to be lesbians and are now bisexual are concerned), and given the difficulty, and for many of us the distastefulness, of enforcing exclusive definitions of community. And yet, the idea and the reality of community are important to us as lesbians, bisexuals, gay men, S/Mers, transsexuals, crossdressers, transgenderists, and so on, for a number of very good reasons, including our political work and our survival in a phobic and violent culture.

When I think about queer politics, I sometimes think that my (queer, political) community includes anyone who has ever felt desire for someone of the same sex and has been motivated to act politically on the basis of that desire. But queer communities' ongoing debates over outing queer politicians who support homophobic policies remind me that sexual identity, desire, or practice is no guarantee of clear analysis or progressive politics. So when I think of these queer people who I don't count as part of my community, and when I think of a few heterosexual allies who are outspoken in the struggle against heterosexism, homophobia, and other forms of sexual fascism, I wonder if the answer is to dispense entirely with a definition of community that rests on the sexual identity of its members. This makes the notion of community rather ambiguous, which may be a good thing.

However, when I think not about my queer *political* but about my queer *social* communities—the ones I engage with when I go to the bar or to a Gay Pride march, or the ones I feel in touch with when I read *GCN* or *On Our Backs*—identity becomes important. This is because of the importance of shared experience (in the sense that we have all felt desire for our own sex, and we are all subject to homophobic repression because of that desire). And at those moments my community includes anyone who identifies as queer. But, as important as identity seems when I think of my social communities as a queer person, identity is no more definitive than it is when I try to define my political communities. My social communities also include, in some abstract way, a host of queers who don't even have the words to identify consciously as queer because, perhaps, they think they're the only one; or because they're 15 and live in a small town, with their parents, their church, and their neighbors looking over their shoulder; or because they're married and have kids and can't yet let their desires surface to consciousness; and so on. At this level community again becomes quite amorphous, not based on shared assumptions, shared identity, or even shared experience (beyond the most basic experience of desire for someone of the same sex, whether or not that desire is even recognized). This broad notion of community is not exactly common ground on which to build a movement, or even a friendship. It appears that to explore the meaning of "community" is not to demarcate clear boundaries, but rather is to become entangled in the complexities of what is indeed a very fuzzy construct. For all its ambiguity, though, this construct is crucially important to many queers. It is also a construct that can be repressive or liberatory, depending upon how it is defined and mobilized.

Perhaps we should focus less on who is in our communities, since this question inevitably leads either to exclusion on the basis of the same oppressive principles we struggle against in other arenas, or to a demarcation so broad and abstract as to be meaningless. Perhaps we should focus more on what we want our communities to be and do, and how we can strengthen them along those lines.

Which brings me back to the controversy over Northampton's Pride March. Among other things, queer communities should be places where we air our differences openly, and where we struggle with each other both to explore the implications of those differences and to build and sustain mutual respect for each other. On this count, the controversy over the Northampton Pride March brought us a long way. The thoughtful and sustained public discussion of bisexuality and the role of bisexuals in queer communities/movements was unprecedented, coming as it did before the publication of any of the bisexual anthologies, and appearing as it did in a lesbian and gay newspaper with a wide readership. My hope is that public discussions of bisexual identity and politics will continue and will broaden to include a wider array of people and positions.

So I think the controversy was useful in sparking open discussion. However—and this is my main regret—the exclusion of bisexuals from the title and the steering committee of the march illustrated and enacted the weakening of queer people's strength that occurs when biphobia takes over. What role did the controversy play in the fact that, by some accounts, attendance at the 1989 march was 3,000 (Siegel, 1990), whereas attendance at the 1990 march was closer to 2,000 (Muther, 1990)?[4]

And what effect did the controversy have on bisexuals and our allies? While some bisexuals did participate openly in the march, some of them carrying a fence and signs that read, "The Bisexual Fence—which side are you on?" (Muther, 1990), how many more stayed home? Or attended, but stayed in the closet as bisexuals? For me, when I entered a new closet as a former lesbian struggling to create an identity out of the social narratives I had available to help me make sense of my experience, being in the closet as bisexual among lesbians and gay men was much more painful than being either a closeted or an out lesbian among straight people. It is a less dangerous closet in many ways, but no less painful—the pain due in large part, I think, to being alienated from a culture and a political movement I defined as necessary to my survival and well-being. How many bisexuals inhabited that painful closet that day? I think about the effect of this controversy on bisexual folks, and I'm saddened by it.

I also think about the effect on our lesbian and gay allies. A lesbian friend of mine did not go to the 1990 Pride march because, she told me, referring to the exclusion of bisexuals, she wasn't proud. Other lesbians expressed similar sentiments. In her article, Bet Power reported that a larger community meeting (the theme of which was "Where Do We Go From Here?") was held in mid-March of 1990 in Northampton, and was attended by more than 300 people:

> Many Lesbians at the meeting spoke of their own sense of discomfort, helplessness and exclusion from the march this year and in past years for a variety of reasons: . . . they are

lovers or friends of Bisexuals; . . . they are themselves Lesbians coming out as Bisexuals; . . . they are Lesbians who are also Sadomasochists; . . . they are Lesbians who also cross-dress . . . they are Lesbians who are coming out as having transgender/ transsexual feelings . . . they are friends of male-to-female transvestites; . . . they are partners/lovers of female-to-males; . . . they are friends of Gay men and straight allies who find this year's Steering Committee and march a hostile, oppressive environment to anyone without Lesbian Separatist convictions. (Power, 1990)

One begins to get a sense of the large numbers and broad range of people who become alienated from queer communities and politics by the exclusion of bisexuals as well as by other exclusions that take place when we engage in gatekeeping. And one begins to see how strong we could be, individually and as a diverse but united political force, if we followed Bet Power's suggestion to "take everyone along with us" on the "road to liberation" (Power, 1990). As Kathy Morgan (1990, p. 5) writes, "By telling bisexuals to go home, we shrink the size of our gay community." The same holds true when we tell the S/Mers, or transvestites, or transsexuals to go home.

Those lesbians and gay men who have not been bisexuals' allies must stop telling us to go home. We are home, and we're here to stay, so let's figure out how we can all benefit from each other's presence so as to expand our communities, foster their diversity, and strengthen our many struggles against all forms of sexual repression. Those lesbians and gay men who have been bisexuals' allies, lovers, and friends deserve our thanks and support. They share with us the knowledge that we all benefit from recognizing how we need and can support each other.

Bisexuals, for our part, must understand that lesbians and gay men, even those who would like us to "go home," are not our enemies. As we work to articulate our experiences, to establish bisexuality as an autonomous and legitimate identity, and to develop a bisexual politic, part of our work is to challenge biphobia in the lesbian, gay, and bisexual communities.

However, we must also continue to confront homophobia and heterosexism in the world at large. And we must do this *openly as bisexuals,* for several reasons. First, we need to work to get bisexuals included in the antidiscrimination clauses and protective ordinances that queer movements are securing for lesbians and gay men. Second, we need to politicize bisexual identity. Most lesbians and gay men who maintain that bisexuals have been absent in struggles against homophobia have actually been struggling alongside bisexuals all the while—but we can't expect them to know that unless we're out, and fighting homophobia, as bisexuals. Finally, we need to let heterosexuals know that a depoliticized, slightly titillating but ultimately nonthreatening conception of bisexuality may have been in vogue in the 1960s and 1970s, but is decidedly out of date in the 1990s—the age of AIDS, bisexual scapegoating, and rising violence against lesbians, bisexuals, and gay men. To this end, we must refrain from making offensive and erroneous claims that bisexuality is universal, or superior to any and all other sexual identities. We must instead embrace sexual diversity while combatting sexual fascism in all its manifestations—including homophobia and heterosexism. And as we do this, we must remember that lesbian and gay liberation is bisexual liberation, in terms of both the institutions that oppress us and the communities and movements that sustain us.

NOTES

1. Examples include the 1986 exchange in *Lesbian Connection* about "ex-lesbians" and their place (or lack thereof) in lesbian community; and Patricia Roth Schwartz's 1989 *off our backs* article about "hasbians"—her term for lesbians who become involved with men. (See Young, 1992 for further discussion.)

2. Thanks to Kim Christensen, one of the march's founders, for information regarding the origins and history of the event.

3. The circumstances surrounding the reversion of the march's title to "Lesbian and Gay Pride March" and the removal of bisexuals from the steering committee involved several votes taken at successive meetings of the march steering committee. The deciding vote was cast at a meeting attended by, among others, 40 lesbians who opposed the inclusion of "Bisexual" in the march title, and who attended the meeting for the purpose of seeing it removed. (See Young, 1992.)

4. Muther's article quotes Sue Krause, a member of the Lesbian and Gay Pride March steering committee, as saying that attendance in 1990 fairly closely matched that in 1989.

Power and Privilege
Beyond the Invisible Fence

Brenda Blasingame

There is no denying that if you choose to be an out, openly self-identified bisexual in the (heterosexual) world, you will be targeted by homophobia and/or heterosexism. On the other hand, if you are not out as a bisexual, you can reap the benefits of heterosexual privilege. There is much ado about bisexuals jumping back and forth over an invisible fence we've supposedly chosen to sit on. So how, then, does the bisexual community go about building alliances with heterosexuals and with the lesbian/gay[1] community?

Alliance-building in bisexual communities is an unusual task. In most communities, building alliances is about reaching across the barriers to those directly across from us on the power scale: i.e., women building alliances with men. Bisexuals are building alliances not only with heterosexuals, but also with our lesbian/gay brothers and sisters, *and* within our own bisexual community.[2] Bisexual alliance-building is therefore a multidimensional task with three basic components, each indispensable to our community's survival.

The first step is to move toward building alliances within our bisexual communities. Many communities are united by a commonality of the oppression. This is not so in our community, partly because of the different ways people identify as a bisexual: gay-identified, queer-identified, lesbian-identified, or heterosexual-identified. Some people are bisexual in an affectional manner only; some are bisexual both affectionally and sexually; and some are bisexual only sexually. Since there are so many ways to express our bisexuality, the first step toward alliance-building is to work internally to accept all members of our own community. It is imperative that we build alliances across our own differences; otherwise, alliance-building outside will fail. Acceptance of the diversity of bisexual labels within our community will allow us to pursue alliance-building with decisive strength in the heterosexual community and what many of us consider our own lesbian/gay community.[3]

The second component in this process is building alliances between bisexuals and the gay/lesbian community. For the gay-identified bisexual this may be the hardest and most risky place to build alliances. Let's face the facts: there is not yet a red carpet rolled out with a flashing welcome sign to accept bisexuals into the gay/lesbian community. Bisexuals who are out in the gay/lesbian community, as I am, confront the ugly façade of the community's internalized oppression expressed as biphobia. This form of internalized oppression is horizontal hostility, because it is occurring within a group of like people.

Horizontal hostility generally works like this: when an individual or community is subjected to daily hostility and negative images of themselves (e.g., a lesbian or gay person experiencing homophobia), it is nearly impossible to shield one's inner self from emotional penetration of the negative messages. We therefore come to devalue ourselves and believe the stereotypes about ourselves. Many of us do not have places to heal ourselves from this hurt. As the hurt grows, we may find ourselves lashing out at those closest to us in our community. Often, we channel our anger, hurt, and pain into judgments of each other, much in the way those who have oppressed us have done. Without interruption that cycle will repeat itself indefinitely, possibly causing a community to split internally. The divisiveness caused by horizontal hostility benefits those who oppress us, because it prevents us from building alliances needed to fight the oppression.

It is important to note here that bisexuals can only experience biphobia from the lesbian/gay community. Oppression from the heterosexual community is called heterosexism. Within the lesbian/gay community bisexuals may experience exclusion or prejudice, but this is different from the systematic mistreatment of lesbians and gays throughout our country. The common oppression of heterosexism affects both gay and lesbian individuals, and bisexuals who choose to be out as such or are in a same-sex relationship. When we all come to the table to build alliances, we must acknowledge where there are differences between someone who identifies as bisexual and someone who identifies as gay or lesbian.

I do not believe that I or anyone else chooses our sexual orientation—we either accept or deny the reality. However, we bisexuals do have an implied choice in the gender of our relationship partners. Owning this choice does not make us any less queer. To own this choice is fundamental to our building alliances with our lesbian and gay family members. Lesbians and gays may perceive a bisexual's refusal to acknowledge potential privilege as another arm of heterosexism, and therefore a major barrier to our working together. We are all responsible for the privilege that heterosexism gives to opposite-sex couples and takes away from same-sex couples. Whether bisexuals claim the privilege does not change the fact that it is present and given.

In building alliances in the gay/lesbian community we must keep power, privilege, access, and choice in mind while holding on to our right to be included in that community. Our strength lies in our ability to recognize our common oppression and our differences, without allowing these differences to divide us.

Finally, the way in which heterosexual-identified bisexuals use their power and privilege illustrates the third element of our alliance-building. The choice to identify heterosexually affords privileges that people should not take lightly or misuse. To be an ally to gays and lesbians, heterosexual-identified bisexuals should use these privileges as a vehicle to speak out against homophobia and heterosexism. The outside world perceives and treats opposite-sex couples as heterosexual. External perceptions change only if people openly admit to being bisexual and speak out as such.

In the same way that we must acknowledge the differences between bisexuals and lesbian/gay people, we must also accept the different levels of privilege afforded to heterosexual-identified bisexuals versus lesbian/gay and queer-identified bisexuals. The heterosexual-identified bisexual may be choosing to be in an opposite-sex relationship while being open about their bisexual identity, or they may choose to hide their bisexuality, which would lead to an assumption of heterosexuality.

As a queer-identified bisexual choosing same-sex partners, I feel and recognize an alliance with heterosexual-identified bisexuals. I expect them to own their access to power and privilege as I own mine within the lesbian/gay community. A bisexual who leads a heterosexual-identified life will enjoy heterosexual privileges unless that individual continually chooses to openly identify as bisexual.

Privilege is not to be taken lightly, but rather to be positively transformed into a force against heterosexism. The heterosexual-identified bisexual who does not publicly self-identify has an implicit role as an ally to all gay and lesbian people as well as to those bisexuals who choose to live out of the closet. Being an ally carries with it the responsibility to speak out in the heterosexual community against homophobia and heterosexism. The heterosexual-identified bisexual who is not out has the safety to say and do things that the rest of us cannot. To not speak out or educate is to deny a part of oneself, and is a misuse of power and privilege.

Using privilege to educate and gain equity for all is an important step toward the eradication of heterosexism. We must be simultaneously working to end heterosexism/homophobia within the heterosexual community, biphobia in the lesbian/gay community, and our own self-judgments within the bisexual community. We must all become allies to each other and ourselves—embracing the difference and rejoicing in our sameness, using both as a source of strength for liberation.

I believe in the right to identify as we see fit. But this right carries with it the responsibility for how we use power and privilege as it relates to our self-identity. In building alliances as bisexuals the first step is moving toward a true understanding of our own community and diversity within. We must continue to examine how we have chosen to live and what we do with our choices. Bisexuals can be catalysts toward the acceptance of all types of relationships. Because we understand many sides, it is incumbent upon us to name our identity and acknowledge whatever privilege we receive from that identity. The bisexual movement is about creating a society that accepts the relationship of a man and a man, a woman and a woman, a woman and a man; about creating a society that accepts the choice not to be in a relationship with another person at all, or with more than one person. Any choice, every choice, should be respected, protected, and given equal access, power, and privilege. Each of us, no matter how we identify, must see our responsibility in the bigger picture of the movement to end heterosexism and biphobia. We must take conscious action.

NOTES

1. The terms lesbian/gay and gay/lesbian are used interchangeably in this essay to denote the equality of these two groups.

2. The term "heterosexual" in this piece refers to the larger community of heterosexuals or heterosexual-identified bisexuals. The word "straight" is not used because of its implied negative connotations.

3. As a part of the larger lesbian/gay/bisexual community, we still need to work continuously to accept the many types of diversity within the community itself, including diversity of ethnicity, religion, class, and gender. However, for the sake of this essay, the writer is specifically referring to the diversity of bisexual identities.

Which Part of Me Deserves to Be Free?

Dajenya

In October 1991, an article appeared in the Lesbian Gay Bisexual Alliance Newsletter *at San Francisco State University. The author, a self-described African-American dyke, expressed the viewpoint that no one has the right to equate the gay/lesbian/bisexual struggle for civil rights with that of the African Americans because the "gay/lesbian/bisexual agenda seems trivial" compared to the history of torture, lynchings, etc., perpetrated against African Americans. She also cited racism within the gay/lesbian/bisexual communities as another reason that her "agenda as an African American takes precedence almost always."*

Being an African-American/Jewish bisexual/lesbian myself, and having heard (too) many versions of the "my struggle is more important than yours" argument, I hastened to reply. Unfortunately, the newsletter folded before my reply could be printed. The following is an excerpt from my reply.

I agree that the oppression of Africans and African Americans by Europeans and European Americans has been murderously horrific, from slavery, colonialism, and lynchings, to genocide through poverty and medical neglect. And surely racist oppression has been perpetuated by some members of sexual minority groups.

But I am equally aware of the murderously horrific oppression that has been perpetrated against lesbians, gay men, and bisexual people. As queers, we have also been lynched, burned at the stake, gassed in ovens, and beaten to death, in addition to other forms of discrimination and oppression. And, sadly, homophobic oppression has been committed by African-American people as well as by whites.

Personally, I am unable to separate out the various ways that I am oppressed (as a woman, as an African American, as a bisexual lesbian, as an impoverished single mother) and say that one oppression is worse than the other, or that I desire one form of liberation more than another. I do not want to experience threats to my life, my child custody, or my job security because of racism *or* homophobia. I don't want to be oppressed for *any* reason!!!

Given the sad fact that there is racism, sexism, homophobia, and biphobia in the African-American community *and* in the lesbian/gay/bisexual communities (as elsewhere), I try to confront and struggle against these manifestations of oppression wherever and whenever I encounter them. I am equally committed to the struggle against the horrors of military and biomedical warfare, and I am aware of the urgency of the struggle to preserve environmental conditions that allow life on earth to continue. *All* of these struggles are truly matters of life and death. Thus, my own personal choice is to support *all* liberation movements wholeheartedly, even while confronting oppression within each movement. Ultimately, I will never feel (or be) truly free until we live in a world where we are *all* free in *every* way to be who we are.

Bisexual Etiquette:
Helpful Hints for Bisexuals
Working with Lesbians and Gay Men

Robyn Ochs

I have recently celebrated my twelfth anniversary as a bisexual activist. Much of my activism has taken place in the Boston area lesbigay[1] community. In most of the lesbian and gay groups I have been involved with, I have been one of two or three out bisexuals. During my decade of activism I have learned a great deal, both from my own mistakes, and from other people's. I have said and done things which I have instantly and thoroughly regretted, and experienced moments of proud accomplishment. At times I have felt like a supplicant, a second-class citizen, a token, a nuisance; at other times an equal, a leader, a decorated veteran, a sister.

What follows are a few suggestions I would like to pass along to other bisexual people who are involved in lesbigay communities.

1. *Respect other people's identities.* Don't say that "everyone's really bisexual." Don't say that bisexual people are somehow more evolved. Think of how frustrated you feel when you hear someone tell you that there is no such thing as a bisexual, or that bisexuals are really lesbians or gay men in transition, or that we are really heterosexual tourists out for sexual adventure at the expense of lesbians and gay men.

2. *Don't raise your own self-image at the expense of other people.* Examples of bad ideas taken from real life: a t-shirt that says "Monosexuals bore me"; a button that says "Gay is good but bi is best." Please.

3. *Avoid the trap of weighing and measuring oppression.* Avoid thinking of oppression and liberation as a zero sum game. There is, unfortunately, plenty of oppression to go around. Fortunately, there

is also enough liberation to go around. Don't say that bisexuals are more oppressed than lesbians or gay men. We are ALL oppressed. Each of us experiences oppression differently. A married bisexual experiences homophobia differently from a bisexual in a same-gender relationship. Out people experience oppression differently from closeted people. Some people are members of more than one oppressed group, and as such have their own unique experience of oppression. And bisexual men have an experience that is different from bisexual women. It is OKAY to have a different experience of oppression. Oppression, however it manifests, still hurts, and we have a common interest in working together to end it.

4. *Respect separate space.* There is a time when coalition building is in order, and a time when we need to get together in our own identity groups to do our own empowerment work. All members of oppressed groups have the right to take space when they feel it necessary, and we need to respect that.

The difficulty, of course, lies in determining when separate space is appropriate and when it is not. My personal belief is that any event in which lesbians and gay men get together is already by definition a coalition event. And I believe that I, as a woman-centered bisexual feminist, have a lot more in common with most lesbians than do many gay men. However, when an event is explicitly a gay male- or lesbian-only event, we need to respect other people's space. (I want to make a distinction here between a lesbian event—an event that is by lesbians, or primarily for lesbians—and a lesbian-only event. I am speaking of the latter.) This is a bit more complicated than it may seem, but I have developed a personal guide for my own use, and I'll give a couple of examples of its application.

In Boston, there was a group called Dyke Dialogue, organized by Val Seabrook, a (wonderful) African-American lesbian. A few lesbians who regularly attended the group complained that the group should be open to lesbians only. In this instance, to determine whether my presence was appropriate, I asked Val, the group's founder and organizer. She told me that the group was for all women, and that bisexual and transgender women were welcome. In this situation, it was totally appropriate for bisexual women to participate. Any lesbians unhappy with the group's composition were free to remove themselves and start their own, exclusive group.

My second example concerns a bisexually-identified woman active in her local lesbigay community who was looking for support as a queer parent. The only group listed in her local newspaper was a lesbian mothers' group. She called the contact person for the group, asked whether bisexual women were welcome, and was told that they were not. Disappointed, but respecting the organizers' wishes, she resolved to start a second group for lesbian and bisexual moms.

In short, communicate. This indicates to others that you are respectful of their existing concerns and space, and that you want to join, not invade. Additionally, you may in the process acquire some allies. But one thing is certain: lesbians and gay men need to feel that there are places and times when their space will remain inviolate. There do need to be limits to inclusion, and inclusionary politics and separate space can exist simultaneously.

5. *Be a good citizen.* Don't insist on being included in a given group unless you are willing to put your energy into that group. While bisexual women and men have been active in the lesbian and gay community from the start, remember that few of us have been publicly identifiable as bisexual. Most of us have simply done the work, sent our money, attended the events, and not corrected people's assumptions about how we identify. I can think of dozens of rallies and pride marches I have attended, along with other bisexual activists, only to read in the gay or straight press that "hundreds of gay men and lesbians rallied to. . . ." This invisibility has allowed many lesbians and gay men to assume that there have been few, if any, bisexual people in the movement. (Sounds a lot like the perceptions of heterosexuals about lesbigay people, doesn't it?) Therefore, when we join a group as out bisexuals and begin asking for explicit recognition as bisexuals, many people have the impression that bisexuals have suddenly appeared out of nowhere and are trying to muscle and whine our way into their movement, riding on the coattails of their hard-fought battles. Remember this when you enter a new group. Be a good citizen. If you want to be recognized as part of the community, don't just show up and tell

them what to do. Join the group. Show your commitment as an out bisexual. Then express your concerns.

6. *Choose your battles.* This has been a hard one for me personally. Is it always important to have every sentence end with "and bisexual"? Is it important to point out this omission every time? Sometimes it may be more constructive, and less physically exhaustive, just to be your wonderful, out, bisexual self.

7. *Listen.* Rather than always being on the defensive, I have been trying hard to listen to the fears, concerns, and perspectives of my lesbian and gay male friends. I've been surprised at how much I learn when I stop defending myself long enough to listen well.

8. *Remember.* Underneath it all, we all want the same things. We want respect. We want understanding. We want to be heard, and to be acknowledged. We want to feel safe. Accord others the same respect that you are demanding for yourself.

NOTE

1. A convenient abbreviation for lesbian/gay/bisexual, lesbigay is a term I first heard from Warren Blumenfeld.

Essay for the Inclusion of Transsexuals

Kory Martin-Damon

I'm a female-to-male transsexual, Cuban-Venezuelan, first-generation American, child of alcoholics, bisexual. This combination of characteristics that comprise who I am also wove into my personality an element of isolation and an inability to fully communicate with others verbally. Early on I felt an intense desire to write because I felt I was at least competent in this medium. It was not until I recognized my transsexuality that I began to understand my self-imposed self-exclusion from various groups of people, whether they were purely political, sexual-political, social, or religious.

Since I didn't seem to belong anywhere, I didn't try. Not until after high school did I begin realizing the issue of gender was at the core of my anger and dissatisfaction with myself. Before this realization, I tried to be what everyone else believed I should be—a woman living the stereotype of a woman. The process of accepting my transsexuality demanded that I first break away from the stereotypes of femininity and masculinity that were part of my childhood cultural indoctrination.

Being honest about sexuality and gender issues was not easy for me. Nothing in my upbringing lent me insight into how to talk about these topics, let alone how to feel comfortable about them. The parameters of sexuality were outlined to me by the Catholic Church. I was taught that one performed the "sexual act" for the sole purpose of procreation, and of course, only in a heterosexual, monogamous relationship. As far as gender was concerned, woman was created from the rib of man.

What I learned about gender, I learned from my Cuban community, where extremes in gender dichotomies were the norm. Femininity and masculinity were specific and narrow. Women behaved one way; men behaved another. This usually meant that women

241

wore mostly dresses or skirts, used makeup, shaved their legs and armpits, and wanted a family before a career. Women who found the initiative to live outside the norm became targets of pity and ridicule. It would not have occurred to many people that women might willfully choose to live single or childless lives, since such would surely lead to unhappiness.

The roles of men were limited also, but the limitations were much more subtle. For example, men were expected to handle stress well, and to always be dependable, employed, and in control. A man's worth was measured by his ability to provide for his family. If a man were unable to work because, for instance, he was emotionally unbalanced, and he became dependent upon his family for his survival, he would be taken care of at all costs, but he would also be a source of silent shame. Men behaved rigidly toward one another too. There was physical affection between males of the same family, but primarily between younger and older males.

I learned about sexual orientation from the same source where I learned about gender: my community. Gays were a source of derision, their depiction extreme as only a community of extremes could portray. Gay men were regarded as effeminate, as psychologically crippled by internalized guilt about their homosexuality, and as having little value for the community. The Cuban community was less inclined to speak about lesbians, although stereotypes existed. Lesbians were abominations—a source of anxiety, disgust, anger. Although it was considered sick for men to be gay, men could live without women, but women needed men to be complete.

This was the cultural knowledge of gender available to me when I began dealing with the emotions and discomfort triggered by my transsexuality. At first I believed that my inability to feel comfortable as a female was due to gender role rigidity. There was also guilt rooted in religious beliefs that I still held as personal truths; guilt rooted in my reluctance to (even inadvertently) place blame on my parents; guilt rooted in my feminist ideals and the fear that I was betraying everything I believed.

During this time I did not see myself as transsexual. The only transsexuals I had ever heard about were genetically-born men who had altered their sex. It would be years before I learned that genetically-born females could be transsexuals too, and that there had always been female-to-male transsexuals woven into the history of many cultures of the world. Because of my ignorance regarding female-to-male transsexuals, and because of my strong attraction to women, I assumed I was a lesbian. I had not yet heard of bisexuality, although I knew of my attraction to men. I chose to pursue only women because my rebellion against patriarchy included all men (at the time), and because the lesbian community afforded me a niche in which I felt partly liberated from the gender rigidities of my upbringing.

However, when I identified as a lesbian, I felt I was somehow deceiving myself and others. The persona I became when I left the privacy and safety of my home was incongruous with my self-concept. I played the contented woman at work, at family gatherings, and with friends, while inside I identified more and more with men. I could not understand how I was a feminist when, in my fantasies, I was always a man. I could not understand how I had breasts and a vagina, when, in my head, I was a man. As further confusion, in many of my fantasies I was a male enjoying sex with both men and women.

While I was still part of the lesbian community, I attempted to broach the subject of sex with men with my lesbian friends. Almost all of them refused to even talk about it. Those who were willing to talk were contemptuous, although I learned years later that some of these very women had been secretly having sex with men all along.

I learned about transsexuality when I was in college, while housesitting for one of my cousins. HBO presented an hour-long program called "What Sex Am I?" about transsexualism, transvestism, and other transgender issues. It was the first time I ever heard the medical/psychiatric term for what I am: "gender dysphoric." All at once I felt pain, horror, repulsion, anger, self-pity. But overlying these emotions was an awareness, a realization, a self-discovery: This is what I am; this is why I don't seem to belong anywhere. From then on it became a matter of what was more important to me, what I was willing to sacrifice. Either I could live in society as a gender-dysphoric woman, or I could attempt to change my gender and risk most everything I valued: my family, my friends, my home, my stability. Two years later I made my choice and began seeking information on transsexuality, searching for others like me in the hope that I would at last be part of a community.

Although I found a few transsexual friends in South Florida, there was no transsexual community for me to join. Transsexuals tend to disappear into society, to clothe our lives in secrecy in an attempt to attain some sense of normalcy and privacy. From the moment we decide to pursue transition, i.e., to leave one gender-reality for another, we become fairly public. Our lives are dominated by psychologists, surgeons, pharmacists, and the general emotional turbulence that accompanies our radical life choices. At times I feel like a white rat in a maze, at the end of which is the completion of all the operations, the analysis, the dependency.

Once I met other transsexuals, I noticed that many of them were clearly homophobic. My experience has been that homophobia is more prevalent among female-to-males (FTMs) than among male-to-females (MTFs). I can only conclude that, in attempting to become men, FTM transsexuals adopt stereotypical behavior. This behavior includes homophobia, gender chauvinism, changes in specific speech patterns (e.g., changing word emphasis in sentences), body language, and, sometimes, decreased expression of emotions. One FTM told me proudly that he no longer cried; he equated this behavioral change to the injections of testosterone that induce masculine traits in FTMs. Since the inception of this essay I have spoken to other FTMs who have shared with me that they rarely, if ever, cry anymore. I have learned from MTFs that the ingestion of estrogen produces, as one friend of mine put it, "an upheaval of emotions" within them. I do not think I cry more or less than before. Testosterone can change the emotional map of an individual, but much of the change that occurs in FTMs transitioning from one gender to another is psychological. We are becoming outwardly who we have always been inside. This brings a great sense of relief, a tremendous sense of belonging within oneself. Unlike people who are not transgendered, this is the first time in our histories when we exist.

Aside from the strong identification with the gender community into which we are transitioning, there are other reasons for homophobia within the transsexual community. These reasons stem from the general population's misconceptions about transsexuality.

The first misconception involves the belief that transsexuality, especially among MTFs, is a "symptom" of homosexuality. Gender identity becomes confounded with sexuality and is equated with "immoral" sexual choices. Transsexuals get called "faggot" by the mainstream and, in turn, refute that accusation by aligning with homophobia.

Transsexuals are no different from anyone else in how we deal with anger and resentment. We often blame gay men for the fact that society alienates us. It is easier to blame someone for our ostracization than to come to terms with the reality that we will always be set apart, if only because of our physiology.

The second misconception about transsexuals is that we change our genders in order to become straight men and women. The truth is, we become women and men to align our bodies with how we perceive ourselves. Most transsexuals happen to be straight simply because our little society mirrors society as a whole—a great percentage of people are, appear to be, or identify as straight. By the time I first began the journey that has led me to who I am today, I had internalized this misconception as truth. I could not understand my feelings of bisexuality in terms of being transsexual. For a time, I believed that bisexuality was simply the outward manifestation of my internal gender confusion. I fully expected to lose my interest in men and to lead a straight lifestyle. On the contrary, I am just as bisexual as I ever was. The process of transitioning into a new gender also necessitated redefining myself as a sexual being.

This last misconception carries with it a hidden justification: that transsexualism becomes a credible, acceptable condition if its purpose is to "correct" homosexuality by creating, as it were, straight men and women. Add to these beliefs religious convictions, and one begins to understand how deeply these ideas are internalized.

Homophobia within the transsexual community could also be the result of how transsexuals are treated by many in the gay, lesbian, and for that matter, the bisexual communities. Coming out as transsexual to my gay and lesbian friends was by no means a nurturing experience. They told me I was betraying women everywhere who had fought hard to gain what little rights they had. They told me I was sick, that I was nothing more than a self-mutilator. They told me I was a traitor, a coward, a sneak. Instead of accepting myself for what I truly was (a lesbian), I was crawling back into the closet, coming out later in another guise.

Many reactions I encountered among gays and lesbians were similar to those among bisexuals I later met. Besides the comments about betraying all women or my inability to ever be a man because I wasn't born one, I also encountered resentment. One woman I met in the bisexual community told me that I had no right deceiving everyone into believing I was a male. Although reactions from individual bisexuals were often candid and frank, if not always pleasant, reactions from bisexual groups were more insidious. During a 1991 meeting of BiNet (formerly the National Bisexual Network) held in Seattle, the monitor proposed that there be media representatives of each sex: male, female, and transgendered. The response from the group included titters, giggles, and scattered comments about the pronoun "it."

As for my straight friends, a large percentage of them automatically expected (and still expect) me to lead a straight lifestyle "when all operations are done and out of the way," as an acquaintance once said. He was, of course, assuming that I would get all the operations done.

Overall, the gay, lesbian, straight, and bisexual communities devalue transsexuals because of the choices we make. When transsexuals fully transition, though for all practical purposes we are men and women, we are not always believed as the gender we present to the world. Transsexuals are not born; we are made. As such, we are somehow less than real, less than legitimate. We are accepted as spectacles, as topics of talk shows and films, but nothing serious. This attitude sets up a caste system that cheapens and demoralizes everyone, including genetically-born men and women.

In the same way sexual orientation is not a matter of choice, transsexualism is not a matter of choice. Whether we go through with transitioning or not, we will still be gender dysphoric. The only choice lies in how we address our gender dysphoria.

I have lived in Seattle now for five years. Not long after I first contacted the bisexual community in 1991, I found out that the Seattle Bisexual Women's Network had voted on the issue of allowing male-to-female transsexuals to attend the women's group meetings. They decided that MTFs would be allowed to attend only on certain nights, excluding the nights for new members. I understand that this is no longer the policy of SBWN. I also understand that the decision was based on consensus, that full inclusion would not be allowed unless all members voted in favor. Nonetheless, the old policy implied that MTFs were accepted as women only on certain nights of the week.

The bisexual community should be a place where lines are erased. Bisexuality dismisses, disproves, and defies dichotomies. It connotes a loss of rigidity and absolutes. It is an inclusive term. Heterosexuality and homosexuality (even if reality is not always practice) are exclusive and unilateral, referring only to the attraction to one gender. Transsexuals, despite the gender of our choice, have been two genders. Many of us will always have the genitals we were born with, whether by choice or because of aesthetics or finances. Setting aside our individual sexual orientation, where do we as transsexuals belong? Where does a male-identified person with female genitals belong?

Since beginning my transition into the male gender, I have met several FTMs who are gay-identified. Rarely does one come across a gay-identified FTM who has found a partner in the gay community. It is much more prevalent for a straight-identified FTM to find a "straight" woman to be his partner. Part of me would like to say that women are more understanding than men, but that has not always been my experience. Perhaps it is the gay community's reliance upon phallocentric sex as the core of its identity that makes FTM transsexuality so threatening.

If the world were perfect there would be no labels to wear. We would simply be human beings enjoying the company of other human beings. In my struggle to identify as a human being I have often dropped labels such as "bisexual" and "transsexual," as every little word boxed me tighter into a mold I did not fit. Bisexuality is a catchall phrase. Most of us are not always 100% bisexual. We are gay or straight, depending on whom we choose to love. Bisexuality gives us the freedom to choose whom to love. If asked, I say I am bisexual. If I were to say I am gay or straight, it would in some sense be a lie, even if I choose to identify either way for the rest of my life. Similarly, I am both genders and neither. As one FTM said at a meeting I currently attend at Ingersoll Gender Center,

"I never knew what it was like to be a woman, even though I gave birth to six children. But I also don't know what it's like to be a man."

Despite how we choose to identify ourselves, the bisexual community still seems a logical place for transsexuals to find a home and a voice. Bisexuals need to educate themselves on transgender issues. At the same time, bisexuals should be doing education and outreach to the transsexual community, offering transsexuals an arena to further explore their sexualities and choices. Such outreach would also help break down gender barriers and misconceptions within the bisexual community itself.

One example of outreach might include distributing information about bisexuality to all gender centers, which can be found in many major cities. Information packets should include books, videos, directories, and everything else currently available to the bisexual community at large. Many gender centers sponsor peer groups in their area, which provide a good opportunity to reach transsexuals. Outreach could include visiting these groups where possible (some groups are confidential due to the desire for anonymity), organizing guest speakers, and holding panel discussions on bisexuality.

Finally, those who do outreach to the transsexual community must realize that the MTF and FTM groups do not jointly hold regular meetings. Except in some political efforts, transsexuals transitioning in opposite directions do not often associate with one another. This has been my experience both in South Florida and in Seattle. Mixed groups are often merely informational, directing prospective members to their "proper" support groups.

All of us who challenge gender realities do so in our quests to find our true identities and belonging. In writing this essay, I have asked myself earnestly why it is necessary for the bisexual community to be inclusive of transgendered people. Why can't those who are transgendered set up their own communities?

Transsexuals have existed on the fringes of a society already rife with little cliques surviving on the edge of the law, cliques that rely more on silence and defensive posturing than they do on actual change. Those transsexuals who want to bring about changes in social attitudes are only small voices who have yet to be heard because they have yet to be given legitimate acceptance by any major political force. If the bisexual community turns its back on transsexuals, it is essentially turning its back on itself. For in singling out any group as undesirable, it is adhering to the old, patriarchal idiom of "we" and "they," thus nullifying its purpose by asserting that only some life choices are valid. The inclusion of transgendered people can only empower any movement (such as the bisexual movement) that seeks to bring about changes in social mores and gender norms. No other group of people has broken so many gender rules and barriers, or redefined so many gender roles.

If Half of You Dodges a Bullet, All of You Ends up Dead

Orna Izakson

When Adolph Hitler began his European rampage, his first targets were queers. When Hitler went after the Jews, he murdered people with the tiniest percentage of Jewish blood. Solomonic arguments didn't work; you couldn't say "just kill the quarter of me that's Jewish and let the other three-quarters live."

In November 1992, the state of Colorado and the city of Portland, Maine approved measures amending their constitutions to deny lesbians, gay men, and bisexuals the same protections as other groups targeted for discrimination. Those who would criminalize same-sex sexual activities don't care how often or exclusively you do it. Bisexual folks suffer from these laws just as surely as the lesbian or gay man who never, ever, has an opposite-sex sex partner. Queer-bashers don't care that sometimes bi folks sleep with opposite-sex partners. In their eyes there is no such thing as half-queer.

It is not my intention to accept our oppressors' definitions of our identity, but it is unrealistic—and conceivably life-threatening—to ignore the way they codify their bigotry. As long as there is bigotry none of us is safe.[1]

Bisexuals and Jews occupy a middle ground in the spectrum of oppression: we are oppressed by the same forces that oppress lesbians, gay men, and people of color. But because bisexuals sometimes have different-sex partners, or because many Jews have white skin, we are not as visible in sharing those forms of oppression. Nevertheless, we often are ostracized by communities whose oppressions we share simply because we appear able to dodge some of the bigotry. Queers and Jews with African, Arab, Asian, or Hispanic blood face a double oppression, for their sexualities or culture and for their overt skin color. This essay, however, focuses on the less visible oppression of Jews and queers whose skin color doesn't give us away.

The charge levied against us by those who should be our allies—lesbians, gay men, people of color—looks only at our surface: Because bisexuals sometimes have opposite-sex lovers we are half-straight, emphasis on the straight; although Jews may have a historical claim to oppression, our invisibility as such equals white-skin privilege.

Pitting oppressed groups against one another is a proven method of consolidating power. When lesbians and gay men blame bisexuals for consorting with the enemy, when people of color call Jews the enemy, they waste precious energy that should be devoted to fighting homophobia and racism by isolating a natural ally.

White-skinned queers and white-skinned Jews have white-skin privilege. But that privilege is only skin deep and is granted *only as long as we are quiet, as long as we behave.* The "privilege" we gain by behaving is illusive, and the costs of behaving are high.

BEHAVING OURSELVES: PASSING, ASSIMILATING, WHITEWASHING

There are two ways to "behave"—passing and assimilating. Passing is pretending to be something you're not (Christian, straight), living your real life in secret. It is a form of fear-driven self-censorship based on historical—if not specifically personal—experiences of discrimination. Assimilation is trying to become something you're not, expunging the things that make you Other in an attempt to melt into the mainstream.

Five hundred years ago, as Columbus embarked upon the colonization of a continent and the genocide of its people, another kind of genocide was taking place: the Spanish Inquisition, which took the lives of millions of Jews, queers, and women (see Daly, 1978, ch.6). Many Jews persecuted during the Inquisition tried passing as Christian, performing their religious ceremonies in secrecy and altering their appearance for protection. But the inquisitors made their accusations with absolute malice and little truth, accepting testimony of witnesses under extreme duress who would name names if only to stop the torture. Trying to pass was very risky business.

Jewish men had particular difficulty passing in Nazi Germany because circumcision was at that time an almost exclusively Jewish practice. Hitler put physical labels on people to single them out for slaughter: the yellow star reading "Jude" for the Jews; the pink triangle for gay men; the black triangle for women who would not submit to patriarchal authority.

The U.S. of the 1990s is different in this regard. Queerness and Judaism are not as visible for targeting as is skin color. Lesbians are increasingly likely to wear power suits to their corporate offices, just as straight women often wear denim and flannel. The Great American Melting Pot has assimilated many Jews, and outside a few urban centers such as New York and Los Angeles it is fairly rare to see Jews dressed traditionally.

But the fear that convinces people to hide continues. Many Jews I know feel scared about seeming "too Jewish," too "out" as Jewish: if we are visible, we could be dead. Many bisexuals feel either "too queer" or "not queer enough." All of us get trampled by mainstream society if we try to fit in, strangling in our conflict between wanting to stop the oppression and not wanting them to know it's us they're talking about.

Passing, with its ever-present threat of exposure, is one way to hide. Jews hide in our closets with our Shabbat candles, call in sick on Yom Kippur. Bisexuals hide our same-sex lovers from our co-workers, our opposite-sex lovers from our lesbian/gay comrades.

Another way to avoid getting caught is to simply erase the part of us that could get us caught. So we assimilate, try to be like the society around us, try to be "normal." Jews change our names from Wasserman to West, from Rothstein to Ross. Queers protect our armed forces jobs by not publicly admitting to behavior deemed "incompatible with military service."

The urge to assimilate permeates all levels of oppressed groups. In my predominantly Jewish, private New York City grammar school, social hierarchy was based on lack of ethnicity. The kids who were picked on the most were the ones who went to Hebrew School, whose parents were religious or spoke with an accent.

But assimilating hurts us. Cutting ourselves off from the strength and support of our culture, we float adrift in a society that doesn't want us or wants us dead. We whitewash ourselves and pay the

price of being lost. But we still are in danger: we have given up the
strength of identity and community to grasp forever for a safety that
is elusive, partly because it is based on a lie.

It is no wonder that we try to pass or assimilate. Just as looking at
Glamour is enough to make women hate the reality of our bodies;
walking around in a straight, white world can lead to a self-imposed
suppression of difference. It becomes easy to let people make their
assumptions: she's got long hair so she's straight; this is America so
she must be Christian. The problem with passing is that we live in
the real and constant fear of discovery. The problem with assimilating is that we may forget we have reasons to be afraid.

VISUAL VIBRATIONS

Bisexuality challenges the necessity of duality: it's about claiming both. Do you want a female lover or a male lover? Yes. Anti-
Jewish oppression functions in a similar way, as the intersection of
several kinds of oppression, including racism, classism, and
religious discrimination. Anti-Semitism is difficult to pin down,
precisely because it includes more than one form of discrimination.

For many of us, understanding the concept of "both" is sort of
like looking at bright purple abutting bright yellow: since the two
are opposites, looking at them together creates a kind of visual
vibration that is very difficult to focus on. Bisexuality and Jewishness are like that. One of the challenges for bisexuals, Jews, and our
allies is to constantly keep looking at both colors/sides, despite the
fact that our socialization makes this very difficult to do.

During the summer of 1992 I was describing incidents of anti-
Semitism I had experienced to a woman who studies oppression.
When I described reactions to my appearance, she said I had experienced racism because I look Latina. When I described reactions to
my New York-Jewish mouth (full of sound and fury signifying my
culture), she said I had experienced classism—since, presumably,
aristocrats have no passion.

The discomfort of seeing *both* results in the dismissal of groups
who cannot be neatly labeled as one or the other. Rather than ex-
pending energy to focus on several sides of us despite the visual and
psychological "vibration," some just deny the concept, returning to

either/or. In those cases Jews are perceived as either victims or oppressors; bisexuals are seen as either straight or queer. If we walk down the street with a same-sex lover, we're seen as lesbian/gay; if we walk down the street with a different-sex lover, we're seen as straight.

IN THE END WE ARE ALL WE'VE GOT

Behaving has its dangers because, historically, it doesn't work. Those who pass or assimilate may be discovered, may live forever in fear of exposure, or may simply face the ongoing hurt of self-censorship and denial. But by owning our identity, we solidify our community and our visibility, and turn fear into strength.

We must build our communities with open doors, and not leave our allies in lonely and dangerous isolation. A straight person who stands up for queer rights—and therefore stands out—can get bashed if s/he doesn't fall back on "but I'm really straight."

By looking at both Jewish and bisexual histories, we learn what the oppression of relatively invisible people looks like. We also learn that the most effective way to fight that oppression is by reclaiming a visible identity, not by whitewashing ourselves.

This is a historical time for all of us who are politically, sexually, culturally, or chromatically Other to recognize how oppressions overlap, and how the perceived need to pick one issue divides all of us in the same struggle—against patriarchy, homophobia, sexism, and denial. It is time for all of us to stop ranking oppression, and stop vilifying and marginalizing those who should be our allies.

All we have to work with is each other. Just as we breathe the air that the dinosaurs once breathed, just as the molecules in our bodies were once cucumbers or honey or old growth forests, everything gets recycled. We are all we've got: to work with, party with, fight with, cry with, laugh with, sleep with, and love with. There is too much work to do to ostracize those who suffer what we suffer, to fight the messenger rather than the King himself. We are family of circumstance and not always of choice, but we are the best we've got.

And so we love each other and wish love for each other, regardless (to the extent possible) of gender and sex. This is my hope in the politics of bisexuality, and it is my hope for anyone who is born with or chooses to share the burden and be my family.

NOTE

1. The story of Passover teaches that as long as any are oppressed none is free; as long as there are those who are enslaved as we, the Jews, were enslaved in Egypt, we are all enslaved. It is therefore incumbent upon all of us to fight oppression everywhere.

Why You *Must* Say "and Bisexual"

Nishanga Bliss

It still happens. I'm sitting at a coalition meeting one night and the topic of discussion is queer invisibility. One of my sisters raises her hand and says, "Gays and lesbians are sick and tired of being ignored, overlooked, not included." I'm leafing through my favorite 'zine, reading the editorial (by the bisexual editor) about Coming Out Day, when "gay and lesbian people are supposed to come out to someone they haven't yet." Gay and lesbian this, lesbian and gay that. Every time I hear it, it's a slap in my queer face.

It amazes me that we're still excluded after all the years of organizing. Bisexuals have fought alongside lesbians and gays for queer liberation since Stonewall and before. Many of us have been in gay or lesbian closets and many of us have been out. After countless teach-ins, educationals, bisexual speakers' bureaus, bi pride stickers, the publication of *Bi Any Other Name* and several other books, classes at two major universities, regional, national, and international conferences, a national bisexual network (BiNet), and our very own magazine (*Anything That Moves—ATM*), it still happens. From people who know how painful it is to be ignored, how degrading assumptions can be, from the people who coined the phrase "Silence Equals Death," it still comes, or rather, it still doesn't, those two simple, beautiful, words: *and bisexual.*

After all the education, pain, love, and publication, ignorance is no longer an excuse. Is it simple viciousness? No. At the root, it is fear. Bisexuals disrupt the categories, scaring gays, straights, and even, sometimes, ourselves. When we come out, it makes people remember things they didn't want to: dreams, fantasies, lovers long forgotten, episodes, and even thoughts that don't fit. This is the sort of personal history that most monosexuals and closeted bisexuals must edit out when they construct their coming-out stories—the stories they tell themselves, and the world, about who they are sexually and how they got to be that way.

Bisexuals are working to define our sexuality inclusively, in a way that does not force us to deny whole aspects of our existence. It is a way of understanding sexuality that admits that people, like everything else in the universe, are involved in a constant process of change. In defining ourselves in this way, we unsettle. We disturb. We get under the skin, hinting that there is more to life than the married-monogamous-lesbian or gay thing or the bar scene or whatever rut someone might be stuck in. We scare ourselves, too, disturbing even our own categories, constantly needing to reinvent ourselves to keep up with our ever-shifting attractions, actions, loves, and desires.

Similarly, transgendered people disturb our rigid notions of male and female. The greater the challenge to established categories a group of people possess, the greater their marginalization—and their potential to transform.

The very way we bisexuals unsettle lesbians and gays is the way we will unsettle the status quo. If you look at the Kinsey studies with an inclusive eye, you find that 40% of the population is behaviorally bisexual. Bisexuals are working to organize these people: to create a space for them to finally be safe, to come out in. Add that 40 to the 10% gay and lesbian population and you get 50% queer. If we don't rise up and take power then, when will we? The real fear, expressed in fear of bisexuals, is the fear that we queers have of our own power.

We are not sure we want to give up our status as the special 10%, as a minority. We do not want to see, to know, the other 40% because that would force us out of our cozy community, out of the gay ghettoes, and make us work with people who may be very different from us, save for the fact that they are queer. It's called coalition politics, and it is very difficult. When what constitutes your differences is what you usually have in common, it's scary. The same fear haunts many efforts at multicultural organizing: the fear of the other because of what they bring up in the self, and the fear of what would happen if we really could work together. But we must work together. Gays and lesbians need to realize that the gay community is not now and has never been homogeneous and to adjust their attitudes and language accordingly.

Our presence has been consistently edited out of history, consciously or unconsciously, by the powers-that-be in the queer community. Acknowledging the true diversity of queer people could threaten the existing lavender hierarchy. It might even threaten the very notion of hierarchy itself, because it would begin to blur the categories: men, women, straights, gays, even bisexuals—one day, the terms themselves will become obsolete.

So unless you are, for some reason, *specifically* referring only to the gay, the lesbian, or the lesbian and gay communities, please remember to embrace the rest of your brothers and sisters by saying "Lesbian, gay, bisexual, and transgendered." When referring to men who sleep with men: "Bisexual and gay men." Women who sleep with women are "Lesbian and bisexual women." Sounds like a mouthful? Try "queer." Saying "queer" is the best way of being all-inclusive.

I'm not asking you to honor the bisexual in yourself. I'm sure you will come to do that in your own sweet time, if that's your destiny. It will be enough if you honor your friend, your ex-lover, your roommate, your mother, and the rest of that 40% of the population. I'm asking you to honor them, and me, and to pay your respects to the power and the numbers our movement will have when it is truly inclusive. Start by saying it: "and bisexual." Or better yet, "Bisexual and. . . ." It's only one step, but it's *something. . . .*

Directions

Our Visionary

Voices

OVERVIEW

Liz A. Highleyman

. . . many of the usual boundaries of a sexually dichotomous society are looking very porous. It appears that gay politics has dared to speak the name of a persecuted minority that banded together in recent decades. Bisexual politics will dare to speak the name of what some believe is humanity itself.

—Salem Alaton, 1993

A key aim of this book is to explore both how one's experiences and beliefs influence one's identity as a bisexual person, and how one's experiences as a bisexual person can influence and inspire one's politics. Are there particular types of theoretical models that bisexual writers are especially likely to adopt by virtue of their experience as bisexuals? As we will see, there are indeed common threads that connect the visions of the bisexual theorists represented in this section.

Bisexual theory is just beginning to pass its infancy. Bi people have produced theoretical writings in the past, but only recently has a body of self-conscious theoretical writings about bisexuality by bisexuals come into being. Some bisexuals in the early 1970s spoke of breaking down categories of gender and sexual orientation. Yet this work often came from a male, heterosexually-identified per-spective that promoted sexual liberation without analyzing how women and non-heterosexuals were oppressed by gender and sexual identity hierarchies.

With the expansion of the bi movement in the 1980s and with the greater influence of lesbian feminism and closer ties to the gay and lesbian movement, writings about bisexuality shifted. Much of the work done during this period was introductory, of the "Bi 101" variety (see Hutchins and Ka'ahumanu, 1991). A great deal of writing was devoted to personal narratives, coming out and "second coming out" stories, expressions of the pain of exclusion from gay and lesbian communities, and attempts to convince gay men and lesbians to recognize and respect bisexuals.

Much of this writing reflected an identity politics perspective; that is, politics related to membership in distinct groups based on ostensibly immutable characteristics and emphasizing the rights of oppressed minorities. In this respect, bi writings have closely mirrored the work of the majority of gay men and lesbians. In the latter half of the 1980s some gay men and lesbians, especially within academia, began to question identity politics and the very concepts of gender and sexuality, most notably within the context of the essentialism/social constructionism debates. Bisexual writings followed a similar trajectory, evolving from tales of personal experience and into in-depth critical examinations of theoretical concepts.

This collection represents one of the first attempts to bring together the visions of bisexual people for the bi movement and for humanity as a whole. How do our experiences as bisexuals lead to unique theories informed by a non-monosexual perspective? Bisexuality compels us to move beyond accepted paradigms and to explore new ways of looking at the world. Rebecca Kaplan, for example, examines how a bisexual politics that critiques dualistic thinking can lead us to a broader understanding of how other forms of bipolarity and categorization can limit us. Annie Murray discusses how bisexuality can help us challenge societal imperatives. Just as we need not make either/or choices about our sexuality, we do not need to do so with regard to our relationships.

A common thread in many of these essays is their emphasis on moving beyond distinct identity categories and questioning the very nature, even the existence, of categories such as gender and sexual orientation. Several writers believe that the concept of *bi*sexuality is too narrow, based as it is on the notion that there are two distinct sexes/genders. Jill Nagle proposes that "genderism" (the insistence that there are two and only two sexes/genders) is the basis for sexism, monosexism, and heterosexism. As Naomi Tucker points out, if the existence of bisexuality means that gender need not be a determining factor of sexual preference, then bisexuals should argue against rigid gender constructs. Sunfrog discusses how the radical praxis of "gender blur" can serve as an important component of personal and societal liberation.

Another common theme is identity politics. While some writers (for example Susanna Trnka) regard identity-based organizing as a necessary tool given current societal realities, and others (for example Mykel Board) regard this type of organizing as inherently destructive and regressive, the writers here all hope to see humanity ultimately move beyond schemes of categorization that limit our full potential as multidimensional beings.

A large proportion of the theoretical writings by bisexuals to date have come from a quite similar perspective: that of formerly lesbian-identified, feminist, bisexual women activists, the majority of whom have been white and middle class with academic backgrounds. This trend was also evident in the production of this anthology. There is a relatively coherent body of work from the perspective of bisexual women (see Weise, 1992). Many of the writings by women have focused on the "lesbian/bisexual debate." Issues of who gets to define whose identity and who gets to be included in whose community have been extremely important (and often painful) for many lesbians and bisexual women. With this anthology we are witnessing a shift in emphasis away from this debate and toward less parochial, more all-encompassing ways of thinking about identity and community.

Bisexual men, on the other hand, have not put forth a coherent body of political/theoretical writings about bisexuality (although bi men have contributed to the body of "gay" men's writing). For this section I solicited contributions from bi men whose work would provocatively delve into the theoretical aspects of bisexuality. One writer, Sunfrog, has close ties to a gay male community (the radical faeries) while the other, Mykel Board, disavows allegiance to any community defined solely on the basis of sexual orientation. The two essays here are not intended to be representative of all bi men's thought, but rather to show the range of its diversity.

To conclude this section, Starhawk declares that pleasure is sacred and worth struggling for, positing the erotic pulse of the Earth as a power that holds the universe together and connects us to all living beings. She argues, as do the other writers in this section, for blending and blurring, for appreciating all aspects of our being rather than limiting ourselves to those that fit neatly within distinct categories.

Unlike the mainstream segment of the gay and lesbian movement, bisexuals have not restricted the project of deconstructing identity-based categories to academicians. Rather, bisexuals both within and outside the organized bi movement have made this project an integral part of how we make sense of the world and live our lives as bisexual, pansexual, omnisexual, multisexual, "just sexual," androgynous, genderfucked, bi-gendered, non-gendered, gender-indifferent, or "don't label me" human beings seeking to create communities with those with whom we find common cause, even (or maybe especially!) if our labels don't happen to coincide.

Your Fence Is Sitting on Me:
The Hazards of Binary Thinking

Rebecca Kaplan

Bisexual theorists have increasingly recognized binary thinking as a source of bi oppression and have proposed alternative models. Such discussions have focused primarily on the binary divisions of gay/straight and man/woman. I would like to explore some problems of binary thinking through a variety of examples. I will discuss the limitations of some new proposed models, which reject only part of binary thinking, retaining either categorization or bipolarity, which are themselves problematic. I then explore how a non-binary view of the world can be expanded as a political tool for addressing a wide range of problems.

Binary thinking is a constraining mode of thought, which divides the world up into two discrete boxes. This highly pervasive form of thought leads to the erasure of bisexuals, and perpetuates oppression in many other ways. Identifying as bisexual[1] in a culture in which bisexuality is marginalized can lead to the development of particular political views about that marginalization. The rejection of the gay/straight binary, which denies the existence of bisexuals, can lead to the questioning of other forms of binary thinking.

The impetus for this article came several years ago while I was reading a conservative critique of a particular left-wing paper. The paper had carried an editorial opposing United States intervention in the Persian Gulf. The conservative critic faulted the paper for failing to describe "the two sides of the issue." Since I myself had at least four separate opinions on the Gulf War, I was particularly struck by the notion of "the two sides of the issue." This phrase is

---

Title thanks to the cool bidude wearing this sign on his head at the 1993 March on Washington.

very common; lack of bias is supposedly demonstrated by reporting "both sides." The belief that there are "two sides" keeps us from exploring opinions and vantage points other than the two which are presented. If only one view is depicted, we may notice that some potential opinion has yet to be expressed, but not when two are given. Binary thinking discourages us from conceiving of other solutions. Once *two* options are given, we cease to seek other alternatives. The illusion of choice serves to uphold the status quo. To me, the acceptance of the two boxes as representing all possible options is the greatest evil of binary thinking.

Binary thinking is the notion that things are most naturally divided up into two discrete categories. Binary thinking is the combination of *bipolar thinking* and *categorical thinking*.

Bipolar thinking is the notion that traits can be described in reference to two extremes or poles, with people falling along a one-dimensional line between them. The Kinsey scale, which describes human sexual orientation on a seven-point spectrum, from exclusively heterosexual (0) to exclusively homosexual (6), is one example of a bipolar model. Bipolar models necessarily define the two poles as opposites. On the Kinsey scale, the more one is attracted to women, the less one is attracted to men, and vice versa. Within a bipolar model it is possible to have people who are neither strictly homosexual nor strictly heterosexual, but these people still must be defined in terms of how "close" they are to being hetero- or homosexual.

Categorical thinking is the notion that items can be divided into discrete, discontinuous groups. One example of categorization is the use of boxes on census forms for race, in which people must check *one* box out of several options. This approach allows for the existence of a number of groups, and allows for the differences between them. However, categorization does not allow for overlap, and it does not account for people who fall between groups (i.e., people of mixed heritage). Furthermore, such systems are rarely exhaustive, and almost always leave some people with no box in which to put themselves.

Binary thinking combines the two ideologies of bipolarity and categorization in that it requires exactly two oppositional groups (bipolarity), and it requires that those groups be discrete and discontinuous (categorization). Dividing people into gay and straight is one example of binary thinking.

Categorization is a function of the human mind. We categorize things in order to be able to name them, so we can talk about them. But the categories are often defined by the communication needs of the ruling classes. Decisions about what racial categories exist, about what is good and bad, about what is legal and illegal, even about what is possible and impossible, are made by those with power. It is important that we examine why certain methods of categorization have developed, and whose interests they serve. One such example is the use of the category "insane." The label "insane" has been used to condemn people of whom those in power disapproved: homosexuals, women who would not allow their husbands to rape them, enslaved people who tried to run away, people who spoke out against oppressive government actions, and others whose conduct threatened the existing order.

What is the purpose of the words we use to describe sexual orientation? For example, if I meet someone, there may be some reasonable cause for me to want to know something about their sexual preferences. Words like "lesbian" arise because they do have a useful purpose. They help predict certain behaviors, such as whom someone is likely to be interested in dating, and they have important political meaning within a heterosexist society. But they are also dangerous, because they allow a dominant group to define an "other" who may then be oppressed. Even if I agreed that it is useful to have words to name the sex(es) to whom someone is erotically attracted, I would not have to use the categories homosexual and heterosexual. I could just as easily divide the world up into gynosexual (attracted to women), androsexual (attracted to men), and bisexual (attracted to both). The division into hetero- and homosexual may serve to reinforce heterosexism by defining non-heterosexual people as a fundamentally different group, to whom all social ills can then be attributed.

Categorical thinking serves to obscure differences within a category, creating an illusion of similarity among all group members, and an illusion of dramatic difference between categories where many similarities exist. Most of the problems with categorical thinking arise because people forget that the categories are the constructions of our minds, rather than some essential reality. When something does not quite fit the boxes, we alter it to make it fit rather than altering our conceptual categories. It is as if we have overlooked the fact that the categories are merely our shorthand for describing and understanding complexities in the world. The point is to think about where certain forms of categorization come from, and to realize that we can change the categories rather than letting them change us.

People's desire to see binaries where there are none also leads to flagrant misrepresentations of scientific data. One example of this tendency is the misinterpretation of the work of Alfred Kinsey. Kinsey collected data about the sexual behaviors and fantasies of a huge number of individuals. He firmly believed that such behavior varies greatly, and that people cannot be divided into boxes on the basis of one element of their sexuality. Kinsey clearly stated his intent in his first study, on men, in 1948:

> Males do not represent two discrete populations, heterosexual and homosexual. The world is not to be divided into sheep and goats. Not all things are black, nor all things white. It is a fundamental of taxonomy that nature rarely deals with discrete categories. Only the human mind invents categories, and tries to force facts into separate pigeon-holes. The living world is a continuum in each and every one of its aspects. The sooner we learn this concerning sexual behavior, the sooner we shall reach a sound understanding of the realities of sex. (Kinsey, 1948)

Despite this, many people read some small excerpt from Kinsey, collapse together all the people on one side of some arbitrarily chosen point on the scale, call all people on one side "gay" and call all people on the other side "straight." In fact, it is this reading which gave rise to the oft-cited 10 percent figure. By collapsing together all people at 5 or above on the Kinsey scale, some activists calculated that 10 percent of adult Euro-American males (Kinsey's population under study) are "gay."

The belief that discrete categories exist naturally and transculturally (essentialism[2]) often underlies categorical thought. Essentialism can be contrasted with constructionism (also known as deconstructionism or postmodernism) which holds that categories are products of a particular culture, and do not describe an intrinsic, eternal reality.[3]

The essentialist versus constructionist debate is important to the question of categorical thinking, in that categorical thinking is often upheld by an unstated essentialist philosophy. Steven J. Gould, a scientist and anti-essentialist, explains the problems of attributing essential natures to categories of natural phenomena, and the importance to Kinsey of continua and antiessentialism:

> Many taxonomists[4] still viewed the world as a series of pigeon-holes . . . defined by their "essences," fundamental features separating them from all others. Variation was a nuisance at best—a kind of accidental splaying out around the essential form, and serving only to create confusion in the correct assignment of pigeon-holes. . . . Taxonomists like Kinsey, who centered their work in evolutionary theory, developed a radically different view of variation. Islands of form exist, to be sure: cats are not a sea of continuity, but come to us as lions, tigers, lynxes, tabbies and so forth. Still, although species may be discrete, they have no immutable essence. Variation is the raw material of evolutionary change. It represents the fundamental reality of nature, not a mere accident about a created norm. Variation is primary, essences are illusory. Species must be defined as ranges of irreducible variation. . . . [Essentialism] leads us to neglect continua and to divide reality into a set of correct and unchanging categories. It established criteria for judgement and worth: individual objects that lie close to the essence are good, those that depart are bad, if not unreal.
>
> Antiessentialist thinking forces us to view the world differently. We must accept shadings and continua as fundamental. We lose criteria for judgement by comparison to some ideal; short people, retarded people, people of other beliefs, colors and religions are people of full status. (Gould, 1982)

Of course, we bisexuals are by no means the first to point out the problems of binary thinking. Race, gender, and a variety of other traits have also been subject to challenges about binarity. The case of gender is fairly parallel to some of the discussions of sexual orientation. In the bad old days, gender came in only two flavors, masculine and feminine. You were either one or the other. Later some social psychologists developed a bipolar gender scale, with questionnaires that elicited responses about conformity to social gender roles. Each person could then be rated on a continuous scale, with extreme masculinity on one end and extreme femininity on the other. Of course, this scale required that masculinity and femininity be oppositional traits that cancel each other out. If someone had many masculine traits and many feminine traits, they would fall in the middle, together with people who had few feminine traits and few masculine traits. In 1974, Sandra Bem formally challenged this bipolar notion of gender, and proposed instead two independent scales, one that expressed degree of masculinity, and one that expressed degree of femininity. This model allowed for subjects to score high on both scales, and allowed for the various gender traits to be posited non-oppositionally. (After all, why should high nurturance cancel out a desire to play sports?)

The mind/body binary is the forerunner of many of the oppressive binaries in common use today. This binary is highly analogous to the culture/nature and male/female binaries, with nature and body being attributed to women, and culture and mind being attributed to men in much of philosophy. Once binary divisions are made, they are often also put into a hierarchy, with one group (men/culture/mind) being defined as good while the other group (women/nature/body) is defined as bad or evil. Other essays such as Kathleen Bennett's *Feminist Bisexuality: A Both/And Option for an Either/Or World* (1992) have further explored the origins of binary thinking.

Binary thinking is nothing new, nor is it unique to only one culture. One example can be found in an ancient Jewish prayer, recited to mark the end of the Sabbath, which blesses g-d for distinguishing between "light and darkness . . . between the sacred and the profane" (traditional *havdalah* service).

As demonstrated by a prayer thanking g-d for clear, easy binary distinctions, the desire to divide, to differentiate between good and evil is a powerful one. We want to know what is good and what is bad. And we would like the answers to be easy. Even *Cosmopolitan* magazine gets in on the act with articles such as "Good Girls, Bad Girls: Which Are You?" (*Cosmopolitan,* 1991). Binaries are everywhere. This form of thinking is so pervasive that we often do not even notice that we are using it. Finding a non-binary way of thinking about sexual orientation and other facets of life requires an active, conscious effort.

OTHER MODELS

Bisexual authors have suggested a variety of other models to move beyond the gay/straight concept of human sexuality. One such approach, which leaves binary thinking firmly in place, is to simply replace the gay/straight divide with a queer/straight divide. This approach unites bisexuals with gays and lesbians (and in some cases with transsexuals and other sex radicals) as "queer." These united "queers" are still contrasted with the oppositionally-defined "straights." Now bisexuals get to belong to a group, but humanity is still divided into two discrete boxes.

Michael Storms sought to escape the notion that attraction to men must be oppositional to attraction to women. His model is similar to Bem's model of masculinity/femininity. Storms (1980) uses a two-dimensional grid that measures attraction to members of the same sex on the horizontal axis, and attraction to members of the other sex on the vertical axis. I find this approach appealing, because it also allows for measures of different degrees of sexualness, and because it does not assume that attraction to members of the same sex cancels out attraction to members of the opposite sex.

Robyn Ochs and Marcia Deihl (1992) eloquently point out that part of biphobia arises from people's need to have clearly defined, binary categories in which to group their reality. They state, "Biphobia is . . . the fear of the space between our categories" (p. 69). They then go on to explore an alternative model of sexual orientation, one that does not necessitate having two discrete groups.

> In answer to the question, "are you gay or straight?" bisexual activists have begun to challenge this artificial polarization and create a lifetime identity that need not change with the gender of our lovers. Honesty demands flexibility, and by dissolving the barriers created by old static categories, all of us can focus less on our differences and more on our common

goals of political empowerment. Bisexuals are not fence sitters. There *is* no fence. Instead of a fence, we see a field, with mostly lesbian and gay people on one side and mostly heterosexual people on the other. Since we *are* men and women, since we *are* "gay" and "straight," we are in the middle. Sometimes we travel toward one end or the other—in a day, in a year, or in a lifetime. (Ochs and Deihl, p. 75)

Unfortunately, their proposed model is highly problematic. They eliminate the categorical element, but maintain the bipolar one. Ochs and Deihl still posit the poles of humanity as heterosexual and homosexual. They still lump lesbians and gay men into one category, and heterosexual women and men into another category. They still see bisexuals as "in between." It is still we bisexuals who must do the traveling, between two static poles of straight and gay. Our orientations are still being defined within an oppressive model. Ochs and Deihl start with the biphobic model of two discrete sides with a fence in the middle, and all they remove is the fence.

Other bisexual theorists have described a "choice C" or trinary model (Rust, 1992). In this model bisexuals are a distinct, unique group with a sexual orientation that is fundamentally different from heterosexuals or homosexuals. People may be divided up into three discrete categories: hetero, homo, and bi. This trinary model is based on several worthy motives: a desire to promote the formation of bisexual community identity, to oppose the notion that we are "between" gay and straight, to oppose the idea that we have simply not made up our minds or chosen a "real" sexual orientation *yet.* By seeing bisexuals as a group separate from hetero- and homosexuals, one can see that having a sexuality that is not predicated on gender distinctions may be fundamentally different from one that is. Bisexuality can be seen as different from, not a combination of, an exclusive attraction to men and an exclusive attraction to women.

Thus, the "choice C" model has much to support it. Nonetheless, I feel that the "choice C" model is ultimately oppressive and problematic. Politically, it may reinforce the idea that bisexuals are some bizarre group of "others," worthy of hatred or at least avoidance. Conceptually, it maintains the idea of dividing people up into discrete boxes based on the gender(s) of their sexual partners. It eliminates the bipolar part of binary thinking, but keeps the categorical element.

All of the prominent models of sexual orientation that I have seen also share two additional problems: they do not account for traits other than sex/gender that may also be important in determining people's attractions, and they do not account for which specific sexual acts people prefer.

WHAT SHOULD WE DO ABOUT IT?

I do not want to be in box C. I do not want a "both/and" world, in which I am seen as gay and straight, but the sex(es) of my lovers is still a question of important public interest, and possibilities are still restricted to two categories. I do not want to be in the middle of a field with gays/lesbians on one end and hets on the other, even if there is no fence. Once we rule out putting people in boxes to predict their behavior, we may find ourselves needing to ask the more scary, but honest question, "Are you interested in me?" rather than "What is your sexual orientation?"

I propose another model that allows us to make sense of our sexuality, yet reinforces neither categorization nor bipolarity. Consider electron shells in atoms, which are clusters about certain locations in three-dimensional space. When drawing diagrams of atoms, electrons are represented as clouds that fall at certain distances and directions from the nucleus. In reality, electrons are constantly in motion. The actual location of an electron is portrayed in terms of probability. Clouds are drawn, depicting the areas within which it is highly probable that the electron will be found.

With regard to the people to whom one is attracted, I prefer to think in terms of probability clouds. I may be attracted to many different people, yet I do see "islands of form" (Gould, 1984) or patterns that repeat with greater frequency than others. People may fall into clusters I call "types" (for some people, these "types" may be genders). Yet each type I perceive is not a group of identical individuals, nor is each category totally discrete from the others. Nonetheless there are clusters of traits that tend to fall together in my, and others', attractions.

As bisexuals, we are necessarily prompted to come up with non-binary ways of thinking about sexual orientation. For many of us, this has also prompted a move toward non-binary ways of thinking about sex and gender. As we try to create a broader bisexual politic, I believe it is vital to take this non-binary perspective to other, perhaps less obvious, arenas.

Binary thinking (and categories in general) works to distance ourselves from others, and from traits that scare us. Lesbian writer Marilyn Murphy explores the use of categories of "old" and "disabled" to further our denial about our own aging, or disabilities:

> What I am learning is that old Lesbians/old women, and even old men, live on a continuum of able-bodiedness. . . . I realize now that I have constructed two imaginary compartments, "The Disabled" and "The Old." Into these compartments I have hidden from myself my fears of dying, physical suffering and pain, debilitating diseases, loss of sight and hearing, bodily integrity and attractiveness. As long as the walls of my compartments were intact, I never had to worry that disease, disability and death happened to ordinary, regular kinds of people, people like me. . . . It occurs to me that we will not be able to accept and love our infirm selves, our disabled selves, or our old selves if we are denied or deny ourselves the opportunity to know and accept and love the infirm, disabled and old women who are part of our community. (Murphy, 1991, p. 144)[5]

Deconstructing binary thinking can have many benefits in the arena of politics. The range of political viewpoints that exist in the U.S.A. are often described in binary terms. People are divided into Democrats and Republicans, with all other possibilities eliminated from popular consideration. Barbara Ehrenreich (1992) criticized this sytem, stating:

> Yes, a third party would be nice, and a fourth, and a fifth. I have never understood how a people accustomed to half a dozen varieties of Coca-Cola can put up with two, or by some counts, one and a half, political parties.

The existence of two parties creates an illusion of dramatic difference where none really exists, and implies that there is unity within each party. This false difference gives people an illusion of choice: if people think they get to choose between two dramatically different options, they are less likely to condemn the entire system as inadequate.

Other popular models of political ideologies are bipolar or categorical. The categorical approach allows for multiple parties (such as Democrat, Workers, Green, Republican), but continues the notion of party allegiance, and of clean lines between parties. Other constructs of political ideologies are bipolar, such as the "political spectrum." The common description of the political spectrum describes people as falling along a line from "liberal" to "conservative." People's views may fall anywhere along the line, but can only be measured along one dimension.

Political ideologies may also be better described as clusters, probability groupings. Ideologies may shift and change. What issues count to make someone a "progressive" differ over place and time. Agreeing with someone on one issue does not mean that I will agree with them on other issues. This clustering view can help us to get beyond one of the frequent problems in identity politics: the inability to deal with disagreement. Just because someone is like us in one way does not imply that we will agree on all political issues. And the fact that we may disagree on several political issues does not mean that we cannot work together. We end up needing to ask "Can we work together in this political struggle?" rather than "Are you a member of my box?"

Challenging binary thinking may also lead to more constructive responses in the area of environmental degradation. Learning to see beyond simple either/or divisions would greatly improve our ability to understand and preserve the complexity of the natural world. One eloquent article reads:

The earth was formed whole and continuous in the universe, without lines. The human mind arose in the universe needing lines, boundaries, distinctions. Here and not there. This and not that. Mine and not yours.

That is sea and this is land, and here is the line between them. See? It's very clear on the map. But the map is not the territory. The line on the map is not to be found at the edge of the sea.

Humans build houses on the land beside the sea, and the sea comes and takes them away. That is not land, says the sea. It is also not sea. Look at the territory, which God created, not the map, which you created. There is no place where land ends and sea begins.

The places that are not-land, not-sea, are beautiful, functional, fecund. Humans do not treasure them. In fact, they barely see them because those spaces do not fit the lines in the mind. Humans keep busy dredging, filling, diking, draining the places between land and sea, trying to make them one or the other. (Meadows, 1991, p. 281)

Our task can be to notice binary thinking whenever it surfaces, and to challenge it. The paradigm that we use will define and limit what we are able to perceive. Traveling to the March on Washington in 1993, I drove along a circular highway called 495 that goes around Washington, DC. Along the highway the signs naming the road change from 495 N, to 495 W, to 495 S, to 495 E. An observer might ask, "Why do you keep changing direction, can't you make up your mind which direction you wish to travel?" But I have been traveling in a constant direction, on a constant road, in a constant counterclockwise motion. Anyone using a linear, Cartesian framework to name directions can only describe my movements as a change in direction. They are unable to perceive the constancy of my circular motion. So too with our sexuality. A limited, binary paradigm describes bisexuals as constantly changing their identity with the sex of their lovers. Only by changing the paradigm can we depict what may be a constant direction of our desires.

NOTES

1. I have many problems with the word bisexual; nonetheless, I use it throughout this essay. *Bi*sexual reinforces the notion that there are two and only two sexes, and that our sexual orientation should be described solely in terms of the sex(es) of the people to whom we are attracted. When I write the word bisexual, I intend to refer to people who (a) call themselves bisexual; or (b) experience their desires as not falling along sex categories; or (c) are sexually attracted to people

of more than one sex (be that male, female, or other flavors for which we don't yet have good words).

2. Amanda Udis-Kessler has written excellent articles on the relationship between essentialism and anti-bi sentiment. (See Udis-Kessler, 1990 and Udis-Kessler, 1991a.)

3. In his book *Forms of Desire,* Edward Stein explains the debate between social constructionists and essentalists with regard to sexual orientation.

4. Taxonomy is the branch of science dealing with the classification of plants and animals. Kinsey was a taxonomist, as is Gould.

5. Marilyn Murphy would likely be surprised to find her words being used in support of a bisexual politic. Despite the anti-bi sentiment of some of her essays, she does provide lucid and moving arguments against binary thinking. I feel that her argument is quite applicable, particularly the notion that people project fears about themselves onto categories of "others."

Pimple No More

Mykel Board

Until recently, bisexuality has been little more than a blip in the morass of identity politics. So-called theories of bisexuality have not been theories at all. Instead, bisexuals simply adopted the standard "We're so oppressed" moaning of every other identity group. The loudest call has been for *visibility,* as bisexuals scrape crumbs from the queer table.

I propose a radically different view of bisexuality. I propose a view that will take us away from the narrow self-serving agendas of identity politics. I propose bisexuality as a way of thinking, rather than as an identity. I propose a massive *inclusive* group, rather than a minority within a minority, struggling to be seen.[1]

THE TRADITIONAL VIEW

The standard line is that bisexuals are attracted to males and females. We form a discrete group, contrasting with monosexuals (that is, those attracted *only* to their own sex or *only* to the opposite sex).[2]

The traditional position holds that discrimination against bisexuals exists because of this dual attraction. In order to end this discrimination, bisexuals should unite to work for their rights, as do other oppressed groups.

Many people holding this view go further. They say that because bisexuals face discrimination *mainly* on the basis of the homosexual part of their identity, bisexuals should align ourselves with the homosexual rights movement. Often this alignment becomes a plea for inclusion. "Oh please, let us be a tagline," we beg. "Just add us at the end of your titles and events. We'll be happy. *Lesbian, Gay, and Bisexual.* That's all we want."

Most of the lesbian and gay movement considers bifolks a pimple on the butt of their struggle. In truth, bisexuals haven't made it that far. Most of us *want to be* pimples on that butt.

WHAT'S WRONG WITH THE TRADITIONAL VIEW

Besides allowing bisexuality to be defined as a *minority*, the traditional view suggests a uniformity among bisexuals. A homosexual only has sex with members of the same sex. A heterosexual only has sex with the opposite sex. There is no such consistency to bisexuality.

Some bisexuals are serial; that is, they are attracted only to males at one time and only to females at another. Some have simultaneous multiple relationships with a range of genders. Some have romantic relationships with one sex and purely sexual relationships with the other. These combinations move throughout the sexual sphere. They are not exclusive or static.

A bisexual, during a phase of opposite sex attraction, might not feel oppressed. Should this cause exclusion from *the movement?* It should if that movement is based on oppression—something common to all identity politics.

Identity politics itself is a good chunk of the problem. Because of its narrow focus, it often obscures a wider world view. People ignore solutions that can solve general problems, in favor of solutions that fit their own group. Often they are completely willing to ignore or take away the rights of others in the quest for their own rights. Even when groups make coalitions, these last only as long as each group perceives its goals to be the same as those of the others in the coalition. When this perception ends, the coalition falls apart.

THE BISEXUAL REALITY

Bisexuals are rarely more accepted by homosexuals than by heterosexuals. Homosexuals have so much time and emotion invested in their sexual ("gay") *identity*. They often see bisexuals as a threat to that identity and are less accepting than heterosexuals. Why?

When those who are attracted to the same sex adopt a "gay" identity, they surround themselves with more and more gay friends. They adopt a new lifestyle, often changing their appearance—and even musical tastes—to conform to this new identity. They see themselves as part of a *culture,* with all the artifacts that cultures possess.

During this process, old friends drift away: a few because they are uncomfortable with the new sexual orientation, others because they just don't fit in with the new lifestyle. This narrowing circle of friends makes gay life even more insular. Participants see the world in terms of gays (or more recently *queers*) versus everybody else.

Bisexuals put a chink in this insularity. We don't fit into the us-versus-them bunker mentality. Homosexuals see us as either liars or traitors.

Bisexuals are liars, some say, because they are really heterosexuals pretending to be partially gay. They want to be trendy, hip, sensitive, or politically correct. They are traitors, say others, because they are really homosexuals pretending to be partially heterosexual. They want to make themselves more acceptable to the "straight world." In either case, bisexuals are a threat to the pat identity that has so neatly defined things for *gay* people.

Homosexuals see bisexuals as people trying to steal their culture. Gays resent us because they struggle to "come out" and develop their very clear identity. Then along comes someone who takes a key part of that identity—same sex attraction—and says "I can do this too—but I don't have the same identity as you do."

TOWARD A BISEXUAL POINT OF VIEW

Most bi theorists try to justify the bisexual position in Queer Theory. Some research Great Moments in Bisexual History, spending hours proving that both Einstein and Attila the Hun were bisexual. Instead of copying other identity movements, we should develop a theory of bisexuality that is different. We need a contrast to the gay point of view. Something different from identity politics in general.

Basic to this alternate theory is the concept of a sphere of human sexuality. Masculinity, femininity, attraction to males, attraction to females, passivity, aggressiveness, horniness, disinterest—all are examples of qualities included in this sphere. Although everyone is *somewhere* on some combination of axes, an individual's position is not fixed. A person can be in one place today, another tomorrow, and another in an hour.

Moreover, more of one quality does NOT mean less of another quality. Being extremely masculine, for example, is independent of being extremely feminine. Minor attraction to males does not imply major attraction to females. You can be both—or neither.

Because this sphere is open and fluid, *everyone* has a place in it. This sphere with its many axes is bisexuality. This theory says, *everyone is bisexual.*

Bisexual is to our sexuality what human is to our species. It is inclusive. It is not an identity. Bisexuality, in this way, tears down the walls between various sexual identities. Transsexuals are in the same group (sphere) as leather boys, who are in the same group (sphere) as *Playboy* readers, who are in the same group (sphere) as Jerry Falwell. There are no walls, only a fluid range of possibilities, open to everyone.

Instead of basing sexual actions on a preconceived self-image or identity, people can act in any way they want. Those actions will be consistent with their being bisexual, because they all take place within the bisexual sphere.

Even those rare people who may *never* be physically or emotionally attracted to one or another gender would be in the sphere. They have the *potential* to be attracted to various genders; that potential is reflected in the sphere. They may never act on that potential, but they are free to do so.

Identity politics deny people that freedom of fluidity. If people act in ways counter to their identity, they suffer an *identity crisis.* Identity limits action—and emotion.

THE FOCUS OF A BISEXUAL MOVEMENT

Instead of developing a "bisexual community," I propose a bisexual movement based on building a sexual consensus. Instead of strengthening disparate sexual identities, bisexuals would concentrate on eliminating them.

This would make bisexuals subversive to all sides of the "orientation" war. Those who demand that "lesbians and gays" be included in every piece of civil rights legislation lose their constituency. There are no separate lesbians and gays. The focus shifts from an exclusive "what I am" to an open "what I do."

OBJECTIONS TO THIS THEORY

Having discussed this theory at great length, I have met with several basic objections:

1. *Bisexuality has a specific meaning, with a specific history. You're making up something completely new and calling it bisexual. It'll confuse people.*
First, those of us who call ourselves bisexual are more aware of sexual choices. We see the greater possiblities in the sexual world than do monosexuals or asexuals. We have the ability to be a springboard toward an inclusive, sexually liberating point of view.
Second, it is the *lack* of bisexual visibility that allows us the freedom to use the word in new ways. When people hear *bisexual,* they have less of a preconceived notion than when they hear "gay" or "straight." The movement is very young. That means we can create what we like with a minimum of historical baggage.
Perhaps we could use *pansexual* to describe this theory. Those who feel uncomfortable about using bisexual in a new way might try this term to see if it makes things easier. I choose not to use it because, to me, it sounds jargony and confusing.
People know that bisexuals have more gender options than monosexuals or asexuals. By theorizing a universal bisexuality, we're saying *everyone* has these options—and more.

2. *Why should we destroy someone else's identity? People should be able to think of themselves any way they want to.*
If an exclusive sexual identity is narrow and isolating . . . if it prohibits growth in various directions . . . if it limits actions, puts people in mental ghettos, and creates a new minority group . . . and if these results are undesirable, then an exclusive sexual identity is also undesirable.
Not only is it destructive to the individuals trapped in that iden-

tity, but it is harmful to society in general. Exclusive sexual identities perpetuate the myth of discrete sexual groups, that is, discrete groups whose members share the same set of characteristics. (Lately, some people even claim these characteristics are biological. Similar claims were made by the Third Reich in the 1930s and 1940s.) The existence of discrete groups makes discrimination and stereotyping easy.

3. *Isn't it a tougher goal to convince everyone they are bisexual (pansexual), than to convince them that bisexuals (pansexuals) deserve equal rights?*

If my concept of bisexuality were goal-oriented, then this criticism would be well deserved. It is much easier to convince people to respect the rights of others, than to convince them there *are* no others. But my theory is not intended to convince people; it is intended as a way of looking at human sexuality and sexual politics. From this point of view, it is no more difficult than looking at the world through a telescope rather than a microscope.

There are practical implications, of course. For example, bisexuals would not be content with a law legalizing same-sex marriage. Instead, they would support a law that legalizes marriage among any group of consenting people. Here, as elsewhere, I take an inclusive rather than an exclusive stance.

4. *Wouldn't it be easier to say that people are just* sexual*? Why use "bisexual" to mean what most people mean by* sexual*?*

It may be that all people are *sexual* (have a sexual aspect to their lives). There are asexual people who would debate this. But that is not the point of this theory. That all people are *bisexual* means that we have the entire sphere of sexuality open to us—and we're free to move throughout that sphere. You can be *sexual* by yourself in a cage. I want to remove the cage.

WHERE DOES THIS LEAD?

Right now an increasing number of people enjoy sex with variously gendered partners. They are not part of a queer movement. They view their activities as normal. In much of the world, what we in the U.S. call *bisexual* is the norm.

In Thailand, for example, same-sex sexual activities are common. The idea of *gay* is reserved for *lady boys,* effeminate men who engage only in passive anal sex. In much of the old hippie and current anarchopunk subcultures, bisexuality is a given. Someone who would say they could never do IT with either a boy or a girl is considered strange. The openness of their politics and the value they place on personal freedom makes such limitations impossible. Even people in these groups who say that they are homo- or heterosexual will often say, "I don't deny that someday I might. . . . "

Such people are left out by those who see sexual identity as defined only in terms of oppression. They do not feel oppressed. They have eliminated the sexual divisiveness created by identities. They view people as people, not as gay, bi, or straight.

I'll use an analogy. Some people have earlobes that are attached on the bottom. Some have loose earlobes that enable to you stick your finger between the lobe and jaw. Although these differences exist, we don't divide the world into lobe-attached or lobe-unattached people. There is no lobe check-off on employment forms. Lobe-attached people don't have their own bars or liberation movements. Lobism is not a major problem. The differences still exist. I wouldn't want to eliminate the diversity. But we don't have the categories and the divisions those categories bring.

Sexuality should be like earlobes. We'd still have the same variety, but we would no longer divide the world in the same way. There would be no us and them. Ideally there would not even be words to separate these groups. A world like this would be a world that is sexually free. A bisexual viewpoint can bring that freedom.

NOTES

1. Since this proposal is new, it's bound to be flawed. It's not the answer, but a compass pointing toward the direction I'd like to go. It can only develop through give and take, feedback and revision. The discussion should, and will, continue.

2. Throughout this essay I use *sex* and *gender* interchangeably. That reflects my opinion that there are no discrete sexes or genders. Instead, gender/sex is a spectrum—similar to the one I'll propose for orientation. When I reluctantly refer to *the opposite sex,* I'm speaking about traditional male/female distinctions, often called sexes. In the traditional view, this is different from gender which is more vague and with more possibilities.

Me, Myself, and You:
Identity Politics in Action

Susanna Trnka

A friend of mine doesn't believe in identity politics. "Look at Clarence Thomas, does he represent the interests of most African Americans?" she asks. "And Phyllis Schlafly—you can hardly claim she's promoting women's rights."

True. But it is also true that at the newspaper I write for, I push coverage of bisexual issues *because I am bisexual.* I also attend queer fund raisers, support queer candidates, and demonstrate to protect the rights of gay men, lesbians, bisexuals, and transsexuals *because I am bisexual.*

My politics are a direct outgrowth of my identity as a bisexual person. Clarence Thomas bases his politics in some understanding of who he is (be it as a person of color, as a man, or as a human being, I can only speculate) as does Phyllis Schlafly. Each of our politics comes out of an understanding of our identities.

Part of the common misunderstanding around identity politics is that claiming a connection between identity and politics means that identity *equals* a certain kind of politics. Generally this kind of reductionist thinking assumes that a straight white man will be conservative, while a woman or person of color will be progressive. If this were the case, then Thomas and Schlafly would in fact throw a wrench into the whole equation.

The "identity equals politics" assumption takes for granted *how* you will interpret your identity. Recognizing that you are a woman does not necessarily lead you to recognize the existence of a patriarchy that uses issues, such as your sexuality or your reproductive rights, against you. But understanding patriarchy does alter your understanding of yourself as a woman to take into account the effects of these political forces.

I am involved in radical, "progressive" politics not because I'm a woman or because I'm bisexual, but because of how I understand what it means to be a woman and to be bisexual. My identity is political not because of who I *am,* but because of how I *interpret* who I am and how I link my understanding of myself to the structures of power in the U.S.

I didn't become politically active through a bisexual group, but in a queer women's discussion group where we hotly debated the politics of being queer, staged kiss-ins in local homophobic restaurants, and organized a protest against the homophobic and biphobic blockbuster film *Basic Instinct.* Having found an identity and a community as a queer woman, it seemed logical, exhilarating, frightening, but also necessary, to protect these parts of myself from cultural and political attack.

I later began to explore the political differences between identifying as lesbian and identifying as bisexual, and integrated a broader bisexual outlook into my politics. I recognized the connections between myself and bisexual men, without rejecting my identity first and foremost as a queer *woman.* Through this process, being a woman became for me inextricably tied to being a feminist, and being bisexual resulted in a commitment to queer politics.

A second factor influencing the relationship between identity and politics is social and political context. Not every aspect of identity is necessarily political at any given time. Most people who know me can't escape learning that I'm queer but hardly anyone is aware that I'm an atheist. Both of these are important aspects of how I define myself, but at times one of them is politically salient and the other is not. When I attended (public) high school in Virginia I was surrounded by Christian rhetoric, primarily because the school was run by a principal who constantly reminded his students that "we are all united by our belief in God." Vocally expressing myself as an atheist was how I protected my identity, and how I challenged assumptions about my beliefs.

Once I graduated, however, this part of myself was in a sense "depoliticized." Because I can now believe and practice (or not practice) whatever I choose, and since I no longer feel threatened or alienated because of it, being an atheist is not as "publicized" a part of me, nor something I need to broadcast. The threatening, discriminatory situation in my high school was what brought my atheist convictions to the surface of my identity.

In a similar way, resistance to political and cultural repression has brought sexual identification to the forefront of some people's activism. My bisexuality is not only emotional and physical, but also political, precisely because I live in a society that constructs sexuality as political.

Identity politics has been criticized for focusing too much on the individual and stopping short of integrating the personal with the global or with other people's experiences. Identity politics does begin with your own identity, but it doesn't have to stop there. It can in fact compel you to engage your own experience of oppression in an analysis of the multiple systems of exploitation that cross-cut our society.

As a white, first-generation American, bisexual woman I can look at how the dominant system oppresses me for my differences and use this knowledge to help me learn about the discrimination faced by other groups, such as Latino/Latina immigrants, people on welfare, or the elderly. Our experiences and struggles are not the same and are not interchangeable. But because I understand my own oppression, I am aware of the fact that I live in an unfair, discriminatory society. This awareness of inequality in turn makes me more able and likely to believe that others are discriminated against and to support them in their struggles for liberation.

These connections are not inherent, immediate, or easy. If they were, there would be no need for education and activism. But when we do make such connections, they are grounded in something we are not likely to forget: our own struggles, our own identities, our own lives. Thus they are more likely to last than the political fervor, anger, or pity that often arise from politics based on issues that we perceive as totally unrelated to ourselves.

Our issues as bisexuals are more often than not inextricable from those of the larger queer community. Combating homophobia, promoting domestic partnership laws, fighting job discrimination, and proclaiming the right to define our own sexuality and to consensually love whomever we choose in whatever ways we choose—these issues are also significant to many gay men, lesbians, and other sexual minorities.

Biphobia does exist in the queer community and it must be addressed, but it should not rip our community apart. Racism, classism, ageism, ableism, discrimination against transsexuals and transvestites, also divide the queer community and need to be addressed. But should they splinter us into tiny clusters of activists who can see no further than "our own" issues? It is one thing for each of us to know "our own" issues, and another for us to attempt to build thousands, or perhaps millions, of tiny, fragmented "movements" and hope to get anything done.

An essential yet often overlooked step in identity politics is going beyond understanding the political implications of your own identity to understanding those of others and recognizing the bonds that exist between you and them. Perhaps we can learn from bell hooks (1984, p. 65) when she writes of feminist struggle:

> Women do not need to eradicate difference to feel solidarity. We do not need to share a common oppression to fight equally to end oppression. . . . We can be sisters united by shared interests and beliefs, united in appreciation for diversity, united in our struggle to end sexist oppression, united in political solidarity.

These are the kinds of lessons we need to apply to not only bisexual politics, feminist politics, and queer politics, but also to progressive politics in general.

Throughout this essay I have used personal examples to illustrate how individuals can name their own identity (or identities), recognize and act upon the political implications of their identities, and begin to make connections between "their community" and other communities and groups of oppressed peoples. Exploring our own identities can be a viable and powerful political tool. The role of identity in progressive politics needs to be expanded upon and critiqued, but not thrown away. For it is by beginning with ourselves and looking outward, that we can truly begin to build strong and solid liberation movements.

Forsaking All Others: A Bifeminist Discussion of Compulsory Monogamy

Annie S. Murray

Many people assume that bisexuals are nonmonogamous by nature. When I talk to monosexuals of all flavors about bisexuality, no sooner does "bisexual" cross my lips than "nonmonogamy" crosses theirs, as if the words were directly linked in some huge dictionary network in the brain. I used to respond by trying to erase that link, pointing out that people of all sexual orientations can be either monogamous or nonmonogamous. This is a valid point, but it buys into negative images of nonmonogamy that I would like to dispel. So I take a different tack now, challenging the underlying belief that there is something wrong with nonmonogamy in the first place. With my new response I seek a consciousness heightened by a bisexual feminism, questioning the social and political forces that influence people's personal choices.

A bisexual politic rooted in feminism must examine issues such as monogamy head-on, rather than dance defensively around controversial questions. I like to use the moments when people's anti-monogamy assumptions are revealed to encourage them to challenge the system of compulsory monogamy, regardless of the kind of relationships they would like to build for themselves.

This essay discusses monogamy from an explicitly bifeminist standpoint. One could easily instead defend the choice of nonmono-

---

I would like to thank Robyn Ochs, who taught the course on bisexuality at MIT, for which I submitted an earlier version of this essay. I thank her for her helpful comments and especially for her friendship and cheerful openness to criticism. I would also like to thank my beloved Rebecca Kaplan, a wonderful bifeminist friend without whose persistent ideas and encouragement this essay would have been abandoned.

gamy on libertarian grounds: if someone wants to have multiple sexual partners, and is open and honest about it, and isn't hurting anyone, then why not? But a bifeminist perspective delves deeper into the origins and perpetuation of compulsory monogamy as a political institution. We all need to examine carefully the choices we make whenever we believe we are acting freely. It is this questioning that the libertarian defense lacks. Are we reacting? Are we assimilating? How do we argue for what we believe? Our choices are political, and our explanations for our choices have political impact. Accusations of nonmonogamy are hurled at bisexuals, much the way the accusation of lesbianism is hurled at feminists. Before we bisexuals get our backs up sputtering denial, let's be sure we have critically examined the expectation of monogamy.

THE INSTITUTION OF MONOGAMY

Monogamy is such a powerful social norm that it is rarely questioned. It is practically invisible. It is not perceived as something that needs explanation, because it isn't perceived at all. It is non-monogamy that stands out, and nonmonogamous people who are asked to explain themselves. However, precisely because the norm of monogamy is so powerful, it is vital that we question it. To begin, we need a definition of monogamy.

Bisexual activist Rebecca Kaplan and I co-facilitated a workshop on nonmonogamy at the National Conference Celebrating Bisexuality in Washington, DC in 1993, and have since conducted a few more such workshops. We begin these workshops by asking different people about the rules and definitions of their monogamous relationships, and we have heard a pile of different answers. For some, monogamy means one can have casual sex outside the relationship, but not any emotional attachment. For others, it means love and intimacy are okay, just no sex. For some people the emphasis on monogamy applies to one's own behavior, for others it applies to one's partner's behavior. For some people, it means one couldn't even have lunch with or fantasies about anyone who could ever be a prospective sexual partner.

John McMurty (1975, p.171) defines monogamy as the "formal exclusion of all others from erotic contact with the marriage partner." This means your partner can't have erotic contact with anyone but you. I would add to this definition that you can't have erotic contact with anyone else either. If we can set aside for now the question of whether "erotic contact" means lunch or sex or love, we have a working definition. Once you have selected one person with whom you enjoy erotic contact, you must prohibit that person, and yourself, from choosing to have erotic contact (even of a different sort) with any other person.

Monogamy is one of the few contracts in which relations with other parties are relevant to the partnership. If your company doesn't want you working for anyone else, it must state this exclusivity specifically in your contract. Otherwise, you can assume it is acceptable to take jobs with other employers too (though not on company time, of course). I find it strange that in sexual relationships, the exclusive arrangement is the default, and the open arrangement is the marked case. Furthermore, an employee's commitment to a company isn't automatically questioned just because the employee does some work for someone else. You can coach Little League and your boss will never worry that you will leave the carpentry business. The threat appears only when you do some work for a competitor. Are all other people are considered competitors to a sexual relationship?

When I ask monogamous people why they do not choose non-monogamy, many tell me they would fear losing their partner to someone else. But when I ask nonmonogamous people why they do not choose monogamy, they often give the same answer. Allowing a lover to date other people may make you afraid that your lover will leave you for someone else. But in a monogamous relationship, it is the potential, unexplored (or covertly explored) relationship that is threatening; even a mild sexual interest in someone else can be enough to end a monogamous relationship. Both types of relationship require constant negotiation and compromise, and both types of relationship can be equally challenged by jealousy and rejection.

When I ask people why they think monogamy is the cultural norm, most mention that it may be the "natural" way that we form relationships. We have all heard the "natural" argument before, and we know where it gets us. Heterosexuality is supposed to be "natural," too. Why is it that what feels natural to some must be imposed on all? As McMurty (1975, p.168) points out, "if it were truly 'natural,' of course, there would be no need for its rigorous cultural prescription by everything from severe criminal law, to ubiquitous housing regulations." In the standard Christian marriage vows, couples commit to "forsaking all others." We don't commit to eating and sleeping. We don't need to commit to what comes naturally.

Our current norm of the monogamous couple is clearly tied to the institution of marriage. This institution is one that benefits men at women's expense, guaranteeing every man the full control of at least one woman. Marriage is based on a model of property rights (such as exclusive ownership) rather than a common partnership. Furthermore, within this system, a man can know that he is the father of any children his wife bears. The nonmonogamous woman is a threat to such a system. How would one determine patrilineage when a nonmonogamous woman bears a child? How could one maintain a system in which power and property get passed from father to son? In the heterosexual world, monogamy serves the patriarchy by enabling patrilineage.

We cannot fault women for participating in this system, as it has offered many of us protection from sexism elsewhere in society. By allowing one man full access to her body, a woman can obtain his protection from other men. She can deny responsibility, and avoid other men's anger, for refusing them erotic contact (having at her disposal such defenses as "My husband would never allow it"). By keeping paternity unambiguous, monogamous women can encourage their husbands to be invested in the welfare of their children. (Often for similar reasons, women will follow the custom of giving children their father's name.) For women whose marriages give them access to financial support, a monogamous system is a guarantee of continued financial security.

By offering these protections, monogamy becomes a central element in sexual power relations. The picture is further complicated by some deeply ingrained beliefs about sexual differences between men and women. Women are supposed to naturally contribute monogamous energy and commitment to their relationships, while men supposedly express (or struggle against) an instinct for nonmonogamy and "spreading their seed." This double-standard is rooted in a system in which men control women and their sexuality. (That is why there are such terms as "wife-swapping," but not "husband-swapping." The "ownership" does not apply equally in both directions.) For men to behave nonmonogamously does not threaten this system, so it is more acceptable for men to have premarital intercourse, solicit the services of prostitutes, or seek extramarital affairs. Women who engage in these behaviors are called "sluts," a word used to keep women's sexual behavior in line. (Again, it is relevant that there is no equivalent word for men.)

As we work toward a feminist world, why should we hold monogamy as an ideal? After all, monogamy contradicts the feminist goal of women's control of their own bodies and decisions about their own sexual agency. I am skeptical of a system which takes as an ideal putting decisions about my body into the hands of a sexual partner, male or female. It may feel safer; it may be easier; but it is not empowering. I need to be able to say "yes" and "no" for myself. The problem is that a woman is at risk in a world where her "no" is not respected. Empowering solutions would make people listen to that "no." Protective solutions (such as compulsory monogamy) don't let the question ever be asked of her.

We each have two decisions to make in considering the issue of monogamy. The first is whether we should choose to be monogamous in our own relationships. The second is whether we should participate in the promotion of the monogamous norm. In the past, increasing women's sexual availability has not served women well. Increasing men's sexual access to women is certainly not central to a feminist agenda. Instead, we feminists tend to focus on reducing that access and increasing women's safety. Monogamy as a norm, like heterosexuality and homosexuality, increases our safety by creating entire classes of "safe people," people who are unquestioningly denied sexual access. Bisexuality and nonmonogamy both undermine these classes of safe people.

"SAFE" PEOPLE

People often encounter uncomfortable (at best) moments when they need to say "no" to unwanted sexual advances or energy. Relationships with friends or co-workers are easier when we know this situation won't come up. Within a heterosexual context, it is easy for women to develop very intimate friendships with other women, since there is clearly no possibility of a sexual dynamic developing. Lesbian and gay identities provide that same "freedom." This phenomenon partly explains the easy interactions between some lesbians and gay men. Warren Blumenfeld, a gay author, notes that he enjoys the ease of interaction that safe people offer:

> With lesbians, it is a given that our relationship will not be sexual, so I find that there is the possibility of a solid friendship developing, free from the tension of sexual feelings. (Blumenfeld, 1992, p. 241)

Sexual feelings supposedly *get in the way* of deeper friendship. Negotiating sexual feelings is awkward. It is easier when external, uncontrollable factors will do that negotiating for us, such as when people are the "safe" gender, or already have a sexual partner. Nonmonogamy exacerbates this problem, especially when combined with bisexuality. Bisexuals have all encountered this awkwardness already. How many of us have come out to someone in a way that made that person no longer on the other side of a safety net? A woman may come out as lesbian or bisexual to a straight woman friend, for example, only to have the friend worry about being hit on. Not only is the sexual dynamic automatically absent with someone who is a "safe" person, but the sexual dynamic is presumed to be automatically present with someone who is not.

Nonmonogamous bisexuality forces people to make active, conscious decisions about when and whether to become sexual with someone. A nonmonogamous bisexual can never know, just based on their own relationship status and someone else's gender, that there will be no sexual feelings with a given person. (Of course, variables other than gender, such as race, age, size, and ability, can still put whole classes of people "out of bounds." This issue could fill several more essays.)

People who have experienced a transition (such as a change in sexual orientation) so that groups previously considered "out of bounds" are suddenly potential sexual partners, know the difficulty of consciously considering sexual dynamics. But this conscious consideration is important. When we control the decisions about our own desires, we can examine our desires with our politics in mind.

Giving up the safety net of "safe people" requires a constant evaluation of the status of your relationships. To choose nonmonogamy is to decline a particular protection, and involves some risks. It demands the self-awareness to know what you want, the strength to ask for it, the sensitivity to hear a refusal, and the power to refuse what you don't want and have that refusal be respected. Maintaining successful nonmonogamous relationships requires these abilities. Oddly enough, many view nonmonogamy as an inability rather than an ability.

THE STEREOTYPE: BISEXUALS CAN'T BE MONOGAMOUS

Almost every reference to bisexuals in the mainstream media portrays us as nonmonogamous and dissatisfied. As a typical example, one *Newsweek* cover article (Gelman, 1987) entitled "A Perilous Double Love Life," focused on the bisexual as nonmonogamous, unreformable, and dishonest with himself (almost all references pertained only to men) and his lovers. The bisexual was thus a dangerous link, spreading AIDS from the homosexual community to the unsuspecting heterosexual community.

Even some of the less vicious images of bisexuals still assume we need multiple partners. In 1987, *The Boston Phoenix,* a weekly newspaper that prints fairly explicit gay and lesbian personal ads, refused to allow a bisexual man to place a personal because of this stereotype. The classified advertising manager, Neil Kosak, explained the paper's position: "The personals are for people looking for longterm, monogamous relationships . . . we don't allow [bisexual ads] because the connotation is sexual." Amy Silberman, the senior classified lines representative, expressed the stereotype even more bluntly: "If you're bisexual, it's implicit in the meaning that you're not monogamous" (*Bay Windows,* 1987).

Two misguided lines of logic lead people to this stereotype. The first argument is fairly straightforward: Since bisexuals are sexually attracted to both "male" and "female" qualities, it is impossible for them to be satisfied sexually with only one person. If we examine any characteristic other than gender, it is quickly clear that this reasoning is flawed. If someone is attracted to both blondes and brunettes, would it be impossible for them to be satisfied with only one person? If they like redheads, too, would they always need three lovers? Since when have we expected the object of our affections to exhibit every last quality that attracts us? Anyone who has ever been in a monogamous relationship knows there will be some qualities that attract you that are not found in your partner. This does not mean the relationship is unsatisfying, or that we need to seek those qualities elsewhere. The ability to be attracted to different kinds of people does not equal the necessity to simultaneously date one of each kind.

The second faulty argument is a logical error that stems from how we determine people's sexual identities. As Orlando commented in an article in *Ms.* (October 1978, p. 60): "The world would define me not by my own sexuality, but by my lover's gender." People's sexual identity is defined by the gender of their sexual partner, rather than by any potential for intimacy. If we ignore people's potentials, those who have only one lover would never need to call themselves bisexual. Only people with multiple lovers of differing genders would need to "resort" to this term. So, when people identify as bisexual, others may assume they must have multiple lovers.

I have encountered an additional attitude, mostly in gay and lesbian communities, that also explains the strong association between bisexuality and nonmonogamy. To some people, bisexuality represents an inability to decide, or a lack of courage to commit. They believe nonmonogamy, too, stems from indecisiveness and lack of commitment. Bisexuality and nonmonogamy are accepted only as stages en route to a new consciousness in which we truly reject heterosexuality. Here's how they view bisexuals: We begin as unenlightened heterosexuals, with a partner of the opposite sex. In our first stage toward enlightenment, we take up a same-sex lover. We later drop our opposite-sex lover. Along the way, we are in a bisexual, nonmonogamous "phase." Those of us "still" in that phase are supposedly less mature, or less developed in terms of our sexual identity, than people with a single, same-sex lover. This kind of biphobic logic forms the basis of the statement made by Jean

O'Leary, then Executive Director of the National Gay Rights Advocates, when asked about whether bisexuals belong in the gay rights
movement:

> [Bisexual] people are very important [in the Gay Rights
> Movement]. When we say there are 20 million Americans that
> are Gay people or have the potential of being Gay, we're not
> saying there's 20 million people who are out of the closet and
> ready to get married to their lifemate. We're saying there's 20
> million out there at different phases of this coming out pro-
> cess; some of them are still married to heterosexuals. (North,
> 1989)

Beneath all three of these attitudes lies the assumption that both
bisexuality and nonmonogamy can only be unconscious, apolitical
choices, rather than intentional political ones. To counter such negative attitudes, we need to publicly discuss the political thinking
behind our behavioral choices. Unfortunately, when we speak publicly as bisexuals we have not been responding this way.

THE TYPICAL RESPONSE: WE CAN BE MONOGAMOUS!

Many bisexual women, especially those coming from a lesbian-
feminist background, are quick to point out (as I used to) that
bisexuals, too, are capable of monogamy. There is a subtle anti-non-
monogamy flavor to these protests. Rather than jumping to defend
the choice of nonmonogamy, we delicately note that it is not pecu-
liar to bisexuals, as in the following statement written by bisexual
writer Lisa Orlando (1984):

> Other gay people will be forced to recognize that as a group
> bisexuals are no more "promiscuous" or incapable of commit-
> ment than anyone else (like many stereotypes of bisexuals, this
> also runs rampant in the straight world).

Remember the straight feminists who would carefully point out
that most feminists were not, in fact, lesbians? Lesbianism was
embarrassing to the women's liberation movement because it made

feminists' motives seem sexual (or anti-male). Rather than use the opportunity to examine their own heterosexual choice, and the sexism inherent in lesbian-baiting, some straight women tried to downplay the lesbian presence, and lesbians were appalled at the homophobia behind their denial. Similarly, many monogamous bisexual feminists try to downplay the presence of nonmonogamy in bi women's communities. Nonmonogamy is often associated with the word "promiscuity" in ways that reveal a fear of pro-sex attitudes and sexual motives. One such example came from a longtime bisexual activist who had been interviewed for the biphobic *Newsweek* article mentioned above. She was justifiably furious at its unbalanced portrayal of bisexuals, and she wrote:

> During my interview, I devoted considerable attention to a definition of bisexuality . . ., emphasizing that bisexuals are *not* by definition promiscuous, nonmonogamous, or sexcrazed. Some bisexuals may be so, but then too are some heterosexuals and some homosexuals.
>
> I discussed my own lifestyle, which is monogamous. (Ochs, 1987)

While it is true that people of all sexual preferences may choose to be monogamous or nonmonogamous, to constantly and defensively point out this fact, in the absence of explicitly validating nonmonogamy as a choice, indicates a certain discomfort with the issue of nonmonogamy, and a belief in the superiority of the monogamous norm. This point is subtle, but I believe it is an important one. Consider how different our response is when people dismiss our bisexual identity as "merely a phase." When we hear this accusation, we reply, "Some bisexuals are going through a phase. As are some lesbians, some gay men, and some heterosexuals. But there's nothing wrong with going through a phase. Every stage of our life, and every choice, is part of our growth and development." Every relationship that lies behind us can be considered a phase, as can our previous homes, our old jobs, or our years as students. We do not need to view our earlier phases with regret, nor scorn phases simply because they are not permanent. We cannot assume we were less committed in the past than we are now to today's choices. And we should never assume that someone whose current choices resemble previous ones of our own is in the same "phase" we were in when we made those choices. For example, if I think quitting my job was copping out when I did it, I cannot assume you are copping out when you choose to quit your job.

The accusation that our bisexuality is "merely a phase" has prompted some good thinking about the importance of phases in our lives. I would like to see bisexuals be similarly motivated by the accusations of nonmonogamy to examine the institution of monogamy, both within bisexual communities and in the cultures that surround us. If we want to make such an examination clearly, we should avoid making stereotyping statements such as: "Some of us are monogamous and tenacious; others are promiscuous and restless" (Ochs and Deihl, 1992, p. 68).

HOW DOES A BISEXUAL PERSPECTIVE OF MONOGAMY RELATE TO A LARGER BIFEMINISM?

Bisexuals have a particular perspective from which to examine cultural norms such as monogamy. As we watch many of our gay and lesbian brothers and sisters rush to accommodate mainstream values, let's examine the insights offered by our own experiences about individual roles in sexual relationships. A bisexual political perspective is informed by our ability to observe how we act when we are intimate with men and with women. Do we have different expectations of our male and female partners? Do we have different expectations of ourselves with male partners as opposed to female partners? Do we expect that women should be more "faithful"? Are we more jealous when our lovers date men or women? Do we assign blame differently according to gender?

Already, bisexuals are forced to question why the existing conventions should govern the types of relationships we choose. We should neither unthinkingly react to, nor unquestionably assimilate, societal mainstream norms. Let's make our choices with our feminist goals in mind, and with an awareness of the sexist origins behind many of our customs. We don't need to shun heterosexual choices of partners or sexual activities, but we know that we are still responsible for regarding these choices with suspicion when we make them. The same is true of our choices about monogamy. Let's not use monogamy as an excuse to avoid examining the erotic dynamic of any relationship, sexual or nonsexual.

Within a framework where open, honest nonmonogamy is a real option, one could still choose to be monogamous. In fact, until nonmonogamy is a valid alternative, one can never know that their monogamy is freely chosen.

Framing Radical Bisexuality:
Toward a Gender Agenda

Jill Nagle

In this essay, I frame radical bisexuality in a model that connects the gender-related oppressions—heterosexism, monosexism, and sexism—within genderism (see Figure 1). Genderism is the artificial channeling of people into two biological sexes, which oppresses those who challenge this duality. My model shows the gender constructs within which bisexuality is (mis)understood, accepted, and rejected as pathological or nonexistent, and also implies that those targeted by gender-related oppression (all women as well as intersexual,[1] bisexual, transgender, lesbian, and gay people[2]) need to work as allies toward dismantling our common, interconnected oppression.

My argument for this model is threefold. First, defining the terms in the model reveals genderism as the conceptual root, or parent oppression of the other three gender-related oppressions (GROs). Second, eliminating any of the other three GROs would not eliminate genderism, but eliminating genderism would eliminate the three "offspring" GROs. Third, the degree to which a particular target group of GRO challenges genderism correlates with that group's audibility and visibility. Each of these premises illustrates genderism's primacy in a slightly different way.

An embryonic form of this essay was published as "Bi, Bi Labels–Hello, Queer Liberation" in the Winter, 1990 issue of *BiFocus, the Newsletter for Philadelphia's Bisexual Community.* I expanded upon those ideas in a handout entitled "Live Theory and Clear Practice: A Thinkbook for Bisexual Activists (and Other Subversive Types)," presented at the April, 1993 National Conference Celebrating Bisexuality. Many, many thanks go to Cheryl Chase, Beth Hackett, Liz Highleyman, Juan Francisco Hulse, Rebecca Kaplan, Henry S. Rubin, Gregory Sax, Ray Schnitzler, and Annie Senghas, whose brilliance and support helped this essay reach its current form.

FIGURE 1

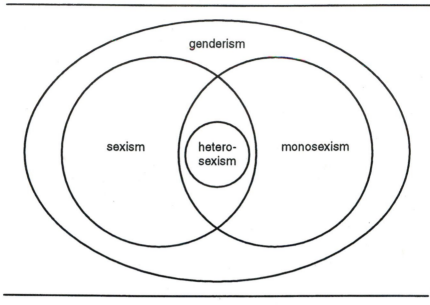

First, I define *genderism* as the notion that it is right and natural to divide people into two and only two mutually exclusive biological sexes (male and female), and the systemic oppression of those who are perceived to challenge that idea. *Sexism* is the perpetuation of particular roles and power arrangements according to the two biologically ordained, (largely) immutable sexes set forth by genderism.[3] *Monosexism* is the perpetuation of compulsory monosexuality; i.e., sexual orientation toward one and only one of the two recognized biological sexes. *Heterosexism* is the perpetuation of compulsory heterosexuality, i.e., mandatory exclusive orientation toward members of the "opposite" of one's own biological sex. So, sexism, heterosexism, and monosexism all *depend conceptually* on genderism, the division of all humans into two and only two sexes. Since the reverse is not true, i.e., genderism is not conceptually dependent on other oppressions, there is an unequal relationship, also known as a hierarchy, among the GROs.

Second, eliminating one GRO eliminates the others contained

within it, but not vice versa. Illustrating this involves a thought experiment. Starting at the center of the model, imagine a society without heterosexism. Same-sex couples have partner benefits, legal marriages, and all the other accoutrements of opposite-sex couples. Children do not torment one another with epithets like "faggot" and "homo." Gay-bashing is nonexistent. Homosexuality is, quite simply, unremarkable.

Monosexism, sexism, and genderism could still exist in such a society. Bisexual people could still be targeted as untrustworthy, confused, fence-sitters, even mentally ill, simply because they refuse to sexually orient toward just one biological sex in a monosexist society. Lesbians *as same-sex couples* might enjoy the same rights and privileges as opposite-sex couples, but could still be oppressed *as women* in a sexist society by rape, sexual harassment, lack of equal access to political and economic power, and all the rest. Finally, elevating homosexual behavior and identity to the same level of social acceptance as heterosexuality would not mean automatic acceptance for those whose gender does not fit into the categories of a still-genderist society.

Now let's move across the model to monosexism. Before envisioning a non-monosexist society, let's identify that which *is* monosexist in *this* society. Just as some feminists and right-wingers have found themselves strange bedfellows in the antipornography movement, each disavowing links with the other, so do some monosexual queers and heterosexuals find themselves on the same side of the monosexist track in rejecting, stigmatizing, or invisibilizing bisexuals. Actual examples of monosexism in this society include the following:

- An AIDS counselor asking a client if she wanted "the lesbian or the straight rap." If she were bisexual, the client's life could be compromised by incomplete information, which the counselor's (and in all likelihood, the agency's) monosexism perpetuated.
- Activists for domestic partnership benefits at a large university limiting their agenda to same-sex couples, arguing that "the straight people can organize on their own behalf" (an example of challenging heterosexism while reifying monosexism). This

approach does not address that, for bisexuals, automatic coverage for nonmarried partners should not be specific to gender.
- Assumptions that bisexual people have not yet decided or realized their "true" orientation, and conclusions that we are actually monosexual (gay when with the same sex, straight when
with the "opposite").
- Separate establishments, recreational areas, bars, clubs, resorts
that welcome only same-sex or only opposite-sex couples.

Thus, monosexism is deeply entrenched, making the world an
often unwelcoming, sometimes hostile and dangerous place for
those who are bisexually identified, inclined, or even curious. This
was evidenced when Kinsey (1948, 1952) revealed that sexuality
was much more continuous than had previously been believed; this
finding was largely ignored. I will come back to this example later.

Now, let's envision a non-monosexist society. It is still commonly acknowledged that there are two biological sexes, but identities and communities are no longer built around attractions to one,
the other, or both. Preferences might be acknowledged, such as for
hairy, smooth, fleshy, or thin partners, but biological sex would be
neither more nor less important to orientation than any other characteristic. There would be no more coming out to parents as lesbian,
gay, or bisexual—it would be as ludicrous as coming out as one
who desires curly-haired or statuesque lovers, assuming such categories were also politically neutral. Obviously, in such a society
there would be no more *hetero*sexism since the sex of one's loves
and/or lusts would be a non-issue. Thus, eliminating monosexism
would also eliminate heterosexism. However, this non-monosexist
society could still permit sexism, as I discussed above.

A non-monosexist society would also be beneficial to those who
currently have monosexual identities (lesbian, gay, and heterosexual). Without monosexism, such individuals could openly experiment with cross-preferential sexual behavior without risking rejection or stigmatization from their communities.[4] They could also fall
in love with someone of any gender without agonizing over having
to change their entire identity.[5] Monosexuality would be optional,
not compulsory.

Moving across another step on the model, let's stretch our minds to envision a society without sexism. Genderist distinctions are still made between women and men, but no power relations automatically follow from those distinctions. Sex is a "neutral" attribute. Women's health and well-being is as high a priority as men's. Women are listened to, respected, and valued. Women, as well as men, are judged by the content of their character, not the shape of their bodies. Women and men have equal access to and control over political and economic resources. Rigid roles are dissolved; women and men are both strong and gentle, breadwinners and parents, leaders and followers.

In a society without sexism, the direction of women's energy toward men in the form of heterosexual pairings would not be the compulsory cornerstone of sexual relations it is today. Man's role as sexual dominator of woman would not be paramount. Therefore, deviations from these roles in the form of same-sex relationships would no longer be remarkable.[6] In other words, a society without sexism would have no ideological basis for heterosexism.

While a nonsexist society might be *less* monosexist, eliminating sexism would not entirely eliminate monosexism, nor would eliminating monosexism necessarily eliminate sexism. Neither appears to be original or fundamental with respect to the other, though it seems clear that both are rooted in genderism, and that the elimination of arguably either, but certainly both, would eliminate heterosexism.

Finally, let's envision a non-genderist society. In this society, "women" and "men" use the same bathrooms. The sex of a newborn is no longer of paramount concern. Intersexual children are allowed to grow up unmutilated, with no social stigma. The terms "women" and "men" are used loosely, if at all. Thus, some "women" have penises, some "men" wombs and/or vulvas; some people have genitals of both sexes. Although most people are identifiable by their bodies as what we now call male and female, gender presentation is treated with a much more relaxed, playful attitude.

From this final perspective, it is easy to see how, as gender becomes a more fluid aspect of social life, sexism begins to erode. Sexism *requires* genderism's rigid identifying distinctions that create "women" and "men." Without these, it becomes difficult or impossible to enforce a system in which one "sex" has power over another. How do you tell who is supposed to oppress whom? Monosexism also erodes, since it depends heavily on genderist definitions. After all, what if it were unclear which people one's orientation allowed one to be sexual with? And with monosexism and sexism, as I argue above, goes heterosexism.

I have so far argued for a model of gender-related oppressions with genderism as the inclusive paradigm, sexism and monosexism contained therein (though overlapping), and heterosexism within those. To that I add that since sexism, monosexism, and heterosexism are all conceptually rooted in genderism, they are ultimately also *forms of* genderism. Bisexuals are targeted not only by heterosexism from heterosexuals, but also by monosexism, from monosexuals, a group that includes both hetero- *and* homosexuals.

The third and final prong of my argument is that all other things being held constant, there is a relative disparity in access to mainstream resources among those targeted by GRO. Those who challenge genderism the most receive the least mainstream prominence and support. For example, gay men (and to a lesser extent lesbians) enjoy support from organizations (such as Parents and Friends of Lesbians and Gays, the National Gay and Lesbian Task Force), mainstream media (lesbians on the cover of *Newsweek),* and money (many foundations now have specific programs to assist lesbians and gay men). In contrast, bisexuals and transgendered people sorely lack such recognition and support. The road to mainstream acceptance of bisexuals and transgendered people has been slower because of our greater challenge to genderism. Unfortunately, increased mainstream prominence also correlates with increased openly targeted hatred and violence.[7] I am not claiming that silence and invisibility are any better or worse than open hatred and violence. Rather, my point is that the examples above once again attest to genderism's primacy in this culture.

In a similar vein, most brands of feminism challenge sexism, or the hierarchy of gender dualism, but stop short of challenging the gender dualism (genderism) itself. When feminism does take on genderism, it inspires even more vitriolic, unabashedly genderist backlash: accusations of tampering with what women and men actually *are,* or implications that feminism would break genderism's sacred divide between male and female. Tellingly, there are few, if any references in mainstream feminism to the phenomenon of "genderism."

Given the nature of gender-related oppressions, intersexuality is perhaps one of the most direct challenges to genderism a human can embody. The silencing and invisibilizing, indeed, the nonconsensual physical eradication of people's intersexual attributes, attest loudly to the primacy of genderism, relative to other GROs. As Cheryl Chase (President, Intersex Society of North America, personal communication) put it, quoting Peter G. Brown (1993):

> The fact that the phenomenon of intersexuality is essentially unknown outside the small group of surgeons and endocrinologists *whose work consists of suppressing it* is "symptomatic of a society unwilling to accept the truth about its members" [Italics mine].

The most direct victims of genderism's violent manifestations, intersexual survivors of repeated surgical genital mutilation, are only just beginning to name their experience and challenge the deeply held beliefs that continue to justify such mistreatment.

Bisexuals have greater audibility and visibility than intersexuals because we do not challenge genderism as much. But, since we challenge genderism more than lesbians and gays, we are currently less audible and visible than they, even though our numbers may be greater. The deployment of Kinsey's research I mentioned earlier illustrates this hierarchy even further. Kinsey's research was rarely cited for its *bi*sexual content, but more frequently in support of the existence of *homo*sexuals.

To recap briefly, heterosexism, monosexism, and sexism are subordinate to the conceptual parent genderism, as evidenced by the nested meanings of the words themselves, the way their elimination is hierarchically connected, and the correlation between audibility and visibility level and degree of challenge to genderism.

I am aware that prioritizing GROs is at least partially a function of freedom from other more immediately life-threatening oppressions. In choosing to focus on GRO, I am not arguing that GRO supercedes, is the model for, or is the origin of other oppressions such as racism, classism, or religious oppression; I believe oppressions interrelate in ways too complex to explain here. I *am* arguing, however, for a conceptual hierarchy *within* the GROs I named above. While members of different GRO target groups arguably experience their particular oppressions quite differently (bisexual women versus lesbians, for example), my aim is not to prioritize the elimination of any one GRO before any other, but rather to show that all GROs are based and nested hierarchically in genderism, the elimination of which would eliminate the other GROs.

SO WHAT?

Reframing bisexuality in the context of GROs thus relocates bisexuals from having half a foot under a heterosexist rubric with the other freely roaming the fields of heterosexual privilege, to being squarely within the target range of monosexism. Far from being a cop-out, a pathology, or an indecision, radical bisexuality directly challenges deeply rooted monosexism, which simultaneously and substantially challenges the foundations of lesbian and gay oppression. *This starkly contradicts prevalent views of bisexuality as an apolitical orientation.*

However, the notion of bisexuality itself depends on the same genderist paradigm (i.e., two sexes) that I advocate working to eliminate. Therefore, radical bisexuality must embrace a future with gender plurality as well as orientational fluidity.[8] Radical bisexuality recognizes genderism as the root of monosexism, sexism, and heterosexism, by all of which bisexuals can be oppressed, hurt, or limited. So, radical bisexuality per se carries within itself the seeds of its own demise. The label "bisexual" then becomes a provisional paradigm, an idea to get beyond monosexism without remaining stuck under genderism.

Framing radical bisexuality thus makes us natural allies with members of the gender community and with those working to eliminate sexism. In addition, it gives a clear rationale for monosexual queers (i.e., lesbians and gay men) to ally with us, as well as with members of the gender community, since, again, monosexual queers also benefit from eliminating monosexism and genderism.

As perhaps with all labels, individuals need at different stages to claim the bisexual label (such as when first coming out, or when challenging oppression); clean it up (strive to make sense of its multiple meanings); and ultimately throw it out (be willing to relinquish the label in service of a common vision of a nongenderist, or multiply gendered society).[9] At times we may need to hold all of these possibilities open at the same moment. Labels will be a necessary tool for naming and combatting GROs as long as they exist (Schaef, 1981). Yet, awareness of the need for labels can and should coexist with a vision of a nongenderist world in which those labels are optional, not necessary.

NOTES

1. Intersexual means congenital intermingling of male and female sexual and/or reproductive organs. Intersexed infants are routinely surgically altered at birth, sometimes with, but often without parents' consent or even knowledge. For more information, contact the Intersex Society of North America, P.O. Box 31791, San Francisco, CA 94131.

2. I am aware that many people occupy or emphasize different or multiple identities that may change over time. I keep this reality at bay for clarity of argument.

3. If the term "sexism" did not already mean something different, I would reverse the definitions of "sexism" and "genderism." "Sexism" refers to gender roles and power arrangements, constructs better connoted by my definition of the word "genderism." That "sexism" is already used to refer to roles and power arrangements has the effect of obscuring the *primacy of genderism*, which is the central feature of my model. Also, although women are the most obvious targets of sexism, I do not discuss women or sexism explicitly herein, as that has been done very well elsewhere.

4. As an out bisexual during my undergraduate years, I often became the repository of monosexuals' bisexual confessions. Whether straight, lesbian, or gay, my monosexual friends felt terrified that they would be rejected from their larger community if they were revealed, and so swore me to secrecy. They felt that because I was bisexual (often the only out bisexual they knew), I would understand. What they did not understand was my pain about how their closetedness maintained the monosexist myths I was working so hard to challenge.

5. See Clausen (1990) for one lesbian's story of falling in love with a man.

6. Suzanne Pharr (1988) argues that homophobia is rooted in sexism. In reviewing the same, Rebecca Kaplan (1991) takes Pharr's argument one step further and argues that homophobia (which may be used synonymously with heterosexism for my purposes) is simply another offshoot of sexism, rather than a completely separate phenomenon. For example, we do not call the channeling of men and women into doctor and nurse roles in the medical profession "doctorism," though specific *forms* of sexism still need to be named in order to be challenged.

7. It is important to note that bisexuals are indeed explicitly targeted *as bisexuals* by, for example, legislation that the Christian Right is now promoting in many U.S. States and cities to restrict the rights of "homosexual, lesbian, and bisexual" people (see, for instance, Colorado Amendment 2, 1992).

8. Labels such as "pansexual" and "polymorphously perverse" may reflect this view. See Tom Geller (1990).

9. I first heard the "Claim it, clean it up, throw it out!" idea at a gather-in for bisexual practitioners of Re-evaluation Counseling held in conjunction with the 1990 National Bisexual Conference in San Francisco. The presenters were David Jernigan, Rebecca Shuster, and Clare Thompson.

The Natural Next Step

Naomi Tucker

It is logical and necessary for bisexuals to recognize the importance of gender politics—not just because transsexuals, cross-dress-
ers, and other transgender people are often *assumed* to be bisexual,
and not just because some of them are, but because we as bisexuals
are visionary in our need and desire to break down dichotomies, to
create a powerful and diverse body of queers to bash the heterosexual monolith.

If bisexuality says that gender is not a determining factor of
sexual preference, we can take our knowledge one step further to
say that gender should not be a determining factor of oppression.
Then what we have is a new language and perspective with which
to talk about sexism, gender bias in our institutions, the gendered
structure of our society: a new feminist force calling for an end to
dichotomies. It is a natural progression to then say gender need not
be such a rigid social construct. After all, if our sexual identity can
be fluid, why not our gender identity?

Our sexual lives can have a lot to say about gender. When a
woman straps on her dildo and fucks me, is that a traditional gender
role in bed? If a butch leather daddy is a bottom in bed, if I flirt with
an androgynous-looking person at a café without knowing whether
it's a woman or a man, then a serious genderfuck is in action.

I have talked to the bisexual partners of pre-op transsexuals who
feel they have the best of both worlds because their lover embodies
woman and man together. Is that not a connection between bisexuality and transgenderism?

Because sex exposes our instinctual desires and the inexplicable,

An earlier version of this essay appeared in *Anything That Moves: Beyond the
Myths of Bisexuality,* No. 4, 1992.

illogical drives that motivate us, I believe that bisexuality has a great deal to contribute to the world, beyond giving immense pleasure to a lot of people. Bisexuals who have had sex with people of different genders have a broader base of sensual experience: to love a body that reminds you of your own; to love a body that is nothing like your own; or to love a body that has something you have *and* something you don't. Similar things could be said about sex with people of different body shapes and sizes. There is something very powerful about experiencing this kind of diversity in sexuality, which I believe has the potential to carry over into the rest of our lives. Such experiences teach us about both loving ourselves and understanding differences.

Gender may be a different construct for bisexuals than for monosexual people (hetero or homo). We may be freer to experiment with or cross traditional gender lines in fantasy and sex play because we are comfortable with both hetero- and homo-eroticism. We don't restrict ourselves to the notion that we must choose, "same" or "other" in sex. So bisexuals are in a unique position to advocate for sexual diversity around gender issues, because we *feel* gender between our hands and on our skin. We learn genderfuck in the breathless moments under the sheets. We teach genderfuck when we talk about our lives without gendered pronouns, bulldozing people's assumptions about sexuality and gender.

Some of us are bisexual because we do not pay much attention to the gender of our attractions; some of us are bisexual because we do see tremendous gender differences and want to experience them all. Either way, the concept of gender is inextricably a part of our bisexuality. The mere *potential* of sex with more than one gender, whether serially or simultaneously, breaks down the social mores that create gender oppression.

With respect to our integrity as bisexuals, it is our responsibility to include transgendered people in our language, in our communities, in our politics, and in our lives. Bisexuals have been saying to the "gay/lesbian" community, THERE IS MORE THAN ONE WAY TO BE QUEER: INCLUDE US. Bisexuals can choose not to repeat the mistakes of our forerunners, and to take a giant leap forward to embrace others who've been left out of the picture.

Bisexuals should be supporting not only transgender issues but also s/m, nonmonogamy, alternative families, anarchy, sex work, radical feminism, HIV activism, disability awareness, sex-positive environments for women—or any other issues that are negatively targeted or ignored within the lesbian/gay "mainstream" and heterosexual communities.

It's time to get past our discomfort. We can learn from the pain of our own invisibility. There is no excuse for a group that has suffered alienation, as bisexuals have, to use what little power it has to make another group suffer. Unless the bi community embraces the cause of other marginalized groups and fights for their right to live alongside and amongst us, then we have learned nothing from our struggle, or from the past struggles of other liberation movements.

Pansies Against Patriarchy: Gender Blur, Bisexual Men, and Queer Liberation

Sunfrog

John Stoltenberg wrote a provocative book called *Refusing to be a Man* in which he adamantly challenges the cultural codes of masculinity but stops short of subverting those codes in favor of a new understanding of gender. Rather he dick-tates, in alleged feminist dogma, a vacuous and thoroughly phallocentric portrait of masculinity as something to be denounced and avoided by (pro)feminist men. The amorphous conception known as the "men's movement" repeatedly reifies traditional masculinity under the guise of redefinition. At the same time, the "men's movement" perceives feminism as "women's work," an ideological position, project, and movement that men can resent or admire, but in which we can never fully participate.

The emerging bisexual movement has thankfully been shaped by an explicitly feminist vision, but where are the voices of "feminists with penises" in this evolving milieu? John Stoltenberg, while clearly a male feminist, does not go far enough in proposing viable alternatives to the paradigm of male domination that he eloquently denounces. Where are the other "male feminists"? Why are there so few of us? Many gay and bisexual men do not consider feminism, gender politics, and a coherent critique of mainstream masculinity as vital components to their queerness. It should be obvious why heterosexual men often feel threatened by wimmin with a feminist response to sexist remarks and gestures. Shouldn't we expect more of gay and bi men?

The very act of loving other men does affect my gender identity and the manner in which I love other wimmin. Bisexual men have an important choice and responsibility. If we can transcend hetero-sexist power dynamics in our gay relationships, does this enable us to have truly liberatory relationships with wimmin? We can begin by deconstructing the macho straightjacket of mainstream masculinity. I view these possibilities as challenges rather than achievements for bisexual men. New theories of bisexual politics could collapse into a comprehensive radical praxis that changes the way we love, the way we live, and the way we work to change a world that still insists on the dualities and dichotomies of heterosexist assumptions.

The formulation of "queer" as a sexual and political modus operandi offers us the opportunity to celebrate a holistic approach to sexual revolution, a polymorphous convergence of gender conception and choice of sexual partners. I propose the convergence of gender blur and new sexual identities as both a theoretical and practical terrain for constructing notions of a postpatriarchal masculinity. My somewhat conflicting desire is to break free of gender constrictions entirely while acknowledging and fighting the tradition of domination and coercive privilege that is our birthright as men in a bitterly sexist and homophobic society. I want to take the *bi*-polar opposition out of *bi*-sexuality. I want to abolish the Kinsey scale. I want to love men *and* wimmin all the time. I want to commit erotic sabotage in the corridors of corporate power.

I have noticed a tendency among queer and hetero "(pro)feminist" men to espouse a self-congratulatory stance surrounding their gender attitudes. They seem to mistake the queer, feminist, gender-neutral utopia for which many of us strive in every aspect of our social and sexual lives as a given reality of the present. They get defensive at the mere suggestion that they may harbor deeply ingrained and internalized sexism or homophobia. Because the nature of gender socialization is so pervasive, and at times frighteningly subtle in our society, it is dangerous to deny these realities. The first step for any man, regardless of class, race, or sexual orientation in the fight against sexism and homophobia, is to find those seeds of oppression rooted in his own consciousness and to confront them. We often need go no further than the realm of primal fantasy to discover the manner in which masculine stereotypes shape our consciousness. If what we want is to break down the duality of gender, the hierarchical binarism of sexual being, we must first understand how we were indoctrinated as children to accept these codes of social behavior as human nature. I have yet to meet a man who has fully healed from, or who was ever wholly immune to, the baby blue bondage of gender enculturation. Sexism is a social disease of domination. No man (or woman) is immune.

Freedom from oppression based on gender, and the re-emergence of blurred or transgendered identities in an evolving queer counter-culture, should not be mistaken for advocating the abolition of sexual difference. One notion of equality, which simply states that women are no longer legally handicapped in the Monopoly-game swindle of capitalist patriarchy, does not present itself as imbued with an insurrectionary stance toward the competitive, domination-based paradigms of modern civilization. Authentic freedom from inequality is also a freedom from the tenets of authority, coercion, and power that define most social relationships in our era.

My vision of gender blur oscillates between a personal penchant for the pleasures of cross-dressing and a desire to break down the gender-based divisions of labor in my daily life (in the context of a living and co-parenting arrangement with my female partner). While my experience as a parent is literally in its infancy, my belief has long been that one of the most radical contributions men can make to revolution is nurturing and caring for children. We can only hope to alter traditional gender codes by offering children loving examples of people who regularly act outside of strictly prescribed masculine and feminine roles. Because queer parents suffer so much persecution, this is one of the riskiest, most rewarding terrains for living out our critique of patriarchy.

When I cross-dress I utilize the signifiers of fashion in playful and political confrontation of peoples' attitudes and preconceptions. I do not strive for a convincing masquerade or "passing." It is important to note that when I wear jeans, boots, a work shirt, and a baseball cap, that is also a form of cross-dressing or masquerade. I am even less interested in a notion of drag as male appropriation of female power, as it has often wrongly been pigeonholed. Men who attempt to steal from women or stereotype them through transves-tism are accomplices, rather than opponents, of the patriarchy.

A more radical sensibility toward cross-dressing subverts gender codes entirely. A "man" who collapses his own "masculinity" by borrowing visual signs of "femininity," or a woman who inverts this strategy, creates a personal subjectivity beyond the limitations of gender. In many indigenous cultures, gender-benders of this ilk were regarded as a "third gender" rather than as impersonators. These precedents to the "butch" and "fairy" archetypes in our contemporary queer culture challenged the strict duality of sex and gender. Similarly, the modern bisexual movement has dissolved the strict dichotomy between "gay" and "straight" (without invalidating our homosexual or heterosexual friends and lovers). We have insisted on our desire and freedom to love people of all genders. We have refused to be "half-gay" or "half-straight."

Currently, voices within our movement are breaking down borders once again. We are no longer simply bisexuals. We are also autonosexuals, omnisexuals, pansexuals, polysexuals, ambisexuals, trisexuals (because we'll try anything!). While the *real* meaning of these terms is presently implied, exotic, vague, and opaque, their very existence is promising. What all these new terms and sexual identities suggest is an expanding consciousness vis-à-vis sexuality. They are saying: "The limitations of language, the existing terms, do not encompass the enormity and explosiveness of my sexuality. My sexuality exudes a manner of being in the natural world that extends beyond simply loving both genders. It includes the entire scope of sensuality. I also love trees, rivers, the sky, and food. My sexuality is bigger than words." *We are very queer.*

Many of my views regarding gender blur and queer identity have evolved from my experiences with the Radical Faeries, a movement of gay men who meet primarily at gatherings held in rural settings, but also have contingents in gay pride marches and other queer events. While Faerie events are predominately gay male, most gatherings welcome the participation of lesbians, and bisexuals of both genders. However, all Faeries do not agree on the issue of inclusiveness. Biphobia in the Faerie milieu has recently generated a great deal of debate. For instance, influential Faerie Harry Hay, in an address to the Malibu Radical Faerie Gathering in 1992, stated: "In inviting Bi-sexuals [sic] to join and make common cause with us, we have in effect reduced our collective image from that of being a cultural and spiritual minority . . . to being merely a heterosexual variation once again . . . " (Hay, 1992, p. 12).

Though Hay's views represent a common blind spot among our potential gay allies, the prevalent spirit among Radical Faeries distinctly deemphasizes the sectarian squabbling that his comment imbues. "Faeriedom" is a movement of kindred spirits rather than a political organization. We generally emphasize gay liberation accompanied by pagan spirituality, connectedness to the earth, anarchist politics, and frequent festivals or gatherings which celebrate free love in the Faerie community (and are excuses to adorn ourselves in the most lavish drag). As Faeries, we often distinguish ourselves from gay rights advocates and assimilationists, understanding our sexuality as woven into our entire being and shaping our spiritual, political, and psychic view of the world. Faeries reclaim and recontextualize many cultural stigmas of queerness. Faggot, sissy, camp, and queen are sacred words in our lavender lexicon.

Rejecting the notion of an "essential" bisexuality, I do not think bisexuals are naturally inclined to be less sexist or subscribe to non-traditional gender roles. I do think our bisexuality affords us a unique opportunity to incorporate gender blur and feminism into our radical, sexual politics, and that these tenets have immense liberatory potential. I certainly believe many bisexual men could experiment more with genderfuck or be more queer identified. But at this point, I wish more bisexual men would simply come out of the closet. More men are bisexual than readily admit it, though I've recently encountered a flurry of men coming out as bi before ever having sex with a man. A certain locker room ideology of fear lingers with many of us from our youth, a time when being a fag was synonymous with a fate worse than death. This fear prevents innumerable men from coming out, whether they are bisexual or gay. I presently am acquainted with many more bisexual wimmin than men, and I perceive this to be a trend everywhere. Many of us are clinging to those last strands of "heterosexual privilege" (god, I hate that term!) by falling back on the *image* provided by our heterosexual relationships, for emotional security, when the going gets rough. While I am "out" to my parents and my co-workers, I am not "out" to the employees at the post office, the plumber, or my aunts, uncles, and grandparents.

Bisexual brothers: borrowing both from feminism and the Radical Faeries, we can blur our collective masculinity and build an army of lovers who love to change the world. We can begin by listening to our feminist sisters and gay brothers, and by loving and conversing with each other. We can form discussion groups, reading groups, direct action affinity groups. We can visit a gay bar, bookstore, or community center. We can attend a queer or feminist demonstration. We can volunteer our time in the fight against rape and domestic violence. We have nothing to lose but a tradition of male domination.

Disinvesting ourselves from the litany of power afforded to heterosexual men in our culture will not be easy. It includes accepting how we as men have consistently used that power to our advantage and have hurt our friends and lovers in the process. It means aligning ourselves with feminists in the fight against patriarchy. It means coming out to a straight acquaintance who makes an anti-gay remark.

Let's do it, brothers. We have humyn liberation to gain. We have a world of pleasures to win.

The Sacredness of Pleasure

Starhawk

A speech for the National Conference Celebrating Bisexuality, Washington, DC, April 24, 1993.

Hello. First let me say how honored and delighted I am to be here at this conference, and to be able to participate in the important events of this weekend.

We are at a crucial moment in history, a crossroads in which we as a society must make decisions that will shape the next millennium. At this vital moment, I would like to speak to you about questions of the sacred. Native Peoples have asserted the need to honor their ancient sacred traditions as integrally woven into the fabric of their cultural survival and land rights. But most progressive movements have abandoned the terrain of the sacred to Fundamentalists. As a result, we are constantly having to define ourselves against a very narrow view of the spirit.

For centuries, if not millennia, patriarchal religions have held that what is sacred is outside the world, removed from the body, from nature, from material being. The desacralized earth and her human children are thus fair game for exploitation. Although even within the most hierarchical religions there have always been earth-centered currents, the main stream has defined the realm of the spirit as separate and severed from the earth.

But there is another view of the sacred, one held by indigenous peoples of every continent on earth, one that is probably the earliest human understanding of spirit. In this view, the earth is alive, not an object but a being in whose life we each participate. The sacred is embodied, in the web of interconnections that sustain life, in air, fire, water, and earth, in animals and plants and humans, in the cycles of birth, growth, death, and rebirth that move through both nature and culture.

I speak to you out of one particular earth-based tradition, the old religion of the Goddess of Europe and the Middle East, called Wicca or Witchcraft. The period of the Witch persecutions of the sixteenth and seventeenth centuries is one of the great undigested traumas of Western culture. They involved the torture and judicial murder of hundreds of thousands to millions of women and men over a period of 400 years. Eighty percent of the victims were women. Many of the men who were killed were targeted because they were gay.

The burnings can be seen as a war on women, but they were also very much a war on all the remaining cultural and healing traditions that stemmed from the ancient understanding of the earth as living being. And they were a war on sexuality. Most of the charges against Witches were of sexual misconduct and perversion—in the Churches' terms. The infamous Witchhunter's manual, the *Malleus Maleficarum* states that "all witchcraft comes from carnal lust, which is in women insatiable." The fear and horror that are still associated with that time have left us with a deep fear of any sexuality that steps outside the narrow bounds defined by the authorities. The burnings left us with a fear of women's power, and a half-conscious sense that any woman who takes charge of her own sexuality is dangerous and possibly demonic.

The Burning Times were also the time of the African slave trade and the conquest of this continent with the enslavement and destruction of its native peoples. They too were defined as dangerous and demonic, in need of control and Christianizing even if it killed them. Everywhere the consciousness of the earth as a living being was attacked and nearly but never completely destroyed. Now, 500 years later, when the very life support systems that sustain all earth's creatures are threatened, we need that consciousness more than ever.

To say that this earth is sacred is to take a very radical position, for what is sacred cannot be defiled or exploited. What is sacred has a value inherent in itself, that cannot be measured by any other standard or weighed by a profit-and-loss accounting system. If we hold the forest sacred, we cannot clear-cut the last stands of old growth, no matter how many short-term jobs that might provide. If we honor the diversity of living things, we must be willing to preserve other species. If the air is sacred to us, we can't sit by and run our air conditioning as the ozone is destroyed. What is sacred is what we are willing to sacrifice for.

This vision of the earth is also integrally connected to our struggles as lesbian, gay, and bisexual people. For if we experience the earth as living being, then in all honesty I think we have to admit that she's an erotic being. How else do we explain fireflies, mangos, the unfurling of ferns? We are part of an erotic being in an erotic universe, whose deepest purposes seem to be served by getting various creatures to rub against each other in a wide variety of ways. Erotic energy holds the universe together. What is gravity but the desire of one body for another?

When we hold the erotic as sacred, we say that our capacity for pleasure has a value in and of itself, that in fact it is one of the ways in which we connect with the deepest purposes of the universe.

I believe that is the position we as bisexuals need to take. For our struggle is not only about affirming our own right to pleasure, but about affirming pleasure, variety, diversity, fluidity, as sacred values worth struggling for.

In a world in which attempts to change our orientation by coercion and force abound, lesbians and gays have necessarily defended the position that homosexuality is inborn and unchangeable. While that is true for a certain percentage of gay people, just as it's probably true for a similar percentage of heterosexual people, those of us who are bisexual, and honest, have to admit that our sexual orientation sometimes seems to change with the phases of the moon or the level of pollen in the air, or just with propinquity to whoever happens to be around. I honor the lesbian and gay activists who have made their sexual orientation a cornerstone of their identities, and respect the political need for doing so and the strength that comes from that position. But if I'm honest about my own sexual identity, it has something to do with a deep reluctance to be pinned down.

How do we take a firm stand in the shifting sands of our own sexual fluidity? How do we counter the vicious hatred that gets aroused by saying, "I'm gay not because I have to be, but because I choose to be, at least today I do, and I have a right to make that

choice?" How do we hold solidarity with our lesbian and gay
sisters and brothers who do not have the option to pass as straight?

When we say that pleasure is sacred, we take a firm stand on
ancient sacred ground. When we fight for the right to determine our
own erotic choices, we fight for the right of our lesbian sisters and
gay brothers to be who they are. We directly confront our cultural
fear and mistrust of pleasure, saying that we do not lack morality,
we uphold a different morality: one which says that each human
being is the keeper of her or his own body, that inherent in our
body's capacity for pleasure is our moral authority to determine just
what sort of pleasure we want to take. That morality supports our
stance as women when we say that by virtue of our wombs we and
only we can be the keepers of our bodies' reproductive powers. It
supports the struggles of those of us with disabilities to be decision
makers about our particular needs and capacities and to participate
fully in our culture.

To affirm pleasure is to affirm life in its deepest purposes, to
value the intimate connections we make, the moments of ecstasy we
experience. When we claim our sacred right to pleasure, we are
honoring life in its variety, diversity, its endless arrangements and
rearrangements. We are acknowledging our participation in the
deepest erotic purposes of the universe.

To assert this right is to assert the right of the old-growth forest to
remain a forest, not a lumber yard, the right of the sacred mountain
to be inviolate, the right of the stream to flow clean and undammed,
the right of every human infant to be held in loving arms and
nourished by loving breasts.

We must not abandon morality to the fundamentalists. Instead,
we as bisexuals can, out of our unique experiences, define a new
morality based on the honoring of our inner, body-rooted authority,
and the integrity of the earth-body of which we are each a part. Our
issues are linked with all struggles of self-determination being
waged by people around the world. We need to envision a new
world, one with room in it for whales and howler monkeys and drag
queens and grizzly bears and ancient sacred tribal lands and leather
dykes and plentiful rain and happily married couples with two-
point-five children and people who just can't make up their mind
and black-white-red-brown-tan-golden-sepia-chocolate-ivory-ebony

and (who knows?) maybe striped and spotted ones of us. And then we need to do the work that will make that vision a reality.

For the last five years, I've been working on a book that attempts to imagine such a world. It's a novel set in the twenty-first century, called *The Fifth Sacred Thing* [Starhawk, 1993]. I'd like to close by reading just a bit of the manifesto that opens the book, the Declaration of the Four Sacred Things which sets forth the values of that hopeful world:

Declaration of the Four Sacred Things

The earth is a living, conscious being. In company with cultures of many different times and places, we name these things as sacred: air, fire, water, and earth.

Whether we see them as the breath, energy, blood, and body of the Mother, or as the blessed gifts of a Creator, or as symbols of the interconnected systems that sustain life, we know that nothing can live without them.

To call these things sacred is to say that they have a value beyond their usefulness for human ends, that they themselves become the standards by which our acts, our economics, our laws, and our purposes must be judged. No one has the right to appropriate them or profit from them at the expense of others. Any government that fails to protect them forfeits its legitimacy.

All people, all living things, are part of the earth life, and so are sacred. No one of us stands higher or lower than any other. Only justice can assure balance: only ecological balance can sustain freedom. Only in freedom can that fifth sacred thing we call spirit flourish in its full diversity.

To honor the sacred is to create conditions in which nourishment, sustenance, habitat, knowledge, freedom, and beauty can thrive. To honor the sacred is to make love possible.

To this we dedicate our curiosity, our will, our courage, our silences, and our voices. To this we dedicate our lives.

Appendices

Appendix A

Brief Timeline of Bisexual Activism in the United States

Dannielle Raymond
Liz A. Highleyman

The following timeline highlights selected events in the history of the U.S. bi movement since the late 1960s. This list does not begin to include all the groups that have existed during this period. According to the Bixesual Resource Guide, *published by the Bisexual Resource Center, there are currently at least 1410 bisexual groups in 22 countries around the world. Of those groups, 1,182 are spread throughout 48 U.S. states and Washington, DC.*

1968-69: Margo Rila co-coordinates the San Francisco chapter of the Sexual Freedom League, a national social/educational organization, that sponsors a bisexual meeting group.

1969: Maggi Rubenstein begins giving talks on bisexuality and convinces the Center for Special Problems, a counseling agency in San Francisco, to include "bisexual" as a valid sexual orientation in their client assessments.

1972: Quaker Committee of Friends on Bisexuality issues "Ithaca Statement on Bisexuality," which later appears in *The Advocate.*

1972: National Bisexual Liberation Group forms (New York). Produces what is probably the earliest bisexual newsletter, *The Bisexual Expression,* with over 5,500 subscribers in ten U.S. chapters.

1975: Bi Forum (social/educational/support group) forms in New York.

1976: San Francisco Bisexual Center, the longest surviving bisexual community center, opens its doors. A social and educational organization, it offers counseling and support services, and publishes a newsletter from 1976 to 1984.

1977: Bisexual activist Alan Rockway co-authors the nation's first successful gay rights ordinance put to public vote (Dade County, Florida). When Anita Bryant initiates her homophobic "Save Our Children" campaign, the S.F. Bi Center, in coalition with gay and lesbian community leaders, holds a press conference with lesbian rights advocates Del Martin and Phyllis Lyon, and pediatrician Dr. Benjamin Spock.

1978-79: Grassroots bisexual communities grow with the formation of midwestern groups such as Chicago Bi Ways, One To Five, and Bi Women Welcome in Minneapolis, and The Bi Married Men's Group in the Detroit suburbs.

1983: Boston Bisexual Women's Network forms. BBWN's monthly *Bi Women*, currently reaching over 600 women, is the longest–lived bisexual newsletter in the U.S.

1983: BiPOL, the first bisexual political action group, forms in San Francisco.

1984: BiPOL holds the first bisexual rights rally at the Democratic National Convention, San Francisco.

1984: After a two-year battle, David Lourea persuades the San Francisco Department of Public Health to acknowledge bisexual men in their official AIDS statistics, setting a standard for health departments nationwide.

1984: First East Coast Conference on Bisexuality held at the Storrs School of Social Work at the University of Connecticut.

1984: Boston Bisexual Men's Network forms. At its peak in 1988, about 150 people receive their newsletter, *BBMN News.*

1985: Seattle Bisexual Women's Network forms. SBWN is noted for its speakers' bureau educating Seattle city agencies, service providers, and policy makers through the 1980s, and for its ongoing bi-monthly newsletter, *North Bi Northwest.*

1985: Bisexual Connection forms, serving the greater Twin Cities area. Currently 350 members receive their newsletter, *Bi Focal.*

1985: East Coast Bisexual Network forms, the first bisexual umbrella group (name changed to Bisexual Resource Center in 1993). ECBN sponsors annual regional conferences and retreats from 1985 to 1989, drawing participants from ten eastern states.

1986: First out bisexual to be elected co-chair of a Lesbian/Gay Freedom Day Pride Parade Committee (BiPOL's Autumn Courtney, San Francisco).

1987: Bay Area Bisexual Network forms as an umbrella group for the San Francisco Bay Area, with a speakers' bureau, educational forums, and a newsletter. BABN's current membership is 1000.

1987: Seventy-five bisexuals march as a national contingent in the 1987 March On Washington for Gay and Lesbian Rights and form an incipient national bisexual network (later to become the North American Multicultural Bisexual Network and then BiNet USA).

1988: Gary North begins writing and producing a national newsletter, *Bisexuality: News, Views, and Networking,* which would continue publication until 1990.

1988: The Bisexual Committee Engaging in Politics (BiCEP) forms in Boston, devoted to bisexual political activism.

1988: Bi Unity (Philadelphia-based group formed in 1987) successfully lobbies the Philadelphia Mayor's Commission on Sexual Minorities to form a working group on bisexual issues.

1989: South Florida Bisexual Network forms, and develops a membership of 300 by the early 1990s.

1989: New York Area Bisexual Network (founded 1987) initiates a successful letter-writing campaign against a defamatory article in *Cosmopolitan* (October 1989) which had maliciously stereotyped bisexual men as dishonest spreaders of AIDS.

1990: BiPOL sponsors the First National Bisexual Conference (San Francisco) with 450 people attending from twenty states and five countries. National Bisexual Network holds its first membership meeting there, formalizing what becomes the North American Multicultural Bisexual Network (NAMBN).

1990: BiPAC New York (formed 1989) mobilizes a national letter writing campaign to protest Hetrick-Martin Institute/Harvey Milk High School's workshop entitled "Bisexual Men: Fact or Fiction?" The workshop is cancelled.

1990: Susan Carlton (aka Nishanga Bliss) offers the first academic course in the U.S. on bisexuality at University of California, Berkeley.

1991: Bay Area Bisexual Network begins publishing the first and only national bisexual magazine, *Anything That Moves: Beyond the Myths of Bisexuality.*

1991: Some 250 people from nine countries attend the First International Conference on Bisexuality in Amsterdam, an academic conference featuring noted bisexual researchers.

1991: Biversity Boston forms, an all-gender social group.

1992: The Bisexual Connection in Minneapolis/St. Paul sponsors first annual Midwest regional bisexual conference, BECAUSE (Bisexual Empowerment Conference: A Uniting, Supportive Experience) which draws 150 people from several states each year.

1992: Embracing Diversity Mid-Atlantic regional conference in Washington, DC, hosted by AMBi (Alliance of Multicultural Bisexuals) and AMBUSH (Alliance of Multicultural Bisexuals United to Stop Heterosexism, Homophobia, Helms, etc.).

1992: Minnesota's bisexual community works in coalition with lesbian, gay, and transgender groups to pass a State Civil Rights Law granting the most comprehensive civil rights protections for bisexual, lesbian, gay, and transgender people in the country.

1992: Second International Bisexual Conference in London.

1992: BiPOL mobilizes thirteen cities nationwide in a lobbying campaign to include bisexuals in the title and organization of the upcoming March on Washington. Fifty-three high-profile lesbian and gay activists, writers, and political leaders sign a letter of support asking the March committee for bisexual inclusion. Openly bisexual people take key leadership roles in local and regional organizing for the March, and the title is changed to the 1993 March On Washington for Lesbian, Gay and Bi Equal Rights and Liberation.

1993: BiNet USA, Seattle Bisexual Women's Network, and Seattle Bisexual Men's Union sponsor the first Northwest Regional Conference, in Seattle. Attendees represent Washington, Oregon, Alaska, Montana, and British Columbia.

1993: BiNet USA, the Bisexual Resource Center, and the Washington, DC-based Alliance of Multicultural Bisexuals (AMBi) collaborate to sponsor the National Conference Celebrating Bisexuality (second U.S. national bisexual conference). Held in conjuction with the March on Washington, the conference draws over 600 people from the U.S. and Europe, making it the largest bisexual conference to date.

1994: Sheela Lambert hosts the first television show by and for the bisexual community, *Bisexual Network*, which airs for 13 weeks on New York Public Access Cable.

1994: Bisexual communities based in Fayetteville, Raleigh, Chapel Hill, and Charlotte unite to form the North Carolina Bisexual Network (NCBN), which sponsors a South Eastern Regional Bisexual Conference attended by 100 people from 11 states.

1994: New York hosts the International Conference Celebrating Bisexuality in conjunction with the celebration of the 25th anniversary of the Stonewall Riots and the March on the United Nations to Affirm the Rights of Lesbian and Gay People. This third international bisexual conference is attended by 350 people. Hundreds of bisexual individuals and groups march as a contingent in the March on the U.N., and many more march as out bisexuals within other contingents.

Appendix B

Bisexuals and the Radical Right

Dannielle Raymond

The civil rights of bisexuals are under attack. Initiatives that deny protection against discrimination for bisexuals, lesbians, gay men, and transgendered people have been introduced in Idaho, Oregon, Arizona, Maine, Missouri, Michigan, Florida, Nevada, Colorado, and Washington. Although all of these initiatives would affect the lives of bisexual people, half of the ten initiatives explicitly deny bisexuals legal protection from discrimination. For example, the Michigan initiative proposes to amend the state constitution to include the following:

> Neither this state, through any of its branches or departments, nor any of its agencies, political subdivisions, municipalities, or school districts, shall enact, adopt, or enforce any statute, regulation, ordinance or policy whereby homosexual, lesbian or **bisexual** orientation, conduct, practices or relationships shall constitute or otherwise be the basis of, or entitle any person or class of persons to have or claim any minority status, quota preferences, protected status, or claim of discrimination. (bold mine)

The inclusion of the word bisexual in the text of these initiatives is intentional. Brian M. McCormick, staff counsel for The National Legal Foundation, a right wing litigation group, advised the Colorado Coalition for Family Values what language to use for Colorado's Amendment 2, the first such amendment to be passed by popular vote in the U.S. In a letter dated June 13, 1991, McCormick writes:

> The initiative is directed at those who engage in same sex activities. . . . I believe the term "bisexual" should be included for two reasons. The first is that many persons who engage in same sex relations

attempt to . . . appear more "normal" or legitimate by saying that they also engage in heterosexual relations. From a moral standpoint of course homosexuality and bisexuality are indistinguishable. . . . Second, it is possible that if bisexuals are not specifically included, then homosexuals could claim that the amendment does not apply to them because they are bisexual and not simply homosexual.

For more information on the Radical Right, contact the "Fight the Right Project" of the National Gay and Lesbian Task Force, 1360 Mission Street, Suite 200, San Francisco, CA 94103. Voice (415) 552–6448; fax (415) 552–6478. E–mail: rfbngltf@aol.com. Or contact People for the American Way, 2000 M Street NW, Suite 400, Washington, DC 20036. Voice (202) 467-4999; fax (202) 293-2672.

References

Abbott, Sidney and Love, Barbara (1978). *Sappho was a Right-On Woman.* New York: Day Books.

ACT UP/NY Women and AIDS Book Group, Eds. (1990). *Women, AIDS, and Activism.* Boston: South End Press.

Adair, Margo and Howell, Sharon (1990). *Breaking Old Patterns, Weaving New Ties.* San Francisco: Tools For Change.

Adam, Barry (1987). *The Rise of a Gay and Lesbian Movement.* Boston: Twayne Publishers.

Ahmed, Sunny Rumsey (1990). "AIDS Issues for African American and African Caribbean Women" in *Women, AIDS, and Activism,* ACT UP/NY Women and AIDS Book Group, Eds. Boston: South End Press.

Alaton, Salem (1993). "Bi Sex," *The Globe and Mail.* Toronto, Ontario (June 26) p. Dl.

Altman, Dennis (1971). *Homosexual: Oppression and Liberation.* New York: Outerbridge and Dienstfrey.

Altman, Dennis (1982). *The Homosexualization of America.* Boston: Beacon Press.

Anonymous (1989). "S/M Aesthetic," *OUT/LOOK: National Lesbian & Gay Quarterly,* 3 (Winter).

Banzhaf, Marion (1990). "Race, Women, and AIDS: An introduction" in *Women, AIDS, and Activism,* ACT UP/NY Women and AIDS Book Group, Eds. Boston: South End Press.

Barr, George (1985). "Chicago Bi-Ways: An Informal History" in *Two Lives to Lead: Bisexuality in Men and Women,* Fritz Klein and Timothy J. Wolf, Eds. Binghamton, NY: Harrington Park Press, pp. 231-234.

Bay Windows (1987). News Article, September 24, p. l.

Bem, Sandra (1974). "The Measurement of Psychological Androgyny," *The Journal of Consulting and Clinical Psychology,* 42, pp. 155-162.

Benjamin, Jessica (1988). *The Bonds of Love: Psychoanalysis, Feminism, and the Problem of Domination.* New York: Pantheon Books.

Bennett, Kathleen (1992). "Feminist Bisexuality: A Both/And Option for an Either/Or World" in *Closer to Home: Bisexuality and Feminism,* Elizabeth Reba Weise, Ed. Seattle: The Seal Press, pp. 205-232.

Bérubé, Allan and Escoffier, Jeffrey (1991). "Queer/Nation," *OUT/LOOK,* 11 (Winter), pp. 12-14.

Bisexual Lives (1988). London: Off Pink Publishing.

Blatt, Martin H. (1989). *Free Love and Anarchism.* Chicago: University of Chicago Press.

Blumenfeld, Warren (1992). *Homophobia: How We All Pay the Price.* Boston: Beacon Press.

Braindrop, Lily (1992). "Bi and Beyond: A Burgeoning Bisexual Movement Gains Momentum," *The Advocate* (July 30).

Brown, Peter G. (1993). Editor's Notebook. *The Sciences,* March/April, p. 2.

Brown, Rita Mae (1976). "The Shape of Things to Come," *A Plain Brown Rapper.* Oakland, CA: Diana Press.

Butler, Judith (1990). *Gender Trouble.* New York: Routledge.

Butler, C.T. Lawrence and Rothstein, Chester (1991). *On Conflict and Consensus: A Handbook on Formal Consensus Decisionmaking.* Cambridge, MA: Food Not Bombs.

Califia, Pat, ed. (1981). *Coming to Power.* Boston: Alyson.

Califia, Pat (1993). *Sensuous Magic.* New York: Richard Kasak Books.

Chee, Alexander S. (1991). "A Queer Nationalism," *OUT/LOOK: National Lesbian & Gay Quarterly,* 11 (Winter), pp. 15-19.

Christina, Greta (1990). "Drawing the Line: Bisexual Women in the Lesbian Community," *On Our Backs: Entertainment for the Adventurous Lesbian* (May-June).

Christina, Greta (1992). "Are We Having Sex Yet?" in *The Erotic Impulse,* David Steinberg, Ed. Los Angeles: Tarcher.

Clausen, Jan (1990). "My Interesting Condition," *OUT/LOOK: National Lesbian & Gay Quarterly,* 7 (Winter), pp. 11-21.

Corsaro, Kim (1991a). "The Love that Dare Not Speak Its Name: Bisexuality in the Gay/Lesbian Community," Community Forum in *The San Francisco Bay Times,* vol. 12, no. 7 (April).

Corsaro, Kim (1991b). "Bisexuality in the Gay/Lesbian Community: The Controversy Continues," Community Forum in *The San Francisco Bay Times,* vol. 12, no. 8 (May).

Cosmopolitan (1991). "Good Girls, Bad Girls, Which Are You?" (September) p. 246.

Cosson, Steve (1991). "Queer Interviews," *OUT/LOOK: National Lesbian & Gay Quarterly,* 11 (Winter), pp. 14-23.

Daly, Mary (1978). "European Witchburnings: Purifying the Body of Christ," *Gyn/Ecology: The Metaethics of Radical Feminism.* Boston: Beacon Press.

Danzig, Alexis (1990). "Bisexual Women and AIDS" in *Women, AIDS, and Activism,* ACT UP/NY Women and AIDS Book Group, Eds. Boston: South End Press.

de Santis, Marie (1990). "Hate Crimes Bill Excludes Women," *off our backs* (June).

Dreher, Sarah and Brook, Lis (1990). "Visibility? Whose Visibility?" *Gay Community News* (March 11-17).

Duberman, Martin (1974). "The Bisexual Debate," *New Times* (June 28), p. 34.

Echols, Alice (1989). *Daring to Be Bad: Radical Feminism in America, 1967-1975.* Minneapolis: University of Minnesota Press.

Ehrenreich, Barbara (1992). "Who's On Main Street," *Mother Jones* (July/August).

Epstein, Steven (1990). "Gay Politics, Ethnic Identity: The Limits of Social Constructionism," in *Forms of Desire: Sexual Orientation and the Social Constructionist Controversy,* Edward Stein, Ed. New York: Garland Publishing, pp. 239-294.

Faderman, Lillian (1991). *Odd Girls and Twilight Lovers.* New York: Columbia University Press.

Farajajé-Jones, Elias (1993). "MultiKulti Feminist Bis No More?" *Anything That Moves,* no. 5.

Fass, Don (1975). Untitled article, inside front cover, *Bisexual Expression* (January-February).

Foucault, Michel (1984). "How We Behave" (Interview with Alice Springs), *Home and Garden* (February), pp. 61-69.

Fox, Ronald C. (1993). "Coming Out Bisexual: Identity, Behavior and Sexual Orientation Self-Disclosure." Doctoral dissertation, California Institute of Integral Studies, San Francisco. Also presented at the First International Bisexual Conference (Amsterdam, October 5, 1991) and the American Psychological Association annual convention (Toronto, August 20, 1993).

Fox, Ronald C. (1995). "Bisexual Identities," in *Lesbian, Gay, and Bisexual Identities over the Lifespan,* D'Augelli and Patterson, Eds. New York: Oxford University Press, pp. 48-86.

Geller, Tom (1990). *Bisexuality: A Reader and Sourcebook.* Ojai, CA: Times Change Press.

Gelman, David (1987). "A Perilous Double Love Life," *Newsweek,* vol. 110, no.3 (July 13), p.44.

Gibian, Ruth (1992). "Refusing Certainty: Toward a Bisexuality of Wholeness," in *Closer to Home: Bisexuality and Feminism,* Elizabeth Reba Weise, Ed. Seattle: The Seal Press.

Golden, Carla (1990). *Our Politics and Our Choices: The Feminist Movement and Sexual Orientation.* Paper presented at the American Psychological Association annual conference, Boston.

Goldman, Emma (1969). *Anarchism and Other Essays.* New York: Dover.

Gonsalves, Sharon (1991). "Red Cross Needs to Change," *Gay Community News* (July 21-27), p. 5.

Gould, Steven J. (1984). "Of Wasps and WASPS," *Natural History,* 91(12), pp. 8-15. (December).

Greene, Johnny (1974). "Decadence by Invitation Only," *New Times* (April 19), p. 38.

Halperin, David (1990). *One Hundred Years of Homosexuality.* New York: Routledge.

Harris, Craig G. J. (1986). "Cut Off from Among Their People," in *In the Life: A Black Gay Anthology,* Joseph Beam, Ed. Boston: Alyson Publications.

Hay, Harry (1992). "Neither Boy nor Girl: Reclaiming our Ancient Gay Cultural and Spiritual Legitimacy: Third Gender," *RFD* vol. XIX:4.

Hite, Shere (1976). *The Hite Report: A Nationwide Study of Female Sexuality.* New York: Dell Publishing Co.

Hochschild, Arlie (1989). *The Second Shift.* New York: Viking Penguin Inc.

Hollibaugh, Amber and Moraga, Cherríe (1983). "What We're Rollin Around in Bed With: Sexual Silences in Feminism," in *Powers of Desire,* Ann Snitow, Christine Stansell, and Sharon Thompson, Eds. New York: Monthly Review Press.

hooks, bell (1984). *Feminist Theory: From Margin to Center.* Boston: South End Press.

Hurwood, Bernhardt (1974). *The Bisexuals.* Fawcett.

Hutchins, Loraine and Ka'ahumanu, Lani, eds. (1991). *Bi Any Other Name: Bisexual People Speak Out.* Boston: Alyson Publications.

Jones, James H. (1981). *Bad Blood.* New York: Free Press.

Jordan, June (1991). "A New Politics of Sexuality." *The Progressive,* (July), p. 13.

Ka'ahumanu, Lani (1982). "Bi-phobic: Some of My Best Friends Are . . . ," *Plexus,* vol. 9, no. 4 (June), p. 15.

Ka'ahumanu, Lani (1991). "Political Activism: A Brief History," in *Bi Any Other Name: Bisexual People Speak Out,* Loraine Hutchins and Lani Ka'ahumanu, Eds. Boston: Alyson Publications, pp. 359-367.

Kaplan, Rebecca (1991). "Book Review, *Homophobia: A Weapon of Sexism*" (Pharr, 1988) in *The Thistle,* vol. 5, no. 2, p.5. Cambridge, MA: MIT (March 8).

Kinsey, Alfred C., Pomeroy, Wardell B., and Martin, Clyde E. (1948). *Sexual Behavior in the Human Male.* Philadelphia: W. B. Saunders Co.

Kinsey, Alfred C., Pomeroy, Wardell B., Martin, Clyde E. and Gebhard, Paul H. (1952). *Sexual Behavior in the Human Female.* Philadelphia: W. B. Saunders Co.

Klein, Fritz and Wolf, Timothy J., eds. (1985). *Two Lives to Lead: Bisexuality in Men and Women.* Binghamton, N.Y.: Harrington Park Press.

Klein, Fritz, Sepekoff, Barry, and Wolf, Timothy J. (1985). "Sexual Orientation: A Multi-variable Dynamic Process," *Journal of Homosexuality* 11, no. 1/2, pp. 35-50.

Klemesrud, Judy (1974). "The Bisexuals," *New York,* p. 37.

Knox, Louise (1974). "The Bisexual Phenomenon," *Viva* (July), p. 42.

Lawrenson, Helen (1974): "Bisexuality: A New Look at an Old Story," *Playgirl* (July), p. 40.

Lawson, Kay (1989). *The Human Polity. An Introduction to Political Science.* Boston: Houghton Mifflin Company.

Levine, Martin (1979a). "The Gay Ghetto," in *Gay Men: The Sociology of Male Homosexuality,* Martin Levine, Ed. (1979b). New York: Harper and Row, pp. 182-204.

Levine, Martin, ed. (1979b). *Gay Men: The Sociology of Male Homosexuality.* New York: Harper and Row.

Lorde, Audre (1980). *The Cancer Journals.* San Francisco: Spinsters/Aunt Lute.

Lorde, Audre (1984). *Sister Outsider.* Trumansburg, NY: The Crossing Press.

MacKinnon, Catharine (1982). "Feminism, Marxism, Method and the State: An Agenda for Theory," *Signs.*

Maggenti, Maria (1991). "Women as Queer Nationals," *OUT/LOOK: National Lesbian & Gay Quarterly,* 11 (Winter), pp. 20-23.

Mallon, Gerald L., ed. (1991). *Resisting Racism: An Action Guide,* National Association of Black and White Men Together, Washington, DC.

Mann, Jonathan, Tarantola, Daniel J. M., and Netter, Thomas W. (1992). *AIDS in the World.* Cambridge: Harvard University Press.

Marcus, Eric (1992). *Making History: The Struggle for Gay and Lesbian Equal Rights, 1945-1990, an Oral History.* New York: Harper Collins, pp.179-180.

Margolis, Robin (1991). "Three Bisexual Ideologies: What Route Will Our Movement Take?" *The Bisexual Centrist,* 1 (Fall), p. 1.

McMurty, J. (1975). "Monogamy: A Critique," in *Philosophy & Sex,* Robert Baker and Frederick Elliston, Eds. Buffalo, NY: Prometheus Books, pp. 168-171.

Mead, Margaret (1975). "Bisexuality: What's It All About?" *Redbook* (January), pp. 29-31.

Meadows, Donella (1991). *The Global Citizen.* Washington, DC: Island Press.

Mills, C. Wright (1959). *The Sociological Imagination.* New York: Oxford University Press.

Mishaan, Chuck (1985). "The Bisexual Scene in New York City," in *Two Lives to Lead: Bisexuality in Men and Women,* Fritz Klein and Timothy J. Wolf, Eds. Binghamton, N.Y.: Harrington Park Press, pp. 223-226.

Moraga, Cherríe (1983). "A Long Line of Vendidas," in *Loving in the War Years.* Boston: South End Press.

Morgan, Kathy (1990). "Integrity and Bisexual Identity," *Gay Community News* (May 6-12).

Mullen, Phil (1974). "Sexual Reform or Revolution?" *The Gay Alternative* (Philadelphia) No. 6, p. 15.

Murphy, Joseph (1988). *Santeria: An African Religion in America.* Boston: Beacon Press.

Murphy, Marilyn (1991). "And the Walls Came Tumbling Down," in *Are You Girls Traveling Alone? Adventures in Lesbianic Logic.* Los Angeles: Clothespin Fever Press, pp. 141-146.

Murray, Stephen O. (1979). "The Institutional Elaboration of a Quasi-Ethnic Community," *International Review of Modern Sociology,* 9 (July-December), pp. 165-177.

Murray, Stephen O. (1990). "Ruth Benedict," in the *Encyclopedia of Homosexuality,* Wayne Dynes, Ed. New York: Garland Publications, p. 126.

Murray, Stephen O. (1992). "Components of Gay Community in San Francisco," in *Gay Culture in America: Essays from the Field,* Gilbert Herdt, Ed. Boston: Beacon Press.

Muther, Chris (1990). "Despite Bi Controversy, 2000 Celebrate Northampton Pride," *Gay Community News* (May 13-19).

North, Gary (1989). "Drawing a Fine Line: How Gay and Lesbian Leaders Feel About Bisexuals and Bisexuality in the Gay Rights Movement and Organizations," from *Bisexuality: News Views and Networking.*

Ochs, Robyn (1987). Letter to the editor. Copy of letter sent to *Newsweek.* In *Bay Windows* (August 6).

Ochs, Robyn and Deihl, Marcia (1992). "Moving Beyond Binary Thinking," in Blumenfeld, Warren (1992). *Homophobia: How We All Pay the Price.* Boston: Beacon Press, pp. 67-75.

Orlando (1978). "Bisexuality: A Choice, not an Echo," *Ms.* (October), p. 60.

Orlando, Lisa (1984). "Loving Whom We Choose: Bisexuality and the Gay/Lesbian Community," *Gay Community News* (February 25).

Person, Ethel Spector (1980). "Sexuality as the Mainstay of Identity: Psychoanalytic Perspectives," *Signs.*

Pharr, Suzanne (1988). *Homophobia: A Weapon of Sexism.* Little Rock, AK: Chardon Press, The Women's Project.

Phelan, Shane (1989). *Identity Politics: Lesbian Feminism and the Limits of Community.* Philadelphia: Temple University Press.

Porter-Lara, Jami and McMaster, Carol (1992). "Deciding on Community: Women Discuss the Northampton Pride March, '92," *Valley Women's Voice* (March), pp. 1-5.

Power, Bet (1990). "Who Gets to 'Belong' in the Lesbian Community Anyway?" *Gay Community News* (April 8-14).

Queen, Carol A. (1992a). "Strangers at Home: Bisexuals in the Queer Movement," *OUT/LOOK: National Lesbian & Gay Quarterly* 16 (Spring), p. 23-33.

Queen, Carol A. (1992b). "Erotic Power and Trust," in *The Erotic Impulse,* David Steinberg, Ed. Los Angeles: Tarcher.

Reagon, Bernice Johnson (1983). "Coalition Politics: Turning the Century," in *Home Girls: A Black Feminist Anthology,* Barbara Smith, Ed. New York: Kitchen Table: Women of Color Press.

Rich, Adrienne (1980). "Compulsory Heterosexuality and Lesbian Existence," in *Women, Sex, and Sexuality,* Catharine R. Stimpson and Ethel Spector Person, Eds. Chicago: University of Chicago Press, pp. 62-91.

Rubenstein, Maggi and Slater, Cynthia Ann (1985). "A Profile of the San Francisco Bisexual Center," in Klein and Wolf, pp. 227-230.

Rust, Paula (1992). "Who Are We and Where Do We Go From Here? Conceptualizing Bisexuality," in *Closer to Home: Bisexuality and Feminism,* Elizabeth Reba Weise, Ed. Seattle: Seal Press, pp. 281-310.

Schaef, Anne Wilson (1981). "Paradox, Dualism and Levels of Truth," *Women's Reality.* New York: Harper Collins.

Sheiner, Marcy (1991). "The Foundations of the Bisexual Community in San Francisco," in *Bi Any Other: Name Bisexual People Speak Out,* Loraine Hutchins and Lani Ka'ahumanu, Eds. Boston: Alyson Publications, pp. 203-206.

Shulman, Alix Kates (1972). "Was My Life Worth Living?" in R*ed Emma Speaks*. New York: Random House, p. 388.

Siegel, Micki (1990). "Bisexual Invisibility," *Gay Community News,* (February 18).

Starhawk (1982). *Dreaming the Dark: Magic, Sex and Politics.* Boston: Beacon Press.

Starhawk (1993). *The Fifth Sacred Thing.* New York: Bantam.

Stein, Edward (1992). "Conclusion: The Essentials of Constructionism and the Construction of Essentialism," in *Forms of Desire: Sexual Orientation and the Social Constructionist Controversy,* Ed Stein, Ed. New York: Routledge, pp. 325-354.

Stoltenberg, John (1989). *Refusing to be a Man: Essays on Sex and Justice.* Portland, OR: Breitenbush Books.

Storms, Michael (1980). "Theories of Sexual Orientation," *Journal of Personality and Social Psychology,* vol. 38, no. 5, pp. 783-792.

Strega, Linda (1986). Untitled letter, *Lesbian Connection,* vol. 9, no. 2 (September/October), p. 16.

Sumpter, Sharon Forman (1989). "Myths/Realities of Bisexuality," in *Bi Any Other Name: Bisexual People Speak Out,* Loraine Hutchins and Lani Ka'ahumanu, Eds. (1991). Boston: Alyson Publications.

Tait, Vanessa (1991). "Bisexual Battle: Queer Among Queers," *Guardian,* July 17, p. 9. [Also printed as "The Bisexuality Debate," *Boston Phoenix,* August 16, pp. 6-7.]

Thompson, Mark, ed. (1991). *Leatherfolk.* Boston: Alyson.

Townsend, Larry (1989). *The Leatherman's Handbook II: Updated Second Edition.* New York: Carlyle Communications Ltd.

Udis-Kessler, Amanda (1990a). "Bisexuality In An Essentialist World," in *Bisexuality: A Reader and Sourcebook,* Tom Geller, Ed. Ojai, CA: Times Change Press.

Udis-Kessler, Amanda (1990b). "Culture and Community: Thoughts on Lesbian-Bisexual Relations," *Sojourner: The Women's Forum,* vol. 16, no. 4 (December), pp. 11-12.

Udis-Kessler, Amanda (1991a). "Present Tense: Biphobia As A Crisis of Meaning," in *Bi Any Other Name: Bisexual People Speak Out,* Loraine Hutchins and Lani Ka'ahumanu, Eds. (1991). Boston: Alyson Publications, pp. 350-358.

Udis-Kessler, Amanda (1991b). "'A Quiet Stonewal': The Rise of the Bisexual Identity and Movement." Unpublished ms.

Udis-Kessler, Amanda (1992). "Closer to Home: Bisexual Feminism and the Transformation of Hetero/Sexism," in *Closer to Home: Bisexuality and Feminism*, Elizabeth Reba Weise, Ed. Seattle: The Seal Press, pp. 183-203.

U.S. Bureau of the Census (1990). *Statistical Abstract of the United States. 1990.* Washington, DC.

Vance, Carole, ed. (1984). *Pleasure and Danger: Exploring Female Sexuality.* Boston: Routledge and Kegan Paul.

Walker, Lenore E. (1979). *The Battered Woman.* New York: Harper and Row.

Weeks, Jeffrey (1985). *Sexuality and Its Discontents.* New York: Routledge.

Weise, Elizabeth Reba (1991). "The Bisexual Community: Viable Reality or Revolutionary Pipe Dream?" *Anything That Moves,* 2 (Spring), pp. 20-25.

Weise, Elizabeth Reba, ed. (1992). *Closer to Home: Bisexuality and Feminism.* Seattle: The Seal Press.

Williams, Walter L. (1986). *The Spirit and the Flesh: Sexual Diversity in American Indian Culture.* Boston: Beacon Press.

Wilson, Ara (1992). "Just Add Water: Searching for the Bisexual Politic," *OUT/LOOK: National Lesbian & Gay Quarterly,* 16 (Spring), pp. 22-28.

Wiseman, Jay (1992). *SM 101: A Realistic Introduction.* San Mateo, CA: Self-published.

Wofford, Carrie (1991). "The Bisexual Revolution: Deluded Closet Cases or Vanguards of the Movement? " *OutWeek,* 84 (February 6), p. 33.

Wolf, Deborah (1980). *The Lesbian Community.* Berkeley, CA: University of California Press.

Young, Stacey (1992). "Breaking Silence About the 'B-word': Bisexual Identity and Lesbian-Feminist Discourse," in Weise, Elizabeth Reba, Ed. (1992). *Closer to Home: Bisexuality and Feminism.* Seattle: The Seal Press.

Zandy, Janet (1990). *Calling Home: An Anthology.* New Brunswick, NJ: Rutgers University Press.

ADDITIONAL RESOURCES:

There are a number of periodicals and newsletters by various bi groups around the world. In addition, Bisexual Resource Center produces and distributes several pamphlets. Information about these resources can be obtained by ordering a copy of the *Bisexual Resource Guide* (send $8 to BRC, P.O. Box 639, Cambridge, MA 02140).

Index